Vagueness: A Guide

LOGIC, EPISTEMOLOGY, AND THE UNITY OF SCIENCE

VOLUME 19

Logic, Epistemology, and the Unity of Science aims to reconsider the question of the unity of science in light of recent developments in logic. At present, no single logical, semantical or methodological framework dominates the philosophy of science. However, the editors of this series believe that formal techniques like, for example, independence friendly logic, dialogical logics, multimodal logics, game theoretic semantics and linear logics, have the potential to cast new light on basic issues in the discussion of the unity of science.

This series provides a venue where philosophers and logicians can apply specific technical insights to fundamental philosophical problems. While the series is open to a wide variety of perspectives, including the study and analysis of argumentation and the critical discussion of the relationship between logic and the philosophy of science, the aim is to provide an integrated picture of the scientific enterprise in all its diversity.

For further volumes:
http://www.springer.com/series/6936

Giuseppina Ronzitti
Editor

Vagueness: A Guide

Springer

Editor
Dr. Giuseppina Ronzitti
UMR 8163 "Savoirs, Textes, Langage" (STL)
Université de Lille 3 – Bât.B4
Rue du Barreau – BP 60149
59653 Villeneuve d'Ascq Cedex
France
ronzitti@gmail.com

ISBN 978-94-007-3550-7 ISBN 978-94-007-0375-9 (eBook)
DOI 10.1007/978-94-007-0375-9
Springer Dordrecht Heidelberg London New York

Printed on acid-free paper

Springer is part of Springer Science+Business Media (www.springer.com)

Introduction
Vagueness and...

Giuseppina Ronzitti

Some vital clues that vagueness leaves behind are more or less standardly identified in the literature as *sorites susceptibility*, namely the fact that vague terms allow the construction of paradoxical series of the sorites type, *borderline cases*, the fact that when applying a vague term – say a predicate such as "red" or "bald" – to instances in its range of significance we end up in situations in which it is unclear whether the predicate does or does not apply, and finally the connected phenomenon of the *lack of (sharp) boundaries*, the fact that the border between cases of application of a term and cases of application of its complement is not clear-cut.[1] This is not to say that these characteristics exhaustively and satisfactorily identify what is behind vagueness or how it is best described. In fact for each of the proposed characterizations, taken as singularly or (totally or partially) jointly characterizing vagueness, objections can be raised.[2] Furthermore, as the above-mentioned characteristics are not mutually independent there is also the question concerning whether one of them is more fundamental than the others. This being said, there is no denying that almost all discussion on vagueness centers on trying to "solve", in some sense, the puzzle posed by the soritical type of reasoning, elucidating the nature of the real or apparent phenomenon of borderline cases of application of a term, and characterizing what can possibly be an "unsharp" boundary, in case one joins the party of those who claim that vague terms fail to draw cut-off points.[3]

---

[1]Cf. Rosanna Keefe, *Theories of Vagueness*, Cambridge University Press (2000), p. 6.

[2]The less controversial characterization of vagueness is often indicated as that of vagueness as *sorites susceptibility*. For an argument against such a characterization, see Matti Eklund, "What Vagueness Consists In", *Philosophical Studies* 125, (2005). Stewart Shapiro also expresses some doubts regarding the need of the requisite of soriticality for vagueness. See his *Vagueness in Context*, Oxford University Press, (2006), p. 4.

[3]To be sure, other characterizations have been proposed, and are widely discussed in the literature, as central features of the phenomenon of vagueness, most notably Crispin Wright's notion of *tolerance*. See his "On the Coherence of Vague Predicates", *Synthese* 30, (1975), pp. 325–363.

As it turns out, as a consequence of the obvious pervasiveness of the phenomenon of linguistic vagueness,[4] we meet the sort of problems posed by the soritical type of reasoning and connected phenomena in nearly all contexts. Besides, in many cases, the phenomenon of vagueness does not just occur, but occurs in a way so as to challenge, at least apparently, the fundamentals of a discipline.

This is immediately clear for terms like, for example, the predicate "moral". The possibility of the sorites type of reasoning in these cases can make it difficult to decide where to draw the line between moral and immoral behavior. To repeat an example from Dorothy Edgington,[5] think of the corruption technique consisting in running a soritical series starting with an innocuous present and moving in very small steps to a clear case of bribery. A politician might accept a small box of chocolates offered to him. Also, the small box of chocolates would probably not be counted in any court of law as evidence for corruption. But, the willingness to accept the chocolates may be taken (by the corrupter) as an indication of a possible willingness to accept some other similar, even if slightly more important, gifts and eventually something which clearly will count as corruption. This technique rests on the fact that if a person accepts the first gift considering this as not being immoral, he or she will postpone the decision of refusing the next gift as the acceptance of a slightly more important gift cannot make a qualitative difference, leading to the shift to an immoral behavior.[6]

This example was not meant to overly exaggerate the importance of the phenomenon of vagueness, but only to illustrate how vagueness, and reasoning "by vagueness", may occur outside philosophy classes. In fact, given that almost all words are vague and therefore vagueness tinges almost all contexts, it seems to be possible to speak of vagueness in connection with almost any subject. Nevertheless, the philosophical reflection on vagueness has developed more consistently around some specific topics which appear to be highly responsive (for different reasons) to the threats posed by vagueness. This is the case, in a very straightforward sense, when it comes to philosophical reflections on logic and language. The responsiveness of language is perhaps the more obvious, language being the *cradle* of the debate on vagueness.[7] The responsiveness of logic to the challenges posed by vagueness is also very straightforwardly explained if we consider how the basic notion of "borderline case" is standardly defined, namely as a case which resists the application of the law of excluded middle. The responsiveness of (classical) logic to the

---

[4]Bertrand Russell, in his well-known seminal paper on the topic, remarks that "all language is vague". See Bertrand Russell, "Vagueness", *Australasian Journal of Philosophy and Psychology* 1, (1923), pp. 84–92. Cf. also Timothy Williamson, *Vagueness*, London: Routledge, (1994), p. 2.

[5]"The Philosophical Problem of Vagueness", *Legal Theory*, (2001), pp. 371–378.

[6]Certainly the soritical series for the predicate "innocuous gift" has more dimensions than more standard examples of a soritical series. In the case of the corruption technique it may be argued that already the first gift (a box of chocolates) is indeed a bribe.

[7]We do not mean to imply that vagueness originates in language rather than in the world.

threats posed by vagueness is therefore connected with its being, in a way, under assault.[8]

Beside logic and language, among the fields of inquiry that have become *loci classici* of the debate concerning vagueness we find metaphysics, philosophy of law, linguistics and the philosophical debate on perceptual experience. This volume centers on the mutual relations between *vagueness and* each of the mentioned subjects. This explains the form of the titles of the chapters "Vagueness and ..." We do not mean, though, that these exhaust all the possibilities. The list of chapters might have been longer; due to the pervasiveness of the phenomenon of vagueness it might have been possible to add more topics. We have chosen to limit ourselves to subjects in which the debate on vagueness is well developed. Among the possible topics which are not included the only noteworthy absence is perhaps mathematics, so the reader will not find here a chapter titled "Vagueness and mathematics". Why not? There are essentially two reasons why we did not include a chapter on vagueness and mathematics. First, in a sense there is no chapter to be written on this topic, as the great majority of philosophers maintain that there is no vagueness in mathematics:

> One objection to the view that sorites paradox [...] [provides] evidence that mathematical induction should be rejected is the familiar point of view that mathematics is free of vagueness [...][9]
>
> Mathematics is *the* area of precision. We are not troubled by borderline cases of mathematical concepts.[10]
>
> [...] there is no vagueness in mathematics (or so it seems).[11]

These are just a few examples, but many more are easily found. The fact is that mathematics, it is maintained, *is* the realm of precision. A little less dogmatically one may point out that mathematical terms occurring in the elementary mathematics which is considered in connection with vagueness are explicitly quantitative. Unlike such predicates as "heap", "fat", "bald" whose meaning implicitly involves the idea of a type of measure without any particular measure being specified, mathematical terms like, say, "90 degrees" explicitly indicate a quantity. The possibility of generating a sorites series is blocked, in these types of mathematical cases, because explicitly quantitative terms (unlike implicitly quantitative terms) discriminate adjacent elements of a series of objects in the range of significance of the predicate.

But then, if there is no vagueness in mathematics, why should the fact that we have not included a chapter on vagueness and mathematics be noticed? This has to do with the second reason, namely that mathematics is employed as a tool in the philosophical analysis of the phenomenon of vagueness. And in fact, in this

---

[8]One should remark, though, that on a different understanding of the nature of the phenomenon of borderlineness, such as the epistemicist account, there is no open conflict with classical logic.

[9]Roy Sorensen, *Blindspot*, Oxford: Clarendon Press, (1988), p. 294.

[10]Dorothy Edgington, "The Philosophical Problem of Vagueness", (2002), *Legal Theory*.

[11]Stewart Shapiro (2006), p. 48.

sense this topic features in this volume, in Shapiro's chapter on vagueness and logic dealing with the model theory which is required by the different theories of vagueness. Models use logical and linguistic notions which are precisely defined within the adopted theory. Otherwise said, models of vagueness are not vague (logical-linguistic) objects. This is also true for the fuzzy approach to sets. Fuzzy sets are not, as the terminology could suggest, examples of vague mathematical objects, but, again, a way of mathematically modeling the concept of "indeterminateness", a way of handling "vaguely specified data".[12]

There are certainly (a few) dissenting voices on this subject, philosophers who have attempted to spell out the occurrence of vagueness in mathematics and who maintain that mathematical language is not exempt from vagueness. Bertil Rolf, for example, has claimed that: "[...] it is simply false that all mathematical predicates are purely exact" and mentions the notions of differentiability and continuity which, according to him, "[m]ight have been vague at one stage in the development of calculus".[13]

That said, we think a chapter on vagueness and mathematics in the sense discussed above is possible and remains to be written. However, in this volume we are interested in analyzing and studying how vagueness occurs and matters as a specific problem in the context of theories that are primarily about something else. Apart from the mentioned chapter on *vagueness and logic*, and an introductory chapter on the sorites paradox, we have selected five topics which seem to have most stimulated the efforts of philosophers. A brief description of the chapters, provided by the authors, is as follows:

Chapter 1: Sorites (Dominic Hyde) In a world of change, we see species go from common to rare and yet are unable to point to any moment at which they ceased to be common. We see people grow old and yet cannot nominate any moment at which they ceased to be young. Nonetheless, transitions like these surely must occur at some point, if at all. There must be a change somewhere but no particular point can be singled out as the point of change. Where then are we to draw the line? This puzzling question lies at the heart of the ancient sorites paradox and the more general class of paradoxical arguments that now go by that name. In what follows we look at the various forms the paradox can take and some of the responses that have been pursued.

Chapter 2: Vagueness and metaphysics (Jonathan Lowe) In this chapter, we explore some important questions concerning vagueness that arise in connection with the deployment of certain key metaphysical notions – in particular, the notions of an object, of identity, of constitution, of composition, of persistence, and finally of existence. Various philosophers have argued for or against the view that there can be vague object's, or that the identity and distinctness of objects can be vague, or

---

[12]Cf. Gilles Gaston Granger, "Sur le Vague en Mathématique", *Dialectica* 44, (1990), pp. 9–22.

[13]In Rolf's view Peano's space-filling curve might, then, have been a borderline case of the predicate "continuous curve". See Bertil Rolf, *Topics on Vagueness*, (1981), Lund, p. 55.

that what an object is constituted by or composed of (that is, what its parts are) may be vague, or that an object's persistence-conditions and thus its temporal duration may be vague, or finally that it may even be vague whether or not an object exists at all. We examine the cogency of some of these arguments. We spend more time on the question of vague identity than on any other topic, partly because it has received more attention in the literature and partly because it is either explicitly or implicitly involved in all of the other topics on our list and so is, in that sense, more fundamental than the others.

Chapter 3: Vagueness and logic (Stewart Shapiro) The plan of this survey is to discuss the sort of model-theory that is suggested (or demanded) by the main, rival accounts of vagueness, and to thereby delineate the logic of each. I will try to indicate, in each case, what the logic would be if the account in question were correct. Since the main logical problem facing vagueness is the sorites paradox, the present survey assesses what each account has to say about typical sorites arguments. Nihilistic and epistemicist accounts do not demand any change in the model theory. Supervaluationist and some contextualist accounts require the introduction of partial interpretations and sharpenings. Subvaluationist and some inconsistency accounts are dual to this, and also make use of partial interpretations and sharpenings. The model theories for some many-valued accounts are also sketched, including a boolean valued account that sanctions classical logic. The resolution of higher-order vagueness is also briefly treated.

Chapter 4: Vagueness and meaning (Roy T. Cook) One natural thought to have about vagueness is that the indeterminacy or imprecision inherent in vague expressions is intimately tied to the meanings of these expressions. If this is right, then important tool for studying vague predicates will be meaning theories. There are three critical issues that must be addressed by any such theory: the incompatibility of vague predicates with the 'governing view' of semantic theorizing, the relation between the meanings of vague expressions and the use we make of them, and the fact that vague predicates are open textured. This chapter explores the prospects for dealing with each of these from the perspective of three approaches: contextualist theories, epistemicist theories, and indeterminist theories. We conclude by looking at a variation of the first problem that applies, not to meaning theories, but to formal logics for vagueness: the problem of inappropriate precision.

Chapter 5: Vagueness and observationality (Diana Raffmann) Vague observational predicates like 'red' and 'loud' are associated with at least two distinctive philosophical problems. First, these words appear to generate the most intractable form of the sorites paradox because they permit the construction of sorites series in which neighboring items are indiscriminable, not just incrementally different, on the relevant dimension. While it is at least non-incredible that incrementally different in a sorites series are category-different, the idea that indiscriminable items could be category-different seems beyond the pale. Second, the nontransitivity of the observational indiscriminability relation threatens the coherence of the notion of determinate observational qualities such as shades of color and loudness levels.

In this chapter I examine these two problems and discuss some experimental results that shed new light on them.

Chapter 6: Vagueness and linguistics (Robert van Rooij) This chapter provides a (biased) overview of analyses of vagueness within linguistics. First, the nature of vagueness is discussed, and contrasted with notions such as ambiguity and context-dependence. After that, some reasons are given that could perhaps explain why vagueness is such a pervasive phenomenon in natural language. This is followed with a review of some more or less standard linguistic analyses of gradable adjectives. The chapter is focussed on approaches that take comparison classes into account. Because comparative constructions are ideally formed in terms of gradable adjectives, comparative ordering relations are discussed as well. It is argued that one specific ordering relation is crucial for any analysis of vagueness that wants to capture the notion of 'tolerance': semi-orders. A lot of attention is given to contextuallist' approaches that want to account for the Sorites paradox, because these approaches are most popular within linguistics. In the final main section, the chapter discusses what some people have called 'loose talk'. The main issue here is whether with loose use of language we say something that is strictly speaking false, but true enough in the particular conversational setting, or true, because the conversational setting loosens the requirements for a sentence to be true.

Chapter 7: Vagueness and law (Timothy Endicott) Vagueness in law is typically extravagant, in the sense that it is possible for two competent users of the language, who understand the facts of each case, to take such different views as to the application of a vague law that there is not even any overlap between the cases that each disputant would identify as borderline. Extravagant vagueness is a necessary feature of legal systems. It is a reason to resist the urge to assert bivalence for propositions of law. The challenge – if bivalence is not asserted – is to articulate the principle of the rule of law in a way that is compatible with the possibility of indeterminacy in the application of vague laws.

Contents

Contributors

Roy T. Cook Department of Philosophy, University of Minnesota, Minneapolis, MN, USA, Cookx432@umn.edu

Timothy Endicott Professor of Legal Philosophy, Balliol College, Oxford University, Oxford, UK, timothy.endicott@law.ox.ac.uk

Dominic Hyde University of Queensland, Brisbane, QLD, Australia, d.hyde@uq.edu.au

E.J. Lowe Department of Philosophy, Durham University, 50 Old Elvet, Durham DH1 3HN, UK, e.j.lowe@durham.ac.uk

Diana Raffman Department of Philosophy, University of Toronto, 170 St. George Street, Toronto, Ontario M5R 2M8, Canada, diana.raffman@utoronto.ca

Stewart Shapiro The Ohio State University, Columbus, OH, USA; The University of St. Andrews, St. Andrews, UK, shapiro.4@osu.edu

Robert van Rooij Institute for Logic, Language and Computation, Oude Turfmarkt 141-147, 1012 GC Amsterdam, R.A.M.vanRooij@uva.nl

Notes on the Contributors

Roy T. Cook is an assistant professor at the University of Minnesota, and Associate Fellow of Archée: Philosophical Research Centre for Logic, Language, Metaphysics, and Epistemology, and a Resident Fellow of the Minnesota Center for the Philosophy of Science. He works in the philosophy of mathematics, the philosophy of logic, mathematical logic, and the aesthetics of popular art.

Timothy Endicott is Professor of Legal Philosophy and Dean of the Faculty of Law in the University of Oxford. He has been a Fellow of Balliol College since 1999. He is the author of Vagueness in Law (OUP 2000), and Administrative Law (OUP 2009). After studying Classics and Linguistics at Harvard and Oxford, he studied Law at the University of Toronto and practised as a litigation lawyer in Toronto, before pursuing the DPhil in legal philosophy in Oxford.

Dominic Hyde is a philosopher now working at the University of Queensland, Australia. He graduated from the Australian National University after pursuing doctoral work on the sorites paradox and the associated problem of vagueness under Richard (Routley) Sylvan. He has published a number of articles in the area and recently published a monograph *Vagueness, Logic and Ontology*.

E. Jonathan Lowe, born Dover, England, 1950. Professor of Philosophy, Durham University, UK, since 1995. Educated at Cambridge University (BA History 1971) and Oxford University (Bhil Philosophy 1974, DPhil Philosophy 1975). Research interests: metaphysics, philosophy of mind and language, philosophical logic. Author of 10 books, including *The Possibility of Metaphysics* (1998) and *The Four-Category Ontology* (2006).

Diana Raffman is a professor of philosophy at the University of Toronto. She is the author of a number of articles on consciousness, perception, and linguistic vagueness, several of which draw upon the results of psychological experiments on color perception and categorization using color predicates. She is currently completing a book, *Unruly Words: A Study of Vague Language*, which develops a new theory of vagueness.

Robert van Rooij is a specialist in the formal semantics and pragmatics of natural language. He studied philosophy and linguistics at the universities of Nijmegen (1991) and Tilburg (1992) in the Netherlands. He earned his PhD in 1997 with his dissertation 'Attitudes and Changing Contexts' at the Institut fuer Masschinelle Sprachverarbeitung in Stuttgart (Germany). Since then he is working at the Institute for Logic, Language, and Computation (ILLC) at the University of Amsterdam (Netherlands). He published many articles on formal semantics, pragmatics, and logic in journals like *Linguistics and Philosophy, The Journal of Semantics*, and *The Journal of Philosophical Logic*.

Stewart Shapiro is the O'Donnell Professor of Philosophy at The Ohio State University and a Professorial Fellow at the Arché Research Centre at the University of St. Andrews. His major works include *Vagueness in context* (Oxford, Oxford University Press 2006), *Philosophy of Mathematics: Structure and Ontology* (Oxford University Press 1997), and *Foundations without Foundationalism* (Oxford University Press 1991). He has taught courses in logic, philosophy of mathematics, metaphysics, epistemology, philosophy of religion, Jewish philosophy, social and political philosophy, and medical ethics.

Chapter 1
The Sorites Paradox

Dominic Hyde

What is the most abundant rare species? And what is the least abundant common species? What is the longest short introduction to the sorites paradox and what is the shortest long introduction? The questions are, of course, rhetorical highlighting the puzzlement that surrounds attempts to draw boundaries to the application of vague terms like 'rare', 'common', 'short' and 'long'.

In a world of change, we see species go from common to rare and yet are unable to point to any moment at which they ceased to be common. We see people grow old and yet cannot nominate any moment at which they ceased to be young, and we see societies become unjust and yet cannot nominate any moment at which they ceased to be just. Nonetheless, transitions like these surely must occur at some point, if at all. There must be a change somewhere but no particular point can be singled out as the point of change. Where then are we to draw the line?

This puzzling question lies at the heart of the ancient *sorites paradox* and the more general class of paradoxical arguments that are now so-described.

1.1 The Sorites Puzzle

The name 'sorites' derives from the Greek word *soros* (meaning 'heap') and originally referred to a puzzle:

> Would you describe a single grain of wheat as a heap? No. Would you describe two grains of wheat as a heap? No. ... You must admit the presence of a heap sooner or later, so where do you draw the line?

D. Hyde (✉)
University of Queensland, Brisbane, QLD, Australia
e-mail: d.hyde@uq.edu.au

This chapter reproduces part of my "The Sorites Paradox" in E. Zalta (ed), *The Stanford Encyclopedia of Philosophy* (2005). URL: http://plato.stanford.edu.

G. Ronzitti (ed.), *Vagueness: A Guide*, Logic, Epistemology, and the Unity of Science 19, DOI 10.1007/978-94-007-0375-9_1,

The puzzle was known as The Heap. It was one of a series of puzzles Diogenes Laërtius (1925: ii 108) attributed to the Megarian logician Eubulides of Miletus.

Another was the Bald Man:

> Would you describe a man with one hair on his head as bald? Yes. Would you describe a man with two hairs on his head as bald? Yes. ... You must refrain from describing a man with ten thousand hairs on his head as bald, so where do you draw the line?

This last puzzle was originally known as the *falakros* puzzle and was seen to have the same form as the Heap. All such puzzles became collectively known as sorites puzzles.

It is not known whether Eubulides actually invented the sorites puzzles. Some scholars have attempted to trace its origins back to Zeno of Elea, claiming his paradox of the Millet Seed as a sorites puzzle. However, the evidence seems to point to Eubulides as the first to employ the sorites. Nor is it known just what he had in mind when he formulated this puzzle. Many targets have been suggested, but he is said to have been exclusively interested in logic and the general consensus is that it was for its delightful puzzlement alone that he proffered such a conundrum.[1]

It was, however, employed by later Greek philosophers to attack various positions; most notably by the Sceptics against the Stoics' claims to knowledge. For more on this early history see Long and Sedley (1987) for translations of early texts, and discussions in Burnyeat (1982), Barnes (1982), Mignucci (1993) and Williamson (1994) covering the history of the sorites from antiquity to the twentieth century.

1.2 The Sorites Paradox

These puzzles of Greek antiquity are now more commonly described as paradoxical arguments – that is, as apparently valid arguments with apparently true premises and an apparently false conclusion. While the sorites conundrum can be presented as a series of puzzling questions it can be, and was, presented as a paradoxical argument having logical structure. The following argument form of the sorites was common:

1 grain of wheat does not make a heap.
If 1 grain of wheat does not make a heap then 2 grains of wheat do not.
If 2 grains of wheat do not make a heap then 3 grains do not.
⋮
If 9,999 grains of wheat do not make a heap then 10,000 do not.

∴ 10,000 grains of wheat do not make a heap.

[1] For more on this see Barnes (1982).

The argument certainly seems to be valid, employing only *modus ponens* and cut (enabling the chaining together of each sub-argument involving a single *modus ponens* inference). These rules of inference are endorsed by both Stoic logic and modern classical logic, amongst others.

Moreover its premises appear true. Some Stoic presentations of the argument and the form presented by Diogenes Laërtius recast it in a form which replaced all the conditionals, 'If *A* then *B*', with 'Not (*A* and not-*B*)' to stress that the conditional should not be thought of as being a strong one, but rather the weak Philonian conditional (the modern material conditional) according to which 'If *A* then *B*' was equivalent to 'Not (*A* and not-*B*)'. Such emphasis was deemed necessary since there was considerable debate in Stoic logic regarding the correct analysis for the conditional.

In thus judging that a connective as weak as the Philonian conditional underpinned this form of the paradox they were forestalling resolutions of the paradox that denied the truth of the conditionals based on a strong reading of them. This interpretation then presents the argument in its strongest form since the validity of *modus ponens* seems assured for this conditional whilst the premises are construed so weakly as to be difficult to deny. The difference of one grain would seem to be too small to make any difference to the application of the predicate; it is a difference so negligible as to make no apparent difference to the truth-values of the respective antecedents and consequents. Yet the conclusion seems false.

Thus paradox confronted the Stoics just as it does the modern classical logician. Nor are such paradoxes – sometimes called "little-by-little arguments" – isolated conundrums. Innumerable sorites paradoxes can be expressed in this way. For example, one can present the puzzle of the Bald Man in this manner. Since a man with one hair on his head is bald and if a man with one is then a man with two is, so a man with two hairs on his head is bald. Again, if a man with two is then a man with three is, so a man with three hairs on his head is bald, and so on. So a man with ten thousand hairs on his head is bald, yet we rightly feel that such men are hirsute, i.e. not bald. Indeed, it seems that almost any vague predicate admits of such a sorites paradox and vague predicates are ubiquitous.

As presented, the paradox of the Heap and the Bald Man proceed by addition (of grains of wheat and hairs on the head respectively). Alternatively though, one might proceed in reverse, by subtraction. If one is prepared to admit that ten thousand grains of sand make a heap then one can argue that one grain of sand does since the removal of any one grain of sand cannot make the difference. Similarly, if one is prepared to admit a man with ten thousand hairs on his head is not bald, then one can argue that even with one hair on his head he is not bald since the removal of any one hair from the originally hirsute scalp cannot make the relevant difference.

It was thus recognised, even in antiquity, that sorites arguments come in pairs, using: 'non-heap' and 'heap'; 'bald' and 'hirsute'; 'rare' and 'common'; 'short' and 'long'; 'small' and 'large'; and so on. For every argument which proceeds by addition there is another reverse argument which proceeds by subtraction.

1.2.1 The Conditional Sorites

A common form of the sorites paradox presented for discussion in the literature is the conditional form discussed above. Let F represent the soritical predicate (e.g., ‘is bald’, or ‘does not make a heap’) and let the expression ‘a_i’ (where i is a natural number) represent a subject expression in the series with regard to which F is soritical (e.g., ‘a man with i hair(s) on his head’ or ‘i grain(s) of wheat’). Then the sorites proceeds by way of a series of conditionals and can be schematically represented as follows:

$$\begin{array}{ll} & Fa_1 \\ & \text{If } Fa_1 \text{ then } Fa_2 \\ & \text{If } Fa_2 \text{ then } Fa_3 \\ & \vdots \\ & \text{If } Fa_{n-1} \text{ then } Fa_n \\ \hline \therefore & Fa_n \text{ (where } n \text{ can be arbitrary large)} \end{array}$$

Whether the argument is taken to proceed by addition or subtraction will depend on whether the series is taken to be increasing or decreasing with respect to the relevant quantity (e.g. number of hairs, number of grains of wheat, etc.)

Barnes (1982: 30–32) states conditions under which any argument of this form is soritical. Initially, the series $\langle a_1, \ldots, a_n \rangle$ must be ordered; for example, scalps ordered according to number of hairs, heaps ordered according to number of grains of wheat, and so on. Secondly, the predicate F must satisfy the following three constraints: (i) it must appear true of a_1, the first item in the series; (ii) it must appear false of a_n, the last item in the series; and (iii) each adjacent pair in the series, a_i and a_{i+1}, must be sufficiently similar as to appear indiscriminable in respect of F – that is, both a_i and a_{i+1} appear to satisfy F or neither do. Under these conditions F will be soritical relative to the series $\langle a_1, \ldots, a_n \rangle$ and any argument of the above form using F and $\langle a_1, \ldots, a_n \rangle$ will be soritical.

Of course, F may be soritical relative to one series but not another. If the degree of change between adjacent members of some other series $\langle b_1, \ldots, b_m \rangle$ exceeds the limits of tolerance of the predicate F then condition (iii) above is not met, and though F may be soritical relative to the original series $\langle a_1, \ldots, a_n \rangle$ it will not be soritical relative to the series $\langle b_1, \ldots, b_m \rangle$. For example the predicate ‘is small’ is soritical relative to the series $\langle 1, 2, 3, \ldots, 10{,}000 \rangle$ since it appears true of 1, false of 10,000, and seems tolerant of a difference of 1; however it is (arguably) not soritical relative to the series $\langle 1, 100, 200, 300, \ldots, 10{,}000 \rangle$. The predicate is (arguably) not tolerant of such large changes. We shall say that a predicate is *soritical* just in case it is soritical relative to some series.

In contrast to the usage adopted here and now common in the literature, some logic texts describe multi-premise syllogisms, polysyllogisms, as “sorites arguments” see, for example, Copi (1972: ch. 7, § 5); Luce (1958: ch. 8). Polysyllogistic arguments are similar to sorites as we have defined them in so far as they are chain-arguments, however polysyllogisms need not be paradoxical and sorites as we have defined them need not be syllogistic in form. The usage we have adopted is the more usual these days.

In recent times the explanation of the aforementioned fact that sorites arguments come in pairs has shifted from consideration of the sorites series itself and whether it proceeds by addition or subtraction to the predicate involved. It is now common to focus on the presence or absence of negation in the predicate, noting the existence of both a positive form which bloats the predicate's extension and negative form which shrinks the predicate's extension. With the foregoing analysis of the conditions for sorites susceptibility it is easy to verify that F will be soritical relative to $\langle a_1, \ldots, a_n \rangle$ if and only if not-F is soritical relative to $\langle a_n, \ldots, a_1 \rangle$. Thus verifying that for every positive sorites there is an analogous negative variant.

The key feature of soritical predicates which drives the paradox, constraint (iii), is described in Wright (1975: 333–334) as "tolerance" and is thought to arise as a result of the vagueness of the predicate involved. Predicates such as 'is a heap' or 'is bald' appear tolerant of sufficiently small changes in the relevant respects – namely number of grains or number of hairs. The degree of change between adjacent members of the series relative to which F is soritical would seem too small to make any difference to the application of the predicate F. Yet large changes in relevant respects will make a difference, even though large changes are the accumulation of small ones which do not seem to make a difference. This is the very heart of the conundrum which has delighted and perplexed so many for so long.

1.2.2 Responding to the Conditional Sorites

How might we respond then to the paradoxical nature of the conditional sorites argument described above? The options are clear. One can:

(1) Deny that the problem can legitimately be set up in the first place; that is, logic does not apply to soritical expressions.
(2) Assume logic does apply to soritical expressions but deny that the argument is valid. Iterated *modus ponens* is not valid for the conditional. Since the argument is valid by the canons of classical logic this response amounts to a refutation of classical logic.
(3) Assume logic does apply to soritical expressions and that the argument is valid, but deny one of the premises.
(4) Assume logic applies, and that the argument is both valid and has true premises and so accept its conclusion.

Option (1) is what Haack (1974: ch. 6, § 4) describes as the "no-item" strategy; soritical expressions are beyond the scope of logic. Well known advocates of this approach include Frege and Russell. Frege (1903: § 56) thought that predicates with fuzzy boundaries of application, vague predicates, lack sense and hence cannot figure in sentences having truth conditions. Russell (1923: 88–89) claimed that "all traditional logic habitually assumes that precise symbols are being employed. It is therefore not applicable to this terrestrial life" where vague language abounds. In each case, vagueness is seen as a defect and expressions that are vague are therefore beyond the scope of logic. Since soritical expressions are paradigm cases of vagueness they go the way of vague expressions generally and logic does not apply to them.

This response to the sorites paradoxes owed much to ideal language doctrines popular earlier last century and associated with the demand for logically perfect languages. Ordinary language, in so far as it fell short of perfection, was deemed unfit for serious consideration and vagueness, like so many other phenomena in natural language, was seen as a defect to be eliminated. An obvious problem with this approach is that logic is relegated to a "celestial realm" (as Russell puts it), and the fact that we do logically evaluate everyday discourse speaks against such an approach. The fading of ideal language doctrines and respect for ordinary ways of talking have meant that this approach is no longer viewed as tenable.

Options (2) and (3) both presuppose natural language to be in order as it is and attempt to describe how it is that a logic of vagueness, in particular a logic of soritical predicates, shows us a way out of the paradoxes that beset such language. Having accepted that the conclusion of soritical arguments is false, opponents of the paradox are then divided into what Barnes has described as the radical opponents – those who endorse option (2) and claim that the argument is invalid, and the conservative opponents – those who endorse option (3) and claim that the argument, though valid, has some non-true premise.

Of course these options are by no means exclusive. It may be that the argument is both invalid *and* has false premises thus the sorites paradox is doubly dissolved. No-one has, to my knowledge, pursued such a course and the reasons are obvious. It is difficult enough to resolve the paradox by either route alone; since either will itself be enough to resolve the matter there is no perceived need to engage in the doubly difficult task of convincing an audience that our intuitions are wrong on two counts.

The incredulity with which option (2) is generally met is a measure of the popularity of option (3), given that most theorists these days are concerned to avoid the more hard-nosed options presented by (1) and (4). The conservative opponent typically picks the conditional premises as the place to attack the argument. Though it appears that adjacent subjects in the sorites series are sufficiently similar in respect of F to treat them alike in this regard, appearances are deceiving.

There are a number of accounts of vagueness which take up this option. One is the epistemic view of vagueness, championed by Williamson and Sorensen, according to which classical logic remains completely intact, even in the context of vagueness. According to Williamson (1994), Stoic logicians pursued just such an option. Given their acceptance of the principle of bivalence and their presentation of the argument as invoking a material conditional, they blocked the conditional sorites by claiming that some one conditional is false (since not true) and that there comes a point in any sorites series where the relevant predicate ceases to apply and its negation does. For example vague terms like 'heap' or 'knowledge', though soritical relative to an appropriately chosen series, are semantically determinate so, in spite of appearances to the contrary, there is a sharp cut-off point to their application. The inclination to validate all the premises of a sorites argument (along with the inference pattern employed, which the Stoics accepted) was to be explained via ignorance – more exactly, the unknowable nature of the relevant sharp semantic boundary.

In this way the threat of wholesale scepticism urged by the Sceptics was met by the limited scepticism arising from our inability to know the precise boundaries to knowledge. 'Nothing can be known' was rejected in favour of 'The precise boundaries to knowledge itself cannot be known'. This epistemological response has been elaborated on most notably in Sorensen (1988, 2001) and Williamson (1994, 2000). Though soritical predicates are admittedly indeterminate in their extension, the indeterminacy is not semantic. The conundrum presented by the sorites paradox is an epistemological one which in no way undermines classical semantics or logic.

In the modern era, such a solution was commonly ruled out by definition until recently, as a cursory study of encyclopedia and dictionary entries will reveal. Vagueness was typically characterised as a semantic phenomenon whereby the apparent semantic indeterminacy surrounding a soritical term's extension was considered real. In the absence of any apparent barrier to knowledge of a soritical predicate's precise extension it was generally assumed that there was simply no precise extension to be known. The philosophical landscape has now changed. Williamson and Sorensen have offered an impressive array of arguments defending an epistemological account of vagueness which, if successful, would make possible an epistemological solution to the sorites. (See Keefe, 2000, Chapter 3 for detailed criticism.)

Contextualist accounts of vagueness also make option (3) available as a response to the paradox. Contextualism seeks to account for the apparent lack of sharp boundaries in the extension of vague terms, the central feature driving the sorites paradox, by proffering an explanation as to how such boundaries will never be found wherever one looks for them. Confronted with any pair of items in a series with regard to which the predicate in question is soritical, the predicate is always interpreted in such a way as to not distinguish between them. For example, 'heap' is never interpreted in a context so as to apply to one of an indistinguishable pair of piles of wheat and not the other. This overriding demand produces contextual-shifts along a sorites series whereby the predicate is re-interpreted so as to not distinguish between adjacent items. Vague predicates thus appear tolerant since contextual variation in their interpretation masks any relevant boundaries that may exist in the series. With this understanding of the elusive nature of semantic boundaries, the way is clear to suppose that such boundaries might exist despite their apparent absence.

Raffman (1996) invokes this analysis, retains classical logic in the face of the sorites, and claims the paradoxical argument is accordingly valid but has some false premise. Appearances to the contrary fail to properly account for context by failing to notice that truth can be secured for all the conditionals together only by equivocating on context. Soames (1999) uses context-sensitivity to defend a non-classical tripartite picture of vague predicates, postulating boundaries between the determinate exemplars, the determinate non-exemplars, and the borderline cases. Subsequently coupled with Kleene's strong, three-valued semantics, this non-classical contextualism denies the truth of some conditional premise.

Graff (2000) also pursues an approach that appeals to hidden contextual parameters to account for misleading appearances underwriting the sorites paradox. According to Graff's "interest-relative" account, vague predicates express properties that are interest-relative in the sense that their extensions are determined by what counts as significant for an individual x at a time. For example, 'is a tall building' as used in a context by an individual x expresses the property of being significantly taller for x than an average building. Given the variation of facts over time then the extension of the univocal property expressed by the vague predicate will vary since what is or is not significant for an individual varies over time. Again then, the conditional sorites appears sound only because we fail to heed variation in background factors relevant to the evaluation of the various conditionals. Assertions of their joint truth equivocate on temporal indices.

Another account pursuing option (3) is the popular supervaluationist account. This account is typically presented as modifying classical logic in a conservative way, preserving iterated *modus ponens* and (in one sense at least) all classical theorems while abandoning bivalence. Keefe (2000) defends this account according to which some conditional fails to be true (thus establishing the conditional sorites as unsound) while nonetheless not being false.

Another less conservative, non-bivalent approach is offered by many-valued logics which, like supervaluationism, declare the conditional sorites unsound by virtue of the non-truth of some conditional premise. Some three-valued logics are of this kind, see Körner (1960) and, more recently, Tye (1994). The work of Zadeh (1965, 1975) on fuzzy sets and fuzzy logic can also be employed to pursue such a many-valued response to the sorites by way of infinitely many values.

Many-valued logics can also be developed in accord with option (2), and both Goguen (1969)'s pioneering paper on fuzzy logics and the subsequent work of Machina (1976) do just this. Machina, for example, suggests defining validity as preservation of the lowest degree of truth possessed by any of the argument's premises. The conditional sorites is, on this approach, deemed invalid since *modus ponens* is not unrestrictedly valid for the (material) conditional involved. A similar diagnosis of the sorites paradox was proposed a few years earlier by Goguen.

Paraconsistent logics also fail *modus ponens* for the material conditional. For example, the pioneering paraconsistent logics of Jaśkowski (1948) and Halldén (1949), both proposed as logics of vagueness, fail *modus ponens* for this conditional and so offer responses to the conditional sorites paradox in accord with option (2).

Yet another alternative pursuing option (3), conservative at least to the extent that classical logic remains completely intact, takes issue with the categorical premise, at least the categorical premise of positive sorites arguments. According to Unger (1979) and Wheeler (1979) all such positive, soritical predicates like 'is bald', 'is a heap', 'is a stone', etc. apply to nothing. Negative sorites arguments using predicates like 'is not bald', 'is not a heap', 'is not a stone', on the other hand, are deemed sound, thus conforming with option (4). The response is therefore a mixed response, with different diagnoses offered for different paradoxes.

Indeed, the very soundness of the negative sorites serves to emphasize the falsity of the categorical premise of the corresponding positive version. Each of a positive and negative pair of arguments cannot consistently be counted as sound since the soundness of one counts against the soundness of the other. The validity of sorites reasoning in conjunction with acceptance of the conditional premises serves to show that the predicate in question is either all-encompassing or empty and applying to nothing at all. It applies everywhere in the sorites series if anywhere, and applies nowhere if not everywhere. Unger and Wheeler propose a view in which positive soritical predicates apply nowhere. Given a choice of predicate-extension that is all or nothing, they opt for nothing. The explanation of the non-applicability of such terms lies in the fact of their incoherence. (Like the Barber Paradox then, the positive sorites paradox is taken to establish the falsity of a key existence assumption – that there is a heap to begin with, for example.)

Dummett (1975), on the other hand, pursues option (4) pure and simple. Considering options (1)–(3) as failed responses to the paradox, Dummett feels forced to accept the view according to which positive sorites paradoxes are sound, exhibiting valid reasoning from true premises to a conclusion which is nonetheless false. Sorites-prone terms are intrinsically incoherent. Such a view has also been advocated in Quine (1981) and Rolf (1984). Since it is advocated as an option of last resort, if any of options (1), (2), or (3) can be shown to succeed then the motivation for adopting such a response is blocked. It would indeed be surprising if, contrary to all appearances, soritical predicates were so radically defective; they certainly don't appear so.

Moreover, further claims about the nature of vagueness made in Sorensen (1985) suggest an argument which, if sound, would render Dummett's response untenable by its own lights. So too with the nihilistic response of Unger and Wheeler. Sorensen argues that 'vague' is itself vague, but the argument seems able to be adapted to conclude that 'soritical' is similarly homological – 'soritical' is itself soritical. If so, it would then follow either that 'soritical' is incoherent (Dummett) or that there are no soritical terms (Unger and Wheeler). Thus the thesis that soritical terms are incoherent or empty is, by its own lights, either incoherent or empty.[2]

Sorensen (1985) argues for the vagueness of 'vague' using the sequence of predicates '1-small', '2-small', '3-small', and so on, defined on the natural numbers. For any i, the i-th predicate on the list is defined in such a way as to apply to only those integers that are either small or less than i. Using these disjunctive predicates we are able to construct a sorites paradox for the predicate 'vague' itself. We, however, can adapt his argument to construct a sorites paradox for the predicate 'soritical'. Namely:

The predicate '1-small' is as soritical as 'small' since both predicates clearly apply to 0 and both apply in exactly the same way to all other integers. The same

---

[2]Of course, if one supposes that all and only vague terms are soritical then Sorensen's argument can be invoked without hesitation. The additional argument invoked here makes no such supposition. It is supposed that only vague terms are soritical but not that all vague terms are. For more see § 3.

'1-small' is soritical.
If '1-small' is soritical then '2-small' is soritical.
If '2-small' is soritical then '3-small' is soritical.

⋮

If '$(10^6 - 1)$-small' is soritical then '10^6-small' is soritical.

∴ '10^6-small' is soritical.

holds for '2-small' and '3-small'. Each of these two predicates apply to the integers in exactly the same way as 'small' does; '2-small' has 0 and 1 as clear instances whilst '3-small' has 0, 1 and 2 as clear instances, and since 0, 1 and 2 are all clearly small it follows that '2-small' and '3-small' are as soritical as 'small' itself. However, we eventually reach predicates where the 'less than *i*' clause has the effect of making some integers clear instances of the predicate '*i* -small' whereas they were borderline cases for the predicate 'small' (i.e. cases to which neither the predicate nor its negation clearly applied). Some borderline cases are eliminated. Still further down the series of predicates – at '*k*-small', say – we find that all borderline cases for 'small' have been eliminated and the predicate '*k*-small' is precise. For example, it is clear whether or not to apply the predicate '10^6-small' to any integer; if the integer is less than 10^6 then the predicate clearly applies and if the integer is 10^6 or greater then, since it is clearly neither small nor less than 10^6, the predicate clearly does not apply. Thus the predicate is not soritical – there are numbers to which it clearly applies and numbers to which it clearly does not apply and yet (in violation of Barnes' condition (iii) for soriticality) the predicate is not tolerant since a sharp line can be drawn to its applicability at 10^6. Thus 'soritical' itself satisfies conditions (i) and (ii).

Moreover, 'soritical' also satisfies condition (iii) and is tolerant. To suppose otherwise – i.e. to suppose a sharp line can be drawn to its applicability along the series of predicates ⟨'1-small',...,'10^6-small'⟩ – is to suppose that there is some natural number *i* such that '*i*-small' is soritical whereas '*i*+1-small' is not. The required difference between the two predicates can only be the inclusion of *i* within the extension of '*i*+1-small' whereas it was not included in the extension of '*i*-small'. Yet such a difference is too small to make the supposed difference to sorites susceptibility. Each predicate obviously satisfies conditions (i) and (ii) and, ex hypothesi, '*i*-small' also satisfies condition (iii) whereas it is supposed that '*i*+1-small' does not. So modifying the soritical predicate '*i*-small' so as to include *i* in its extension is supposed to be such as to produce a predicate that draws a sharp boundary (with *i* a satisfier and *i*+1 not) whereas it did not previously do so. But since the only change is to render *i* a satisfier of the new predicate, it must not have been a satisfier of the predicate '*i*-small' in which case '*i*-small' is such that *i* is not a satisfier despite *i*-1 being one (by definition). However, this contradicts our assumption that '*i*-small' is soritical since it would then follow that a line can be drawn between its satisfiers (natural numbers less than i) and non-satisfiers (natural numbers greater than i).

No sharp line can be drawn between those predicates that are soritical and those that are not in the series ⟨'1-small',...,'10^6-small'⟩ and the difference, for any i, between adjacent predicates in the sorites series 'i-small' and 'i+1-small is indiscriminable in respect of their soriticality. Consequently, since Barnes' conditions (i), (ii) and (iii) are all satisfied, 'soritical' is itself soritical.

1.2.3 The Phenomenal Sorites

Dummett (1975) argued for the seemingly self-defeating option of last resort, option (4), because of the existence of particularly virulent versions of the conditional sorites that employ vague phenomenal predicates like 'looks red'. Such paradoxes appear particularly virulent since tolerance seems analytically assured. (See, for example Graff, 2001: 909.) Assuming two objects a_i and a_{i+1} are indiscriminable in respect of colour, if a_i looks red (under normal conditions, etc.) then, since the look of a_{i+1} is the same as the look of a_i, a_{i+1} must also look red. Since this holds for each a_i in the sorites series, we can thus generate the required sequence of conditionals for a standard conditional sorites paradox.

More directly and independently of any appeal to conditionals, a relation of F-indiscriminability, $\sim_F$, appears to permit substitution within the scope of a phenomenal predicate F much as an identity relation would. Suppose we have to hand a series of 10,000 colour-patches $\langle a_1, ..., a_{10,000}\rangle$ gradually (and monotonically) becoming more yellow as we progress along the series, where a_1 clearly looks red and $a_{10,000}$ clearly does not (it looks yellow, say). Furthermore, suppose that just by looking we cannot discriminate between any two adjacent patches a_i and a_{i+1} with respect to their looking red (R), i.e. $a_i \sim_R a_{i+1}$, for all i s.t. $0 < i < 10,000$. Then, since a_1 looks red and a_2 looks the same colour as a_1, a_2 looks red, and a_3 looks the same colour as a_2 so a_3 looks red, ... and $a_{10,000}$ looks the same colour as $a_{9,999}$ so, paradoxically, $a_{10,000}$ looks red.

More generally, for a phenomenal predicate F, if a_1 is F and adjacent members of the series $\langle a_1, ..., a_n\rangle$ are indiscriminable in repects relevant to F, then it seems a_n is F.

$$
\begin{array}{ll}
 & Fa_1 \\
 & a_1 \sim_F a_2 \\
 & a_2 \sim_F a_3 \\
 & \vdots \\
 & a_{n-1} \sim_F a_n \\
\hline
\therefore & Fa_n \text{ (where } n \text{ can be arbitrary large)}
\end{array}
$$

for phenomenal predicate F.

While instances of this form using phenomenal predicates are particularly challenging given the apparent difficulty of applying the phenomenal predicate in question to one but not both of a phenomenally indistinguishable pair, the sorites paradox more generally (phenomenal or otherwise) can also be taken to have this form. It simply makes explicit the assumptions upon which the truth of the many conditionals are said to depend, namely the indiscriminability in respects relevant to F of adjacent items in the series with respect to which F is soritical.

1.2.4 The Identity Sorites

If we continue with our previous example of the colour-sorites we can, it seems, construct a sorites argument that replaces the indiscriminability relation '$\sim_F$' that is said to hold between adjacent colour-patches a_i and a_{i+1} with an identity relation '=' claimed to hold between the phenomenal look of adjacent colour patches a_i and a_{i+1}. Writing b_i for 'the phenomenal look of a_i' and rewording F as 'is as of a red looking thing', the corresponding sorites argument then has the following form:

$$
\begin{array}{ll}
 & Fb_1 \\
 & b_1 = b_2 \\
 & b_2 = b_3 \\
 & \vdots \\
 & b_{n-1} = b_n \\
\hline
\therefore & Fb_n \text{ (where } n \text{ can be arbitrary large)}
\end{array}
$$

for phenomenal predicate F.

Priest (1991) generalises this to a form of the sorites into which *any* sorites, phenomenal or otherwise, can supposedly be cast. It is not simply that the phenomenal look of one colour patch is identical to that of an indiscriminable colour patch but, rather, that they are identical in colour *simpliciter*. 'Being red' is a determinate of the determinable 'colour' so that being indiscriminable in respect of redness, '$\sim_{red}$', amounts to being the same colour. More generally, whenever we have a predicate F there is some determinable D of which F is a determinate so that where items a_i and a_{i+1} are such that $a_i \sim_F a_{i+1}$ we can say that the D of a_i is the same as the D of a_{i+1} – i.e. $D(a_i) = D(a_{i+1})$. For example, 'being bald' is a determinate of 'hairiness of head' and 'being a child' is a determinate of 'maturity', and so if two persons are indiscriminable in respect of baldness (so that the first is bald if and only if the second is bald) then the hairiness of the first is the same as the hairiness of the second, and similarly if they are indiscriminable in respects relevant to being a child then the maturity of the first is the same as the maturity of the second. And so on for other soritical predicates.

Writing c_i for 'the D of a_i' and reworking F appropriately, we can then, according to Priest (1991), recast any sorites in the following form:

$$\begin{array}{ll} & Fc_1 \\ & c_1 = c_2 \\ & c_2 = c_3 \\ & \vdots \\ & c_{n-1} = c_n \\ \hline \therefore & Fc_n \text{ (where } n \text{ can be arbitrary large)} \end{array}$$

Whereas the pursuit of option (2) in respect of the conditional sorites typically focusses on the failure of *modus ponens*, in respect of the identity sorites it is the principle of substitutivity of identicals that is correspondingly at issue.

1.2.5 The Mathematical Induction Sorites

Obvious alternatives to the conditional form of the sorites paradox are also frequently discussed. Dummett (1975), for example, discusses a form that replaces the set of conditional premises with a universally quantified premise.

Let 'i' be a variable ranging over the natural numbers and let '$\forall i(\ldots i \ldots)$' assert that every number i satisfies the condition $(\ldots i \ldots)$. Further, let us represent the claim of the form '$\forall i$(if Fa_i then Fa_{i+1})' as '$\forall i(Fa_i \rightarrow Fa_{i+1})$'. Now the sorites is seen as proceeding by the inference pattern known as mathematical induction:

$$\begin{array}{ll} & Fa_1 \\ & \forall i(Fa_i \rightarrow Fa_{i+1}) \\ \hline \therefore & \forall i Fa_i \end{array}$$

So, for example, it is argued that since a man with 1 hair on his head is bald and since the addition of one hair cannot make the difference between being bald and not bald (for any number i, if a man with i hairs is bald then so is a man with i+1 hairs), then no matter what number i you choose, a man with i hairs on his head is bald.

Whether this is a simple variant of the conditional form of the paradox depends on what account one offers for the quantifier. Supervaluationst responses to the sorites – e.g. that of Fine (1975) and Keefe (2000) – distinguish between the two at least in so far as they claim that the universally quantified conditional premise is false despite no conditional of the conditional form of the paradox being false – some such premise is non-true by virtue of its being indeterminate in truth-value. Nonetheless, such theorists respond to each paradox by denying the truth of some premise – a type (3) response.

1.2.6 The Line-Drawing Sorites

Yet another form is a variant of this inductive form. (See Cargile, 1969: 193; Rolf, 1984: 220.) Assume that it is not the case that, for every i, a man with i hairs on his head is bald, i.e. that for some number i, it is not the case that a man with i hairs on his head is bald. Then by the least number principle (equivalent to the principle of mathematical induction) there must be a least such number, say $m + 1$, such that it is not the case that a man with $m + 1$ hairs on his head is bald. Since a man with 1 hair on his head is bald it follows that $m + 1$ must be greater than 1. So, there must be some number i $(= m)$ such that a man with i hairs counts as bald whilst a man with $i + 1$ does not. Thus it is argued that though a_1 is bald, not every number i is such that a_i is bald, so there must be some point at which baldness ceases. Let '$\exists i(\ldots i \ldots)$' assert that some number i satisfies the condition $(\ldots i \ldots)$. Then we can represent the chain of reasoning just described as follows:

$$Fa_1$$
$$\neg \forall i Fa_i$$
$$\therefore \quad \exists i \geq 1(Fa_i \,\&\, \neg Fa_{i+1})$$

1.2.7 The Forced March Sorites

The foregoing presents the sorites paradox as a paradoxical *argument* and responses have typically addressed a range of logical assumptions appealed to in framing the argument, for example the validity of *modus ponens*, or the validity of inferring '$Fa_n \rightarrow Fa_{n+1}$' from Barnes' condition (iii): $a_n \sim_F a_{n+1}$, etc. But for all their sophistication, modern logical treatments of the paradox will fall short of a convincing response to the problem if they fail to deliver a response to the original puzzle, and the puzzle relies on very little logic.

Recall the original puzzle. We would surely describe a man with one hair on his head as bald. Would we also describe a man with two hairs on his head as bald? Yes. Would we continue to say 'Yes' in response to repeated questioning with ever-increasing numbers of hairs? If not then at some point we must discontinue offering affirmative responses. But any such point would then be distinguished as a cut-off to the application of baldness yet no such cut-off can exist across a difference of merely one hair. So we must continue to affirm the baldness of each successively hairier man until eventually forced to affirm the baldness of hirsute men.

We are simply and ineluctably drawn down the series and asked our response at each point. Unwilling to draw any kind of boundary by offering differential responses, we continue with the same response as originally given. Yet, since there has been a change in the underlying nature of things (from bald to hirsute), we too must surely change our response. Horgan (1994: § 4) brings us back to this simple yet deeply puzzling conundrum via the metalinguistic *forced march sorites*.

Horgan points out, reminiscent of the original puzzle, that if one takes 'Fa_1' to be true then when marched down the sorites series from a_1 to a_n one must paradoxically continue to evaluate as true each 'Fa_i' ($1 \leq i \leq n$). To do otherwise would commit one to a sharp semantic boundary at some point by applying an evaluation other than 'true'. We thus find ourselves on the horns of a dilemma.

Priest (2003) describes a non-metalinguistic variant which brings us full circle and returns us to the original puzzle with which we began. We can generalise his particular example to any sorites series, resulting in the following:

> Is it the case that Fa_1? Some objectively justifiable answer may be offered (e.g. 'Yes'), and so too when asked whether it is the case that Fa_2 and so on. But at some point in the forced march such an answer will no longer be appropriate since it is not appropriate in respect of Fa_n. At that point, wherever it may be, we have committed to the existence of a cut-off point. We have drawn a line where no line seems able to be drawn.

What is the respondent to do? Answering the same to all questions in the forced march leads to paradox, yet changing one's answer at any point leads similarly to paradox. We must recognise the change that undeniably eventuates but are unable to do so at any point.

1.3 Soriticality and Vagueness

Having thus set out and commented upon the nature of sorites puzzles and paradoxes it is easy to see that soritical predicates are vague in the sense that they apparently lack sharp boundaries by virtue of the presence of borderline cases. Soritical predicates appear tolerant so it would seem that there cannot be any sharp boundaries within the predicate's range of significance. Are all vague predicates soritical though?

To be sure, the phenomenon of vagueness is typified by soriticality. The reasons for this presumably are to be found in the fact that vagueness is historically rooted in sorites puzzles and because this is where the challenge presented by vagueness seems most forcefully presented. Yet, one might think, the apparent lack of sharp boundaries or presence of borderline cases can arise for predicates that are not soritical.

If one takes vague predicates to be predicates which fail to sharply partition, in any way, their range of significance then further questions of ordering the range and doing so in such a way as to make adjacent members apparently indiscriminable in respects relevant to the application of the predicate are simply left unanswered. As such, there is no reason to think all vague predicates soritical. One could of course *define* vagueness in such a way that all and only soritical predicates are vague. However there may be broader issues concerning the apparent deviant semantic behaviour of vague predicates, famously exemplified by Frege's worries about concepts that have 'fuzzy boundaries', that motivate our treating some non-soritical predicates on a par with soritical ones – that is, for our treating some non-soritical predicates as vague.

Rolf (1981: 98), for example, cites the possibility of a mathematical predicate having borderline cases without there necessarily being any ordered series of objects in the predicate's range of significance with regard to which it could be said to be soritical. Shapiro (2006: 4) also doubts that soriticality is necessary for vagueness.

Greenough (2003: 270) presents argument to show that the tolerance underlying soriticality follows necessarily from vagueness understood as typified by borderline cases. However, his proof (see assumption 2), seems to rely on a further assumption that vague terms are associated with some dimension of comparison so that the assumed "intolerance" that he makes reference to is a matter of intolerance along some *presumed* dimension of comparison. The step from borderline cases to soriticality is made all the easier for the presumption, as Greenough ingeniously shows, however the presumption requires defence. It may be that an ordering is unobtainable or, given some ordering, it may be that adjacent members of any such series are sufficiently dissimilar to falsify any claims to tolerance on behalf of the predicate. The issue, I think, remains open. Comments to the effect that vague predicates are "typically" soritical, though apparently true, do not settle the matter.[3]

Thus it may be that the analysis one offers of soriticality in response to the sorites paradox holds merely for a subclass of vague terms and cannot yet be said to hold for vague terms in general.

References

Barnes, J. (1982), "Medicine, Experience and Logic" in Barnes, J., Brunschwig, J., Burnyeat, M., and Schofield, M. (eds.), *Science and Speculation*, Cambridge: Cambridge University Press, pp. 24–68.

Burnyeat, M.F. (1982), "Gods and Heaps" in Schofield, M. and Nussbaum, M.C. (eds.), *Language and Logos*, Cambridge: Cambridge University Press, pp. 315–338.

Cargile, J. (1969), "The Sorites Paradox", *British Journal for the Philosophy of Science* 20: 193–202.

Copi, I. (1972), *Introduction to Logic*, New York, NY: Macmillan.

Diogenes Laërtius (1925), *Lives of Eminent Philosophers*, trans./ed. by R.D. Hicks, Cambridge: Harvard University Press.

Dummett, M. (1975), "Wang's Paradox", *Synthese* 30: 301–324.

Fine, K. (1975), "Vagueness, Truth and Logic", *Synthese* 30: 265–300.

Frege, G. (1903), *Grundgesetze der Arithmetik*, Vol. II, in Geach, P. and Black, M. (trans./eds.), *Translations from the Philosophical Writings of Gottlob Frege*, 3rd edn, Oxford: Blackwell (1980).

Goguen, J. (1969), "The Logic of Inexact Concepts", *Synthese* 19: 325–378.

Graff, D. (2000), "Shifting Sands: An Interest-Relative Theory of Vagueness", *Philosophical Topics* 28: 45–81.

[3]See, for example, Keefe (2000: 7).

Graff, D. (2001), "Phenomenal Continua and the Sorites", *Mind* 110: 905–935.
Greenough, P. (2003), "Vagueness: A Minimal Theory", *Mind* 112: 235–281.
Haack, S. (1974), *Deviant Logics*, Cambridge: Cambridge University Press.
Halldén, S. (1949), *The Logic of Nonsense*, Uppsala: Uppsala Universitets Arsskrift.
Horgan, T. (1994), "Robust Vagueness and the Forced-March Sorites", *Philosophical Perspectives* 8: 159–188.
Jaśkowski, S. (1969) [1948], "Propositional Calculus for Contradictory Deductive Systems", *Studia Logica* 24: 143–157. Originally published in 1948 in Polish in *Studia Scientarium Torunensis*, Sec. A II: 55–77.
Keefe, R. (2000), *Theories of Vagueness*, Cambridge: Cambridge University Press.
Körner, S. (1960), *The Philosophy of Mathematics*, London: Hutchinson.
Long, A.A. and Sedley, D.N. (1987), *The Hellenistic Philosophers*, Vol. 1, Cambridge: Cambridge University Press.
Luce, A.A. (1958), *Logic*, London: English Universities Press.
Machina, K. (1976), "Truth, Belief and Vagueness", *Journal of Philosophical Logic* 5: 47–78.
Mignucci, M. (1993), "The Stoic Analysis of the Sorites", *Proceedings of the Aristotelian Society* 93: 231–245.
Priest, G. (1991), "Sorites and Identity", *Logique et Analyse* 135–136: 293–296.
Priest, G. (2003), "A Site for Sorites" in Beall, J.C. (ed.), *Liars and Heaps: New Essays on Paradox*, Oxford: Oxford University Press, pp. 9–23.
Quine, W.V.O. (1981), "What Price Bivalence?", *Journal of Philosophy* 78: 90–95.
Raffman, D. (1996), "Vagueness and Context-Sensitivity", *Philosophical Studies* 81: 175–192.
Rolf, B. (1981), *Topics on Vagueness*, PhD thesis, Lund.
Rolf, B. (1984), "Sorites", *Synthese* 58: 219–250.
Russell, B. (1923), "Vagueness", *Australasian Journal of Philosophy and Psychology* 1: 84–92.
Shapiro, S. (2006), *Vagueness in Context*, Oxford: Oxford University Press.
Soames, S. (1999), *Understanding Truth*, Oxford: Oxford University Press.
Sorensen, R. (1985), "An Argument for the Vagueness of 'Vague'", *Analysis* 45: 134–137.
Sorensen, R. (1988), *Blindspots*, Oxford: Clarendon Press.
Sorensen, R. (2001), *Vagueness and Contradiction*, Oxford: Oxford University Press.
Tye, M. (1994), "Sorites Paradoxes and the Semantics of Vagueness", in Tomberlin, J. (ed.), *Philosophical Perspectives 8: Logic and Language*, Northridge, CA: Ridgeview Publishing Co., pp. 189–206.
Unger, P. (1979), "There are no Ordinary Things", *Synthese* 41: 117–154.
Wheeler, S.C. (1979), "On that Which is Not", *Synthese* 41: 155–173.
Williamson, T. (1994), *Vagueness*, London: Routledge.
Williamson, T. (2000), *Knowledge and Its Limits*, Oxford: Oxford University Press.
Wright, C. (1975), "On the Coherence of Vague Predicates", *Synthese* 30: 325–365.
Zadeh, L. (1965), "Fuzzy Sets", *Information and Control* 8: 338–353.
Zadeh, L. (1975), "Fuzzy Logic and Approximate Reasoning", *Synthese* 30: 407–428.

Chapter 2
Vagueness and Metaphysics

E.J. Lowe

In this chapter, we shall explore some important issues concerning vagueness that arise in connection with the deployment of certain key metaphysical notions – in particular, the notions of an *object*, of *identity*, of *constitution*, of *composition*, of *persistence*, and finally of *existence*. Various philosophers have argued for or against the view that there can be vague objects, or that the identity and distinctness of objects can be vague, or that what an object is constituted by or composed of (that is, what its parts are) may be vague, or that an object's persistence-conditions and thus its temporal duration may be vague, or finally that it may even be vague whether or not an object exists at all. We shall examine the cogency of some of these arguments. Given the immensity of the topic, however, we shall only be able to look at a representative sample of such arguments and arrive at some tentative conclusions concerning them. We shall spend more time on the possibility of vague identity than on any other topic, partly because it has received more attention in the literature and partly because it is either explicitly or implicitly involved in all of the other topics on our list and so is, in that sense, more fundamental than the others. Even so, the sections of this chapter (Section 2.6 onwards) that follow those specifically devoted to the possibility of vague identity are written so as to be intelligible independently of the earlier sections, for the convenience of readers whose primary interests in the metaphysics of vagueness concern these other topics. We shall not, incidentally, have very much to say about the possibility of vague *properties* in this chapter, for a number of reasons. One is that the metaphysics of properties, including the question of their very existence and the question of whether, if they exist, they should be thought of as universals or as particulars (so-called tropes), is an immense and highly contentious subject in its own right. Another is that most of the literature that has a bearing on this topic is framed in terms of questions concerning vague *predicates* and as such either presumes uncritically a straightforward relationship between predicates and properties or else fails to address issues concerning vague properties as such. A third, finally, is that the metaphysical issues that we

---

E.J. Lowe (✉)
Department of Philosophy, Durham University, 50 Old Elvet, Durham DH1 3HN, UK
e-mail: e.j.lowe@durham.ac.uk

G. Ronzitti (ed.), *Vagueness: A Guide*, Logic, Epistemology, and the Unity of Science 19, DOI 10.1007/978-94-007-0375-9_2,

have chosen to focus upon need, in any case, to be considered before any attempt is made to address any concerning vague properties.

2.1 Vague Objects and Vague Identity: Evans's Argument

A good place to begin a discussion of vagueness and metaphysics is with Gareth Evans's classic one-page article 'Can There Be Vague Objects?' (Evans, 1978), whose brevity belies its subtlety and importance. Despite the paper's title, Evans's purpose was to demonstrate, by means of a *reductio ad absurdum* argument, that there cannot fail to be a fact of the matter as to whether an object *a* is identical with an object *b* – so that his direct concern seems really to be with vague *identity* rather than with vague *objects* (A closely related argument was independently developed by Nathan Salmon – see Salmon, 1982, pp. 243–246; see also Wiggins, 2001, pp. 162–163 – but we shall concentrate on Evans's version). It will prove instructive in due course to compare Evans's argument with another notorious 'proof' of a metaphysically contentious doctrine, the Barcan-Kripke proof of the necessity of identity. More precisely, Evans's argument may fruitfully be compared with a closely related proof of the *non-contingency* of identity. It seems not implausible, indeed, that Evans had the Barcan-Kripke proof partly in mind as a model for his own argument, given the obvious similarities between them and the notoriety of the Barcan-Kripke proof at the time at which he was writing.

As has just been said, what is at stake in Evans's paper is the possibility of there *failing to be a fact of the matter* as to whether an object *a* is identical with an object *b*. That this is so seems clear from his opening remark that 'It is sometimes said that the world might itself *be* vague' – for he contrasts vagueness of this supposed kind with 'vagueness being a deficiency in our mode of describing the world', with which he clearly has no quarrel. In other words, his target is what may be called *ontic* rather than *semantic* vagueness – although whether 'vagueness' is really an apt word in the ontic case is a moot point. As we have already observed, is also a moot point whether, in the light of its contents, the title of Evans's paper is apt in representing it as concerning the question of whether there can be vague *objects*. It seems that the real question is, rather, whether there can be objects whose *identities* are ontically indeterminate: that is, once again, whether there can ever fail to be a fact of the matter as to whether an object *a* is identical with an object *b*.

Here, however, another preliminary observation is in order before we turn to Evans's argument itself. This concerns Evans's curious remark that the idea whose coherence he seeks to call into question is 'the idea that the world might contain certain objects about which it is a *fact* that they have fuzzy boundaries'. This remark confirms that Evans's concern is with *ontic* rather than with semantic vagueness, but it is puzzling in its suggestion that the idea of ontic indeterminacy of identity is necessarily connected with the idea of the possession of 'fuzzy boundaries' – by which one assumes is meant 'fuzzy' *spatial or temporal* boundaries. It is true that cases of *semantic* vagueness frequently concern the drawing of such boundaries. For instance, it may be said that our use of the name 'Mount Everest' does not determine a precise spatial boundary between terrain that is part of the mountain so named and terrain that is not. In this case, there are many different ways of drawing a precise spatial boundary all of which are equally consistent with our use of the name: the 'fuzziness' lies not in any boundary that may be drawn, for each boundary that may be drawn is a precise one – rather, it lies in our language, which does not determine that any given one of these precise boundaries must be drawn in preference to any other. But it is far from obvious that ontic indeterminacy of identity would have to be grounded in a genuine 'fuzziness' in boundaries themselves, quite independent of language – as though boundaries could somehow *really* be 'smeared out'. It isn't even clear what could be meant by saying this. Fortunately for the advocate of ontic indeterminacy of identity, however, making sense of such a notion is not crucial to the position that he seeks to defend. As we shall see (in Section 2.5), the most plausible cases of ontically indeterminate identity do not turn on the issue of boundaries at all. However, Evans's assumption – that ontic indeterminacy of identity would have to have something to do with 'really' fuzzy boundaries – is widely shared (see Keefe, 2000, p. 15) and has done much to perpetuate scepticism about the possibility of such indeterminacy.

Now let us turn to Evans's remarkably simple argument. His 'proof' contains just five lines. It begins with the following proposition, assumed for *reductio*:

$$\nabla\,(a = b) \tag{1}$$

Evans indicates that (1) is to be understood as expressing the assumption that the sentence '$a = b$' is of indeterminate truth-value, with the idea of indeterminacy being expressed by the sentential operator '∇'. So, it seems, (1) may read as 'It is indeterminate whether it is true that $a = b$', or, more concisely, 'It is indeterminate whether $a = b$'. And as was implied earlier, we may take this to be another way of saying 'There is no fact of the matter as to whether $a = b$'. For the purposes of *reductio*, (1) is being assumed to be *true*, so it is being assumed that there *is* a fact of the matter as to whether there is no fact of the matter as to whether $a = b$. We shall return to this point later, since it bears on something that Evans says at the very end of his paper.

To explain and justify the next step of his proof, Evans says that '(1) reports a fact about b which we may express by ascribing to it the property "$\lambda x\,[\nabla\,(x = a)]$"' (we use here, for clarity, the more familiar lambda symbol in place of Evans's circumflex). Because Evans takes (1) to report this (purported) fact and expresses the (purported) fact by

$$\lambda x\,[\nabla\,(x = a)]\,b \tag{2}$$

he takes it that (2) follows from (1). I shall assume that (2) may be read as 'b has the property of being such that it is indeterminate whether it is identical with a', or equivalently as 'b has the property of being such that there is no fact of the matter as to whether it is identical with a'.

Next, Evans asserts as a premise this:

$$\sim \nabla\,(a = a) \tag{3}$$

which we may read as asserting 'It is *not* indeterminate whether a is identical with a', or equivalently as 'There *is* a fact of the matter as to whether a is identical with a'. Presumably, what justifies this premise is that it is *true*, and so a *fact*, that a is identical with a, whatever object a might be. For, surely, if it is indeed a fact that a is identical with a, then there is a fact of the matter as to whether a is identical with a – the fact in question being the fact that a is identical with a.

Evans then supposes that, just as (2) follows from (1), so the following follows from (3):

$$\sim \lambda x[\nabla (x = a)]\, a \tag{4}$$

Modelling our reading of (4) on that of (2) above, (4) may be read as 'It is not the case that a has the property of being such that it is indeterminate whether it is identical with a', or equivalently as 'It is not the case that a has the property of being such that there is no fact of the matter as to whether it is identical with a'.

Finally, Evans says that 'by Leibniz's law, we may derive from (2) and (4)' the conclusion of his proof:

$$\sim (a = b) \tag{5}$$

Evans clearly has in mind here the version of Leibniz's law which asserts that if an object a is identical with an object b, then a has any property that b has and vice versa. Contraposing, if a does *not* have some property that b has, then a is *not* identical with b. Now, in lines (4) and (2) respectively it is stated that a does *not* have a certain property – the property of being such that it is indeterminate whether it is identical with a – and that b *does* have this property. Consequently, it may be inferred from (2) and (4) by the contrapositive of Leibniz's law – as above interpreted – that a is not identical with b, which is what (5) states.

Equation (5) itself does not directly contradict (1), so we do not yet formally have a *reductio ad absurdum* proof of the falsehood of (1). To make good this seeming deficiency, Evans makes the following final remark, which has given rise to some puzzlement and a great deal of discussion:

> If 'Indefinitely' and its dual, 'Definitely' ('Δ') generate a modal logic as strong as S5, (1)–(4) and, presumably, Leibniz's law, may each be strengthened with a 'Definitely' prefix, enabling us to derive
>
> $$\Delta \sim (a = b) \tag{5*}$$

which is straightforwardly inconsistent with (1).

The first oddity about this remark is that we were initially prompted to read the sentential operator '∇' *not* as 'indefinitely', but as something like 'it is indeterminate whether'. In fact, the nearest that Evans comes to spelling out exactly how we are to read a formula like (1) is when he says, by way of introducing (1) as an assumption for *reductio*, 'Let "a" and "b" be singular terms such that the sentence "$a = b$" is of indeterminate truth value'. This actually suggests a reading of (1) as 'The sentence "$a = b$" is of indeterminate truth-value'. However, this is a metalinguistic statement, whereas Evans quite explicitly intended his symbol '∇' to be a *sentential operator*, that is to say, an expression that forms a sentence of a given language when it is prefixed to another sentence of the same language. This is why it seems natural to read (1) as was proposed earlier, namely, as ‘It is indeterminate whether (it is true that) *a* is identical with *b*’.

However, another possible reading would be something like ‘It is indeterminately true that *a* is identical with *b*’, where this is seen as being analogous to the modal statement ‘It is contingently true that *a* is identical with *b*’ (compare Parsons, 2000, p. 45 and 204ff). And, indeed, this analogy might superficially seem advantageous if one wants, as was suggested earlier, to draw certain parallels between Evans’s proof and the Barcan-Kripke proof of the necessity of identity. But this reading requires us to understand (1) as expressing, so to speak, a *way* in which it is (supposedly) *true* that *a* is identical with *b* – to wit, ‘indeterminately’, as opposed to ‘determinately’. It is not inconceivable that Evans himself did have something like this in mind (compare again Parsons, 2000, p. 204ff). And, indeed, a reading like this might well be appropriate if *semantic* vagueness were at issue, because a ‘supervaluational’ treatment of such vagueness would supply a reading of ‘It is indeterminately true that *a* is identical with *b*’ as saying that the sentence ‘*a* is identical with *b*’ *is true on some but not all precisifications* of the references of the names ‘*a*’ and ‘*b*’ (compare Lewis, 1988). After all, being true *on some precisifications* is a way of being true. However, we are now taking it that semantic vagueness is *not* what is at stake – and it is not easy to make clear sense of an ‘ontic’ analogue of such ‘indeterminate truth’. We are taking the interest of Evans’s proof to lie in its apparent demonstration that there cannot fail to be a fact of the matter as to whether or not an object *a* is identical with an object *b*. And this is undoubtedly how most other philosophers have viewed it too. So we shall carry on viewing it in this way.

But now the question is whether, if we view the proof in this way, we can make sense of Evans’s final remark, quoted above. At first sight, at least, it doesn’t look as though we can. For if ‘∇’ is read as ‘it is indeterminate whether (it is true that)’, or ‘there is no fact of the matter as to whether’, how could this sentential operator be understood to have a *dual*, ‘Δ’, in the sense familiar in modal logic? The modal operators ‘$\Diamond$’ and ‘$\Box$’ are ‘duals’ in this familiar sense, with each being definable in terms of the other together with negation – so that ‘$\Diamond p$’ is equivalent to ‘$\sim\Box\sim p$’ and ‘$\Box p$’ is equivalent to ‘$\sim\Diamond\sim p$’. Obviously, Evans’s remark, quoted above, that (5*) is ‘straightforwardly inconsistent with (1)’ presumes an analogous equivalence between ‘∇p’ and ‘$\sim\Delta\sim p$’, because only if (1) is thus equivalent to ‘$\sim\Delta\sim(a = b)$’ does it contradict (5*). But if we read Evans’s other operator, ‘Δ’, as ‘it is not indeterminate whether (it is true that)’, or ‘there is a fact of the matter as to whether’, *do* ‘∇’ and ‘Δ’ turn out to be suitably interdefinable with the help of negation? *Is* it the case that ‘∇p’ is equivalent to ‘$\sim\Delta\sim p$’ on this reading? That is to say, is ‘It is indeterminate whether *p*’ equivalent to ‘It is not indeterminate whether not *p*’? (The double negation here is required, of course, since we have elected to read ‘Δ’ as ‘it is *not* indeterminate whether’).

Now, ‘It is not not indeterminate whether not *p*’ is obviously equivalent, by double negation elimination, to ‘It is indeterminate whether not *p*’, so our question reduces to one of whether this is in turn equivalent to ‘It is indeterminate whether *p*’. But then, surprising though this might have seemed prior to investigation, it turns out that our question does in fact have a positive answer. For it seems clear that ‘It is indeterminate whether *p*' is true if and only if 'It is indeterminate whether not *p*' is true. That is to say, it seems clear that, as we have proposed otherwise to express it, 'There is no fact of the matter as to whether *p*' is true just in case 'There is no fact of the matter as to whether not *p*' is true. For if there *was* a fact of the matter as to whether not *p*, this would either be because it was a fact that not *p* or because it was a fact that *p* – and, either way, it would follow that there was likewise a fact of the matter as to whether *p*. We see, then, that even if Evans's operators '∇' and 'Δ' are interpreted in the fashion that we have proposed, they do turn out to be interdefinable with the help of negation in a manner that exactly parallels the interdefinability of the dual modal operators '◊' and '□'.

However, this is by no means enough to confirm Evans's speculation, in his final remarks, that his two operators 'generate a modal logic as strong as S5'. So we are not in a position to endorse his attempt to turn his derivation of (5) from (1) and (3) into an argument with a conclusion that is 'straightforwardly inconsistent with (1)', namely (5*), by 'strengthening' (1)–(4) and Leibniz's law with the prefix 'Δ'. At the same time, it also appears that nothing so ambitious as this is needed in order to turn Evans's derivation of (5) from (1) and (3) into a formal *reductio ad absurdum* proof, given the interpretation of the operators '∇' and 'Δ' now being proposed. For it appears that on this interpretation we can simply *extend* the existing derivation of (5) from (1) and (3) by going on to derive (5*) directly from (5). Recall once more that, as we are now proposing to interpret it, 'Δ' may be read as 'it is not indeterminate whether (it is true that)', or equivalently as 'there is a fact of the matter as to whether'. Now, for the purposes of *reductio*, (1) is assumed be *true*. As Evans himself says, it supposedly 'reports a fact'. And we may agree with Evans that premise (3) is *true* – indeed, that it is logically true. But if the derivation of (5) from these is valid, then it is *truth-preserving*, so that if (1) and (3) are true, so too is (5). But if (5) is true, then it is *true*, and so a *fact*, that *a* is not identical with *b*, in which case there *is* a fact of the matter as to whether *a* is not identical with *b*: which is what (5*) says. So we may extend Evans's original argument by deriving (5*) directly from (5). To be sure, to call (5*) a *strengthening* of (5), given our proposed reading of Evans's sentential operator 'Δ', would be highly misleading. For on this interpretation it is not the case that (5*) entails but is not entailed by (5) and so (5*) is not in this sense 'stronger than' (5). The question at issue now, however, is whether the original derivation of (5) from (1) and (3) may legitimately be turned into a derivation of (5*) from (1) and (3), given the proposed interpretation of the operator 'Δ' – and it seems clear enough that it can. And then all that is further needed in order to turn Evans's original argument into a formal *reductio* of (1), on this interpretation, is the interdefinability of '∇' and 'Δ' that we established earlier, for this allows us to derive the negation of (1) from (5*).

Let us now briefly sum up our findings so far. It seems that Evans's sentential operator '∇' can and should be interpreted as meaning 'it is indeterminate whether (it is true that)', or equivalently as 'there is no fact of the matter as to whether', and that on this interpretation it is, with the help of negation, interdefinable with his other sentential operator, 'Δ', so that '∇*p*' is logically equivalent to '∼Δ∼*p*'. It also appears that, with '∇' and 'Δ' thus interpreted, Evans has no problem in turning his original argument from (1) and (3) to (5) into a formal *reductio ad absurdum* proof of the impossibility of ontic indeterminacy of identity, subject only to the following condition: that his *original* argument – which we shall henceforth refer to simply as 'Evans's argument' – is itself valid. We shall shortly see, however, that there is reason to suppose that Evans's argument is *not* in fact valid.

2.2 Is Evans's Argument Question-Begging?

There is reason to suspect, on closer inspection of Evans's argument, that it is subtly *question-begging*. By a 'question-begging' argument is meant, roughly speaking, one which in some manner already assumes or presupposes something that it is supposed to establish. Now, of course, by no means every question-begging argument can be convicted of containing an invalid step. An argument for a conclusion p that had p as its only premise would be blatantly question-begging, but it does not contain an invalid step: for p certainly entails p. However, an argument can be more subtly question-begging than this. It may be, for example, that the validity of a step in the argument depends in some way upon something that the argument is supposed to establish – and in this sort of case, its being question-begging may well be indicative of its being invalid. Such may be the case with Evans's argument.

Why, then, might we consider that Evans's argument is subtly question-begging? For the following reason (see Lowe, 1994 and Lowe, 1998, p. 63ff and, for further discussion, Noonan, 1995 and Lowe, 1997). The crux of Evans's argument is his use of Leibniz's law in an attempt to show that, on the supposition that (1) is true, a and b differ in their properties and hence that a is *not* identical with b. The property that b is supposed to possess but a to lack is symbolized by Evans as '$\lambda x\,[\nabla\,(x = a)]$'. That b possesses this property is asserted in (2), which is taken to follow from (1). But notice that if it is valid to derive (2) from (1), then it is equally valid, by parity of reasoning, to derive the following from (1):

$$\lambda x\,[\nabla\,(x = b)]\,a \qquad (2^*)$$

(2*) asserts that a possesses the property of being such that it is indeterminate whether it is identical with b. But now we may ask the following question: is this property, $\lambda x\,[\nabla\,(x = b)]$, which has just been attributed to a, the same as or different from the property that was previously attributed to b, $\lambda x\,[\nabla\,(x = a)]$? These 'two' properties 'differ' only by permutation of a and b. So it would appear that, on the assumption that it is indeed indeterminate whether a is identical with b, it is by the same token indeterminate whether these properties themselves are identical – and thereby equally indeterminate whether they are different. (Recall that 'It is indeterminate whether p' is equivalent to 'It is indeterminate whether not p'.) But in that case it seems that the most that can be concluded is that it is *indeterminate* whether a and b differ in their properties and hence not that a is *not* identical with b, but only that it is *indeterminate* whether a is identical with b – which is just what was originally assumed.

If this diagnosis is correct, Evans's argument is question-begging in the following way. The argument attempts to establish, through an application of Leibniz's law, the non-identity of a and b, by showing that b possesses a property that a lacks. And it attempts to derive this conclusion from the assumption that it is indeterminate whether a is identical with b. However, given that assumption, the very property in respect of which b is supposed to differ from a is one such that it is in fact *indeterminate* whether it is different from a property that a must equally be supposed to possess. Hence, the alleged difference in the properties of a and b, required to establish their non-identity, already presupposes their non-identity and hence cannot be used to establish it. The problem arises, of course, from a special feature of the properties concerned, namely, their *identity-involving* character. The properties in question are $\lambda x\,[\nabla\,(x = a)]$ and $\lambda x\,[\nabla\,(x = b)]$, which are 'identity-involving' in that each of them involves the identity of an object – a in the one case and b in the other. But since the properties 'differ' only by permutation of a and b, their own identity or distinctness turns entirely on the identity or distinctness of a and b themselves. Hence, if the latter is indeterminate, as has been assumed, so too is the identity or distinctness of these properties indeterminate – the consequence being that Leibniz's law is powerless to distinguish the objects by means of such properties.

However, although this diagnosis calls into question the ability of Evans's argument to establish its intended conclusion, it does not yet show where exactly the argument can be supposed to go wrong. But it will be noticed that in offering this diagnosis we have said nothing about a crucial step in the argument, namely, the derivation of (4) from (3). (3) seems to be a perfectly uncontentious logical truth, but (4) is the line in which a is asserted *not* to possess the property attributed to b in line (2). Now, as we have seen, given that the inference from (1) to (2*) is valid – which it must be if the parallel inference from (1) to (2) is valid – (1) entails that a possesses a property that is *not determinately distinct from* the property that a is denied to possess in (4). The two claims (2*) and (4) are clearly in tension with each other, because the first attributes to an object a property that is not determinately distinct from a property that the second denies that object to possess. But that a possesses the property attributed to it in (2*) is not an inconsistent claim in itself and cannot be inconsistent with the trivial logical truth (3). Hence, the inference from (3) to (4) must *generate* a tension between (2*) and (4) that did not exist between (2*) and (3). And this implies that the claim made in (4) goes beyond anything entailed by (3). We may conclude that if Evans's argument is invalid, the most plausible place to locate its invalidity lies in the inference from (3) to (4). This suggestion is one that we shall return to shortly.

2.3 Lessons from the Parallel Between Evans's Argument and the Barcan-Kripke Proof of the Necessity of Identity

As was remarked earlier, there is a seeming parallel between Evans's argument and the Barcan-Kripke proof of the necessity of identity (for which see Kripke,

1971) – or, more exactly, between Evans's argument and a closely related modal proof of the *non-contingency* of identity (on these parallels, compare Wiggins, 2001, p. 163 and Keefe, 1995). To say that objects *a* and *b* are *contingently* identical is to say that they are identical but might have been non-identical. This is a supposition that one might attempt to reduce to absurdity by means of an argument formally paralleling Evans's, simply by reading his operator '∇' as meaning 'it is contingent that', on the understanding that 'It is contingent that *p*' is equivalent to '*p* and possibly not *p*'. Thus reinterpreted, Evans's argument may be paraphrased as follows. Suppose that (1) it is contingent that *a* is identical with *b*. Then it follows that (2) *b* possesses the property of being such that it is contingently identical with *a*. However, (3) it is not contingent that *a* is identical with *a*. And from this it follows that (4) *a* does not possess the property of being such that it is contingently identical with *a*. But from (2) and (4) it follows by Leibniz's law that *a* is *not* identical with *b*, which contradicts our initial assumption that *a* is contingently identical with *b* (recalling here, once more, that '*a* is contingently identical with *b*' means '*a* is identical with *b* but *a* might not have been identical with *b*').

One thing to notice about this argument for the non-contingency of identity (hereafter 'NCI') is that it does not need to be supplemented in the way that Evans's argument had to be in order to turn the latter into a formal *reductio ad absurdum* proof, because when Evans's operator '∇' is read as 'it is contingent that' the conclusion (5) directly contradicts the assumption (1). Although the arguments are formally indistinguishable, then, their status as formal proofs is not the same.

Notwithstanding this difference between Evans's argument and the argument for NCI, both may be charged with committing the same error of formal inference. The error, if error it is, lies in the inference of (4) from (3). And, indeed, the Barcan-Kripke proof of the necessity of identity may also be charged with committing an exactly similar logical error (compare Lowe, 1982a). In the latter case, the erroneous step, according to this line of objection, is the inference of '*a* possesses the property of being such that it is necessarily identical with *a*' from 'It is necessary that *a* is identical with *a*'. Since this step – the Barcan-Kripke step, as we shall call it – is much more familiar than, although formally exactly like, the step from (3) to (4) in Evans's proof and the argument for NCI, let us focus on it for the time being. Now, of course, a general complaint may be raised against the Barcan-Kripke step that it moves from a proposition ontologically committed merely to the existence of a certain *object*, *a*, to one ontologically committed in addition to the existence of a certain *property* – and, indeed, to what may appear to be a very strange kind of property. However, general complaints of this sort, for what they are worth, need not at present concern us, either with regard to the Barcan-Kripke proof or with regard to Evans's argument and the argument for NCI. We need have no hostility towards properties in general and – while it must be acknowledged that we cannot, on pain of paradox, suppose every meaningful predicate to express a property – it would be tendentious to respond to the arguments now under consideration by contending that the properties that they invoke simply do not exist. Certainly, if one can find fault with the arguments without needing to deny the existence of the properties, this will be a more satisfactory method of rebuttal.

So what, exactly, might be thought to be wrong with the Barcan-Kripke step? Just the following. Even if it is conceded that 'It is necessary that *a* is identical with *a*' entails that *a* possesses some corresponding property, it may be disputed what property this is – and, of course, there might be more than one such property. One property that *a* might be thought to possess in virtue of the necessary identity of *a* with *a* is the property of being necessarily identical with itself or, more simply put, *the property of necessary self-identity*. This, clearly, is a property that *a* could share with many other things – plausibly, indeed, it is one which it does and must share with every other thing. Obviously, this is a quite different property from the property of being necessarily identical with *a* which, it seems evident, *a* alone can possess. The question then is whether *a* may be said to possess the latter property simply in virtue of the fact that it is necessary that *a* is identical with *a*.

To answer this question, we need to think about the grounds of necessary truths. Some necessary truths are grounded purely in the laws of logic, which are themselves necessary truths (compare Lowe, 1998, p. 13ff). An instance of a logical law need not itself qualify as a logical law, but it will inherit the necessity of the law of which it is an instance. The law of the reflexivity of identity – that everything is identical with itself – is a necessary truth. And an instance of the law, such as the singular proposition that *a* is identical with *a*, inherits that necessity. Hence, it is necessary that *a* is identical with *a*. Against this it may be objected that if *a* is a contingent being, then *a* does not exist in every possible world, whence it cannot be true in every possible world that *a* is identical with *a*. There are various ways to reply to this objection – for instance, by championing a kind of 'free' logic that allows a singular proposition to be true even if its singular terms are 'empty', thus denying that it entails the corresponding existential proposition. According to such an approach, that *a* is identical with *a* may be true even in a possible world in which *a* does not exist, so that even if *a* is a contingent being, it may nonetheless be affirmed that it is necessary that *a* is identical with *a*. Another strategy is to say that, where *a* is a contingent being, the proposition that *a* is identical with *a* is necessary in a restricted sense, namely, in the sense that it is true in every possible world in which *a* exists. But whatever we say, it seems clear that we should say that some sort of necessity attaches to the fact that *a* is identical with *a* and that the ground of this necessity lies in the laws of logic.

What is by no means clear, however, is that the fact that *a* possesses the property of being necessarily identical with *a* – supposing there to be such a fact – is one whose ground could be held to lie solely in the laws of logic. The problem is that it would, it seems, be a substantive *metaphysical* fact of an essentialist character, whereas the laws of logic are properly conceived as being metaphysically neutral. No similar concern attaches to the thought that the laws of logic can ground the fact that *a*, like anything else, possesses the property of being necessarily self-identical. The laws of logic can ground facts about the properties of individuals, but only, it would seem, facts involving properties that are perfectly general in this way. The putative property of being necessarily identical with *a* is not, however, a perfectly general property. On the contrary, it is a property that, if it exists, *a* alone can possess. And the existence of such properties and their attribution to individual objects are matters for metaphysics, not logic. The problem with the Barcan-Kripke step, then, is that it purports to extract a metaphysical fact from a purely logical one. Our proposed objection to Evans's argument and the argument for NCI is just the same: that each of them tries to pull a metaphysical 'rabbit' out of a purely logical 'hat'. This, then, is what seems objectionable about the inference from (3) to (4) in each case.

Here it may be protested that there can be nothing logically suspect about that inference because it simply exploits the formal device of so-called *property abstraction*, which is equally at work in the inference from (1) to (2). However, here we may pose a dilemma for the defendants of the arguments. Either property abstraction is simply a notational reformulation, so that '$\lambda x[Fx]a$' is just an elaborate way of rewriting 'Fa', or else the property abstract '$\lambda x[Fx]$' is seriously intended to denote a *property*, in a way in which the predicate in 'Fa' need not be supposed to do. It should be borne in mind here, as always, that not every predicate can automatically be taken to denote a property, on pain of contradiction. If so-called property abstraction is *not* understood necessarily to involve the denotation of a property, then it may indeed be no more than an elaborate rewriting device with a highly misleading name. But in that case lines (2) and (4) of Evans's argument and the argument for NCI are simply superfluous and we should evaluate the arguments in the form in which they would be left without them. This we shall do in a moment. On the other hand, if property abstraction *is* understood necessarily to involve the denotation of a property, then neither the inference from (1) to (2) nor the inference from (3) to (4) can be construed as a perfectly innocent logical step that cannot be subject to the sort of objection that was raised earlier.

2.4 A Stripped-Down Version of Evans's Argument

Now we need to explore the possibility, just mentioned, of simply *stripping down* Evans's argument and the argument for NCI by removing lines (2) and (4). The problem now, of course, is that the arguments are supposed to involve an application of *Leibniz's law*, construed as the principle that if an object a is identical with an object b, then a has any property that b has and vice versa. And this principle cannot be applied unless properties are invoked in the arguments. The best that one could do instead is to invoke the principle of the substitutivity of identity. But how could that possibly work in the case of Evans's argument? How are we supposed to derive (5) directly from (1) and (3) by means of this principle? It might be supposed that we could assert the following as an instance of the principle of the substitutivity of identity

$$a = b \rightarrow (\sim \nabla (a = a) \rightarrow \sim \nabla (a = b)) \tag{6}$$

and contrapose this to give

$$(\sim \nabla (a = a) \& \nabla (a = b)) \rightarrow \sim (a = b) \tag{7}$$

Then, conjoining (1) and (3) and applying *modus ponens* to their conjunction and (7), we might suppose that we could detach the consequent of (7), which is (5).

One apparent problem with this strategy is that we seem to be using classical truth-functional operators and classical bivalent logic, when the presence of the indeterminacy operator precludes us from doing that (compare Parsons, 2000, p. 47). Thus, for example, the contraposition of (6) to give (7) might be called into question. However, interesting though this line of objection may be, it has the drawback that it will appear question-begging to someone who has yet to be persuaded that the notion of ontic indeterminacy of identity is really intelligible. In any case, such an objection would obviously not be appropriate when the operator '∇' is interpreted as expressing *contingency*, as in the argument for NCI, so let us consider whether it would be legitimate to reformulate *that* argument in this stripped-down fashion. And here we may note that, in fact, the Barcan-Kripke argument in its original Kripkean formulation did not make use of property abstraction and proceeded along lines just like those now under consideration (see Kripke, 1971, p. 136).

The answer that we may give to this query recapitulates one that may be given regarding Kripke's original argument for the necessity of identity (see Lowe, 1982a). In essence, it is this. The principle of the substitutivity of identity is in fact a schema, of the form

$$x = y \rightarrow (Fx \rightarrow Fy) \qquad (*)$$

where the predicate letter 'F' may be uniformly replaced throughout by any predicate and the variables be bound by universal quantifiers or replaced by constants to give a logically true formula. In the case of the argument for NCI, the predicate that would need to be substituted for 'F' in (*) to deliver (6) as an instance of the principle is '$\sim \nabla (a = \xi)$', where 'ξ' marks an argument-place to be completed by the name of an object. (6) is obtained when 'x' and 'y' are replaced by 'a' and 'b' respectively. However, in order to derive (5) from (6), (1) and (3), we must discern this same predicate as present in (3), on pain of falling foul of a fallacy of equivocation. Now, of course, it is an article of faith of Fregean semantics that a proposition like (3), '$\sim \nabla (a = a)$', may be 'carved up' in different ways without this implying that it involves any kind of ambiguity. Thus it is assumed that (3) may equally well be characterized as saying of a that it is not contingent that a is identical with it and as saying of a that it is not contingent that it is identical with itself. However, that these really are just two ways of saying exactly the same thing is not, perhaps, as uncontentious as the Fregean orthodoxy assumes it to be.

Even if we set aside the question of whether the predicates now at issue denote properties, it is clear that these predicates have different *meanings* – 'is not contingently self-identical' and 'is not contingently identical with a' certainly do not mean the same and so it is at least questionable whether, when they are predicates of the same subject term, 'a', the sentences thus formed have exactly the same meaning. When two expressions with *different* meanings are each combined with another univocal expression, to form in each case a meaningful sentence, it would seem surprising that this could result in their forming sentences with exactly the *same* meaning. It is certainly not obvious that 'a is not contingently self-identical' and 'a is not contingently identical with a' are synonymous, but both of these English sentences are supposed to be representable by the same symbolic formula, '$\sim \nabla (a = a)$', which is assumed to be univocal. And the closest English equivalent to this formula, 'It is not contingent that a is identical with a', is assumed just to be another way of saying exactly the same thing. But all of this is certainly open to debate. Indeed, returning to the business about 'property abstraction', it seems that one way of construing this technical device is precisely as a means of *predicate disambiguation*, rather than a means of denoting properties. The idea would be that a formula like '$\sim \nabla (a = a)$' is ambiguous, because it can be parsed as resulting from the combination of the name 'a' with either of two different predicates, with one parsing being read as '$\lambda x [\nabla (x = x)] a$' and the other as '$\lambda x [\nabla (a = x)] a$'. The whole point of avoiding ambiguity in formal logic is that in such logic there should be a one-to-one correspondence between meaning and form, so that valid inferences can be identified as such purely in virtue of their form. The upshot of all this is that the 'stripped-down' version of the argument for NCI, invoking the principle of the substitutivity of identity in place of Leibniz's law, may be accused of involving a fallacy of equivocation which arises from an insufficiently perspicuous logical syntax.

We need to make it clear exactly what, according to this construal, is objectionable about the 'stripped-down' versions of the arguments for NCI and against the indeterminacy of identity. The objection to the argument for NCI is that in order for the conclusion (5) to be derived from (1) and (3) by means of the principle of the substitutivity of identity, the monadic predicate chosen to replace the schematic letter 'F' in that principle will have to be '$\sim \nabla (a = \xi)$', rather than '$\sim \nabla (\xi = \xi)$'. However, (3)'s status as a purely logical truth is plausible only if it is parsed as the result of filling both argument-places of the *second* of these predicates with the name 'a', that is, as saying of a that it is not contingent that it is self-identical. Indeed, if (3) is instead parsed as saying of a that it is not contingent that it is identical with a – which it needs to be if the argument for NCI is not to involve a fallacy of equivocation – then it appears that the argument turns out to be question-begging in a perfectly straightforward way, because (3) so parsed is effectively nothing less than an assertion of the non-contingency of identity. Recall that a here is an arbitrarily chosen object. And what (3) so parsed says of this object – and so, in effect, of any object – is that it is not contingent that it is the very object that it is: in other words, that it could not have been any other object. But this is precisely what the doctrine of the non-contingency of identity amounts to. The alternative parsing of (3) is quite different in its metaphysical import, for on that parsing (3) merely says of any arbitrarily chosen object that it could not have failed to be self-identical. And an exactly parallel objection can be levelled at Evans's argument, namely, that his premise (3), depending on how it is parsed, is either too weak to sustain his conclusion that identity is never indeterminate or else implicitly presupposes it. On the innocuous parsing, (3) says of an arbitrarily chosen object that it is not indeterminate whether it is self-identical, whereas on the question-begging parsing it says of an arbitrarily chosen object that it is not indeterminate whether it is just *that* object.

But precisely what it *means* to assert that an object may have indeterminate identity is that an object may be such that it is indeterminate whether it is just *that* object, as opposed to another.

2.5 A Plausible Example of Ontically Indeterminate Identity

It is one thing to query Evans's argument and quite another to say that there are genuine counter-examples to his conclusion. But there do seem to be some (compare Lowe, 1994 and Lowe, 1998, p. 62ff), which are worth describing here, partly in order to illustrate the point made earlier that ontic indeterminacy of identity need have nothing to do with 'fuzzy' spatial or temporal boundaries and partly to provide material for some remarks about the notion of 'singular reference'. One example involves the capture of a free electron by a helium ion, which thus comes to have two orbital electrons, one of which is subsequently emitted. Throughout this episode there exist two electrons, neither of which begins or ceases to exist during the period of time involved. But, it may plausibly be maintained, there is no fact of the matter as to whether the electron that is emitted is identical with the electron that was captured. This is because, during the period in which both electrons are orbiting the helium nucleus, they are in a state of so-called quantum 'superposition' or 'entanglement'. During this time, there are certainly two electrons orbiting the nucleus, each with a spin in a direction opposite to that of the other: but there is, it seems, no fact of the matter as to *which* electron has the spin in one of the directions and *which* has the spin in the other direction. In fact, nothing whatever differentiates one of the electrons from the other during this time. Suppose, now, that we call the captured electron '*a*' and the emitted electron '*b*'. Then the claim is that there is no fact of the matter as to whether *a* is identical with *b*.

One might imagine that there are in fact two alternative possible courses of events in this scenario. The first is that the captured electron continues to orbit the nucleus and the electron that was previously orbiting it is later emitted. The second is that the captured electron is later emitted and the electron that was previously orbiting the nucleus continues to do so. But our claim is that no fact of the matter can distinguish between these supposedly different courses of events. By this is meant not just that we cannot possibly *tell* which course of events actually occurred, but that it is a misconception to think that there really are these two distinct possibilities. The facts of the matter just amount to this and not more than this: that one electron was captured, two electrons orbited the nucleus for a while, and then one electron was emitted. There is simply no further fact of the matter as to the identity or distinctness of the captured electron and the emitted electron. That this is the proper way to characterize the situation seems to be not only perfectly intelligible but also almost certainly correct. If Evans's argument were correct, this could not be so. But now we have good reason not only to reject Evans's argument as fallacious, but also to reject the thesis that it is supposed to prove – that ontic indeterminacy of identity is impossible. It is not only possible, but also very plausibly exemplified in the domain of sub-atomic particles (see further French and Krause, 2006).

Here, however, the following complaint may be raised. It may be urged that if one is to offer a genuine example of ontically indeterminate identity, then it is important that the singular terms employed – in this case, the names '*a*' and '*b*' – are not terms whose references are vague. They must be 'precise' designators, for if they are not, then it would appear that we are merely dealing with a case of *semantic* vagueness, not genuine ontic indeterminacy of identity. But is it not the case, in the foregoing example, that the names '*a*' and '*b*', introduced as names of the captured electron and the emitted electron respectively, are vague rather than precise designators? For isn't it the case that the manner in which these terms have been introduced leaves it indeterminate whether '*a*' applies to the emitted electron and '*b*' applies to the captured electron? So isn't it just this indeterminacy of *reference* that leaves it indeterminate whether the sentence '*a* is identical with *b*' is true?

This line of objection would appear to be misplaced. Of course, it would not be misplaced if it were *correct* to suppose that there really are two distinct possible courses of events in the scenario, as outlined earlier. For in that case we could quite properly say that the name '*a*' has been introduced in such a fashion that it is left undetermined whether it refers (1) to an electron that is captured and thereafter continues to orbit the nucleus, or (2) to an electron that is captured and is thereafter emitted, or indeed (3) to an electron that is captured and to *another* electron that is later emitted – and similarly with regard to the name '*b*'. But our claim is that *there simply are no distinct possibilities* of the sort now being suggested. To suppose that there are is precisely to suppose that the example under discussion does *not* involve genuine ontic indeterminacy of identity – and as such entirely begs the question at issue. In other words, only if it is already *assumed* that the example does not really involve ontic indeterminacy of identity can it be classified as a case of semantic vagueness arising from our failure to fix precisely the references of the names involved. If this is right, we simply *couldn't* fix the references of these names any more 'precisely', because the facts themselves don't admit the distinctions that would be required for this.

The lesson is that some singular terms may *necessarily* fail to make determinately identifying reference. In our example, the name '*a*' and the definite description 'the captured electron' are such terms. But this is not to say that they are 'vague designators' in the sense required by the preceding line of objection, for a vague designator in that sense is a singular term whose reference *could be* made determinate in principle, or which in other words is capable of 'precisification'. We might, of course, still call them 'vague designators' in *another* sense – implying thereby simply that statements containing them may be of indeterminate truth-value, without any presumption that their references could be precisified so as to eliminate such indeterminacy (On these contrasting conceptions of a vague singular term, compare Keefe, 2000, pp. 159–160). It would be improper to complain, then, that our proposed counterexample to Evans's thesis defeats itself by turning into a harmless case of semantic vagueness, because it can only be seen in that light if it is already presumed that ontic indeterminacy of identity is not involved in the case. And it would be similarly question-begging, of course, to raise a similar complaint in defence of the argument for NCI, by invoking the distinction between 'rigid' and 'non-rigid' designators. Both complaints attempt to rebut a metaphysical thesis by semantic sleight of hand. As such, they repeat the original error of Evans's argument and the parallel argument for NCI: the error of trying to establish substantive metaphysical claims by means of purely logical argument (For further discussion of the issues covered in Sections 2.1, 2.2, 2.3, 2.4 and 2.5 of this chapter, see Cowles, 1994, Hawley, 1998, Heck, 1998, Hirsch, 1999, Noonan, 1982, Over, 1989, Sainsbury, 1989, Thomason, 1982, Tye, 1990, van Inwagen, 1990, p. 244ff, Williamson, 1996, Williamson, 2002, and Zemach, 1991).

2.6 The Paradox of the 1,001 Cats, the Problem of the Many, and Vagueness of Constitution

We shall pass on now from issues concerning vague objects and vague identity to ones concerning vagueness of constitution and composition. For this purpose it will be helpful to focus on an interesting paper of David Lewis's (Lewis, 1993) in which he raises, in slightly modified form, P. T. Geach's well-known paradox of the 1,001 cats, as an example of what Lewis calls, following Peter Unger (1980), the 'problem of the many'.

Geach's original paradox goes as follows. We are to suppose that a certain cat, Tibbles, is sitting on a mat. Moreover, Tibbles is the only cat sitting on the mat. Since Tibbles is a normal cat, she has at least one thousand hairs. Geach continues:

> Now let c be the largest continuous mass of feline tissue on the mat. Then for any of our 1,000 cat-hairs, say h_n, there is a proper part c_n of c which contains precisely all of c except the hair h_n; and every such part c_n differs in a describable way both from any other such part, say c_m, and from c as a whole. Moreover, fuzzy as the concept *cat* may be, it is clear that not only is c a cat, but also any part c_n is a cat: c_n would clearly be a cat were the hair h_n plucked out, and we cannot reasonably suppose that plucking out a hair *generates* a cat, so c_n must already have been a cat. So, contrary to our story, there was not just one cat called 'Tibbles' sitting on the mat; there were at least 1,001 sitting there! (Geach, 1980, p. 215)

A possible solution to Geach's paradox is the following (compare Lowe, 1982b, Lowe, 1982c and Lowe, 1982d). We should say that neither c nor any of the other 1,000 lumps of feline tissue $c_1, c_2, \ldots{}_{,000}$ on the mat *is a cat*, at least in the sense in which *Tibbles* 'is a cat'. For cats and lumps of feline tissue have different and incompatible criteria of identity, which import different persistence-conditions for things of these respective kinds. Thus, c is a cat only in the sense that it *constitutes* a cat, namely, Tibbles – and *constitution is not identity*. Similarly, each c_n *would be* a cat only in the sense that if h_n were plucked out, then c_n would constitute Tibbles the cat. But it doesn't follow that c_n *is* a cat, in this constitutive sense, prior to h_n's being plucked out: because what plucking out h_n does is to bring it about that c_n, instead of c, constitutes Tibbles the cat.

Lewis objects to this solution in the following terms. First, he objects that it is 'unparsimonious' to deny that constitution is identity. He concedes that a persisting object such as Tibbles the cat cannot be identified with the same parcel of matter throughout its existence. But he points out that if we are willing to admit that persisting things have temporal parts, we can nonetheless identify each temporal segment of Tibbles with a temporal segment of the parcel of matter then constituting it. However, of course, those who are not friends of temporal parts will find this objection uncompelling.

But Lewis believes that our proposed solution to Geach's paradox is untenable even waiving his first objection. He remarks:

> So only those who reject the notion of temporal parts have any need for the dualism of things and constituters. But suppose we accept it all the same. At best, this just transforms the paradox of 1,001 cats into the paradox of 1,001 cat-constituters. Is that an improvement? We all thought there was only one cat on the mat. After distinguishing Tibbles from her constituter, would we not still want to think that there was only one cat-constituter on the mat? (Lewis, 1993, p. 26)

Now, as has already been made clear, in advancing our proposed solution we are *not* supposing that Tibbles has many constituters, at least as far as Geach's original version of the paradox is concerned. Rather, c alone constitutes Tibbles, and each of the c_n *would* constitute Tibbles if the appropriate hair, h_n, were plucked out. However, Lewis proposes an amendment to Geach's story, according to which Tibbles is moulting and each of the hairs h_n is loose: they are 'questionable parts: not definitely still parts of the cat, not definitely not' (Lewis, 1993, p. 25). With this amendment, we can no longer insist that c, which includes all of the h_n, is indisputably the one and only constituter of Tibbles. But we needn't be driven to saying that Tibbles has *many* constituters: we can say that she has just *one* constituter, but that it is *indeterminate* whether this is c or a certain c_n. That is, we can say that it is neither determinately true nor determinately false that it is c, as opposed to c_1 or c_{153} or some other c_n, that constitutes Tibbles at present – although it *is* determinately true that just one of them does, because *whichever* candidate were chosen as occupying the role of constituter of Tibbles would exclude all others from that role.

On this view, which seems quite plausible, the definite description 'the constituter of Tibbles' is a *vague designator*. (Such a view by no means implies, of course, that the name 'Tibbles' is likewise a vague designator – at least if one denies, as we are now proposing to, that constitution is identity.) Clearly, the kind of vagueness that we are invoking here is not *ontic*, but is a product rather of what Lewis calls 'semantic indecision' – a phenomenon to which he appeals in his own solution to the paradox – and can be handled by the method of supervaluations. Here it should be added, however, that even if one *were* compelled to say that Tibbles has many constituters – at least 1,001 – it is not clear why this should be deemed *paradoxical* in the way that Geach's original story of the 1,001 cats is. For it is not as though we have some firm pre-theoretical intuition that there is only one cat-constituter on the mat, in the way that we do have such an intuition that there is only one cat there.

Perhaps foreseeing this reply, Lewis has one last objection to our solution to Geach's paradox:

> Further, even granted that Tibbles has many constituters, I still question whether Tibbles is the only cat present. The constituters are cat-like in size, shape, weight, inner structure, and motion ... Any way a cat can be at a moment, cat-constituters also can be ... They are all too cat-like not to be cats. Indeed, they may have unfeline pasts and futures, but that

> doesn't show that they are never cats; it only shows that they do not remain cats for very long. Now we have the paradox of the 1,002 cats: Tibbles the constituted cat, and also the 1,001 all-too feline cat-constituters. (Lewis, 1993, p. 26)

Here we may protest that the concept of a cat is an *essentially historical* concept, a fact which is reflected in the criterion of identity for cats. A cat is a biological object with a certain kind of developmental history – a history which must be consistent with a certain restricted range of possibilities for change. Outside the realms of fairy tale, an object cannot *become a cat* for a few moments, having been something quite different before and going on to become something equally different later. Being 'cat-like' for a moment is by no means a sufficient condition for cathood. Even a friend of temporal parts should acknowledge this, and consequently deny that momentary cat-stages are themselves *cats*.

But, in any case, since we *don't* want to say that there are many cat-constituters in the (amended) Tibbles story, but rather that there is just *one* – although *which* one it is, we acknowledge, is to some extent indeterminate or vague – Lewis's new paradox of the 1,002 cats simply does not arise for us, at least in the terms in which he states it. If the paradox is restated in terms of *candidates* for occupancy of the role of Tibbles' constituter, then our reply will be once more to appeal to the essential historicity of the concept of cathood.

We should mention, finally, that Lewis's own solution to Geach's paradox is to say that there are indeed many cats on the mat but that the many are 'almost one' by virtue of their high degree of overlap – although he combines this solution with a supervaluational approach which allows him to say that there is also a perfectly good sense in which there is just *one* cat on the mat. But while we, too, appeal to supervaluations as far as *cat-constituters* are concerned, we don't with regard to *cats*, and are not compelled to acknowledge *any* sense in which there are many cats on the mat. The only plurality that we need to acknowledge is the plurality of *lumps of feline tissue*, c, c_1, c_2, ..., $c_{1,000}$, each of which is an equally good candidate for exclusive occupancy of the role of being the constituter of Tibbles. Vagueness of constitution is not a heavy price to pay for a solution to the paradox – if indeed a multiplicity of constituters is deemed paradoxical – because constitution was always a semi-theoretical notion concerning which we have no firm pre-theoretical intuitions of sharpness (For further discussion on the theme of this section, see Lowe, 1995, McKinnon, 2002, Sanford, 1993, and Weatherson, 2003).

2.7 Vagueness and Persistence: Perdurance Versus Endurance

Let us proceed next from questions concerning the constitution of objects to ones concerning their persistence through time, which also involve questions concerning their composition – but now their composition by *temporal*, as opposed to spatial, parts. A number of philosophers have argued that *perdurance* accounts of persistence (which invoke the notion of temporal parts) can handle problems of vagueness more satisfactorily than can *endurance* accounts (which don't), and that this is an important and perhaps even decisive consideration in their favour (see, for example, Sider, 2001 and Hawley, 2001). Indeed, such a claim was implicit in Lewis (1993), discussed in the preceding section. Others reply, however, that *both* types of account can handle such problems equally well. This shouldn't be surprising if, as has sometimes been claimed, perdurantism and endurantism as they are usually understood do not really present fundamentally different pictures of the metaphysics of persistence, and are in fact in an important sense 'equivalent' (see, for example, McCall and Lowe, 2003). It should be noted that in what follows we shall not discuss so-called 'stage theory' as a distinct four-dimensionalist account of persistence in rivalry with perdurantism, even though our concern is with four-dimensionalism in general and not just the perdurantist version of it. We shall focus on perdurantism chiefly because it is more familiar and more widely endorsed (Sider, 2001 and Hawley, 2001 both defend stage theory, as it happens).

First let us remind ourselves what the distinction between perdurantism and endurantism amounts to, according to the standard way of drawing this distinction. The perdurantist says that continuant objects persist by *perduring*, that is, by having distinct temporal parts at different times at which they exist. The endurantist denies this, and typically says that such objects are 'wholly present' at each time at which they exist, implying thereby at least that they do not have temporal parts and so, *a fortiori*, do *not* persist by having different such parts at different times at which they exist. The endurantist may well allow, however, that other temporally 'extended' entities, such as processes and events, have temporal parts – including, if they exist, such entities as the 'lives' or 'careers' of continuant objects.

But what is a 'temporal part' of a persisting object supposed to *be*? This is a somewhat tricky and contentious question, especially as some endurantists purport not to be able to comprehend the notion. At the very least, however, such an entity would be something that *coincides spatially* with the persisting object at a certain time (that is, occupies exactly the same region of space) but which, unlike that object, exists *only at that time*. By a 'time' here, one might mean a *moment* or *instant* of time (and that is what we shall assume henceforth), or perhaps just a *period* of time shorter than that of the entire career of the persisting object in question – for we are taking it that we are here concerned only with *proper* temporal parts. How is the persisting object related to its supposed temporal parts? Supposedly, they *compose* it. But the *mode* of composition is something that may be debated. It might be said that the persisting object is a *mereological sum* of its temporal parts, but that is not the only possible account. However, it is a popular one, and so is the one that we shall be assuming henceforth.

Why is *vagueness* supposed to create a problem for theories of persistence? For the following sort of reason. Most persisting things, we ordinarily think, can lose or gain at least a few parts over time, without thereby ceasing to exist (We are not talking here of *temporal* parts, of course, but of *other persisting things* spatially smaller than the things of which, for some time, they are parts). A *mereological essentialist* will deny this, but let us set aside that position as too extreme. The parts in question can be very small and barely noticeable – for example, we should surely allow that a table or a cat could lose or gain a few molecules or subatomic particles without a threat to its continuing existence. But many small changes can amount to a big change, of a sort that surely *should* be taken to bring about the demise of a persisting object. However, it seems problematical to suppose that it is a vague matter *what* or *how many* objects exist at any given time. This might not be problematical if we can make sense of *ontic* vagueness – vagueness 'in the world', as opposed to vagueness in our descriptions of it. But most philosophers think that this notion does *not* make sense. Earlier in this chapter, we saw reason to disagree with them, at least as far as vagueness concerning *identity* is concerned. But we shall set that fact aside for the present. If vagueness is *semantic* – we shall not consider here *epistemicist* accounts of vagueness – then, it seems, it could be a vague matter what or how many objects exist at any given time only if there were semantic vagueness in our expressions for existence, identity and number. But these expressions, it is commonly said, are not capable of harbouring such vagueness, because they are 'logical' expressions and such expressions are not vague (see, for example, Sider, 2001, p. 120, following Lewis, 1986).

So how is this sort of consideration supposed to favour perdurantism? In the following way. Consider the example of a cat – our old friend Tibbles once again – that loses some subatomic particles. It seems that we are bound to be faced with 'borderline cases' of the following sort. On one side of the borderline, we have clear cases of a cat surviving the loss of some subatomic particles. On the other side, we have clear cases of a cat ceasing to exist through the loss of some subatomic particles. In between, we have cases in which we are undecided what to say. But, for the reasons just given, it seems that we shouldn't treat this as a matter of vagueness regarding *what or how many objects* exist at a certain time. It can, then, only be treated as a matter of vagueness regarding how we are to *describe* or *refer to* the objects that *do* exist at a certain time. The perdurantist looks at it this way. A cat is a sum of momentary cat-stages. Tibbles, for example, is such a sum. But of *which* stages is Tibbles the sum? Our general term 'cat' and our proper name 'Tibbles' are semantically imprecise. Our semantic practices do not determine precisely *which* momentary stages are included in the referent of the terms 'Tibbles' or 'that cat'. There is a persisting object identical with *any* sum of momentary cat-stages. Vast numbers of these objects share the vast majority of their temporal parts, differing from one another only in respect of a few parts at either temporal 'end'. Many of these very largely temporally overlapping objects are equally good candidates for being the referent of 'Tibbles' or 'that cat'. Our indecision about whether or not to say that Tibbles has ceased to be is not really a worry about what or how many persisting objects *exist* at a certain time. All the persisting objects that possibly *could* exist, given the momentary stages that there are, *do* exist, because any such possible object is a sum of some of those stages, and *every* sum of any of those stages exists. (*Unrestricted mereological composition* for stages is here being presumed – see Sider, 2001, p. 7.) Our indecision is really indecision over which of these persisting objects to call *Tibbles*.

At this point, we need to look more closely into the question of what, exactly, these 'momentary stages' are, such as the putative 'cat-stages' that compose Tibbles. As we have already indicated, each of them is, supposedly, an object that coincides spatially with Tibbles at a certain moment – and hence is, so to speak, exactly 'as big as' Tibbles, spatially, at that moment – but, unlike Tibbles, it exists only at the moment in question. So, the temporal part of Tibbles at time *t* is something that 'includes' all and only the subatomic particles making up Tibbles at *t*, but exists only at *t*. Why should we suppose that any such thing exists? The perdurantist's answer to this question is, at least in part, that by supposing that such things exist, and by supposing that objects like Tibbles are composed of such things, we can solve the problem for theories of persistence that vagueness supposedly poses. Let it be granted that the problem *is* thus solved. The important question now is whether *only* perdurantism can solve it, in something like the foregoing fashion.

Before we address this question, it is worth confirming that what has just been said about temporal parts seems to apply fully to the important and influential account of these issues presented by Theodore Sider (2001). Sider argues that, for every persisting object *x* and moment of time *t* at which *x* exists, there is an object *z* which is a temporal part of *x* at *t* (see Sider, 2001, p. 138). He says that *z* is what he calls a 'minimal D-fusion of *A*', where *A* is 'the assignment with only *t* in its domain that assigns {*x*} to *t*' (138). Here an 'assignment' is 'any (possibly partial) function that takes one or more times as arguments and assigns non-empty classes of objects that exist at those times as values' and 'an object *x* is a *diachronic fusion* ("D-fusion", for short) of an assignment *f* iff for every *t* in *f*'s domain, *x* is a fusion-at-*t* of *f*(*t*)' (133). A *minimal* D-fusion is 'a D-fusion of [a given] assignment that exists only at times in the assignment's domain' (133). As an example of a D-fusion, Sider says that *he* is a D-fusion (although not, of course, a *minimal* D-fusion) of a function *f* with two times in its domain that assigns to each of those times 'the class of subatomic particles that are a part of me then' (133). We may take it, then, that he would regard as a *momentary temporal part of himself* at a time *t* what we shall later call the 'sum-at-*t*' of all the subatomic particles composing him at *t*, this being understood to be an entity that exists *only at t*. In Sider's terms, this entity is a minimal D-fusion of a function *f* with only *t* in its domain that assigns to *t* the class of subatomic particles that are a part of Sider at *t*.

Now let us return to the question posed a moment ago. We shall see that a plausible answer to that question is that endurantism can in fact solve the problem of vagueness in persistence in a fashion exactly analogous to that offered by perdurantism. Plausibly, indeed, the two solutions are, in a sense, inter-translatable. This is what the endurantist can say. All persisting objects persist by *enduring*. Such objects *have no temporal parts* – they are '3D', not '4D' objects. However, some persisting objects are, of course, *composite* objects, including things like cats. At any given time, such an object is composed of smaller objects, such as molecules and, ultimately, subatomic particles – but it may well be composed of different subatomic particles at different times. Let us say that a persisting object is *constituted*, at any given time, by the sum of its subatomic particles – that is, by the sum of the subatomic particles collectively composing it at that time. Suppose that *S* is the sum of the subatomic particles composing *O* at *t*. Then *O* is constituted by *S* at *t*. Note, however, that we cannot say that *S* is the *temporal part* of *O* at *t*. For, although it is true that *S* coincides spatially with (and so is spatially exactly 'as big as') *O* at *t*, we are not given that *S exists only at t*. Indeed, *S* may well exist at other times, at which it does not constitute and hence does not coincide spatially with *O* – although, in principle, *S* could indeed constitute *O* at two or more different times. This is because *S*, being a sum of certain subatomic particles, exists just so long as all of those subatomic particles do (even if they should happen to be *dispersed* for some of the time). Moreover, the endurantist can say the following, by analogy with the perdurantist. For *any* sequence of times and sums of subatomic particles existing at those times, there is a persisting object constituted at those times by those sums. Vast numbers of these persisting objects will be *co-constituted* at many of those times – that is to say, many of them will be constituted at those times by the *same* sums of subatomic particles. Consider, thus, the example of Tibbles once more. At any time during her existence, Tibbles is constituted by some sum of subatomic particles, and often by different sums at different times. But at any such time, the sum of subatomic particles constituting Tibbles will also constitute, at that time, very many other persisting objects, which differ from Tibbles only in respect of what sums of subatomic particles constitute them at *other* times. What determines which of all these persisting objects we refer to as 'Tibbles'? The answer is that our semantic practices do not determine this precisely and that is why, according to our envisaged endurantist, it is to some extent vague whether or not *Tibbles* has persisted at a certain time. The vagueness does not really concern what or how many persisting objects exist at that time, but only which of these objects, if any, is a candidate for being the referent of the name 'Tibbles'.

As was indicated earlier, there is a translation scheme available between the perdurantist and endurantist ways of describing the situation. The perdurantist takes as his or her building blocks momentary object-stages, each stage being a momentary sum of subatomic particles. By a 'momentary sum of subatomic particles' we mean a *sum-at-a-moment* of subatomic particles, that is, something that could be represented by an ordered pair of a sum of subatomic particles and a moment of time, $\langle S, t \rangle$, and whose existence- and identity-conditions are correspondingly these: if $M = \langle S, t \rangle$, then M exists if and only if S exists at t, and if M exists then M exists *only* at t; and if $M = \langle S, t \rangle$ and $M' = \langle S', t' \rangle$, then $M = M'$ if and only if $S = S'$ and $t = t'$. (Note, incidentally, that what we are now calling a 'sum-at-a-moment of subatomic particles' is effectively what Sider calls a 'minimal D-fusion' of an assignment with only that moment in its domain which assigns to that moment the unit class of a persisting object wholly composed of those subatomic particles at that moment.) For the perdurantist, *every* sum of object-stages is a persisting object. As was indicated earlier, we are assuming here unrestricted mereological composition, because this is a standard part of the perdurantist's strategy for dealing with vagueness concerning persistence. On this view, many persisting objects will share the same stages at many times. Let us say that any two persisting objects that have the same stage as their temporal part at a time *t* are *temporally co-composed at t*. Then, for example, very many of the rival candidates for the referent of 'Tibbles', according to the perdurantist's account, will be temporally co-composed throughout most of their careers, differing only at the 'ends' of those careers.

But this is what the endurantist can analogously say. The endurantist takes his or her building blocks simply to be *sums of subatomic particles*, rather than *sums-at-a-moment* of subatomic particles. And he or she says that for any sequence of times and sums of subatomic particles existing at those times, there is a persisting object existing at just those times which is constituted at those times by those sums of subatomic particles. So, suppose that S is a sum of subatomic particles existing at t and S' is a sum of subatomic particles existing at t'. Then, according to the endurantist, there is a persisting object O which exists at just t and t', and which is *constituted* by S at t and by S' at t'. (Never mind that O may consequently have an *interrupted existence*: nothing prohibits an endurantist from allowing this.) The perdurantist will instead say here that there is a persisting object O which exists at just t and t', and which is the sum of the momentary stages or sums-at-a-moment of subatomic particles <*S*, *t*> and <*S′*, *t′*>. But then it is hard to see in what substantive respect the endurantist and perdurantist accounts really differ. They both agree that O, S, S', t and t' exist. They differ only with regard to how these entities are related to one another. The translation scheme between the two accounts involves the following equivalence principle: <*S*, *t*> is the temporal part of O_p at t if and only if O_e is constituted by S at t. (Here we may read 'O_p' as 'O conceived as a perduring object' and 'O_e' as 'O conceived as an enduring object'.) Of course, it may be said that the perdurantist invokes the existence of the *sums-at-a-moment* <*S*, *t*> and <*S′*, *t′*>, whereas the endurantist does not. That is true, but nothing substantive hinges on this. The existence- and identity-conditions of sums-at-a-moment make it clear that these entities are wholly ontologically dependent upon sums of subatomic particles and moments of time – they are an ontological 'free lunch', to borrow David Armstrong's memorable phrase. It seems, thus, that whether we invoke the perdurantist language or the endurantist language is really just a matter of how we prefer to *describe* the facts of persistence. The underlying facts, it seems, are really just the same, however described.

It will not do for the perdurantist to object that endurantism is somehow forbidden, as perdurantism is not, to inflate the number of persisting objects far beyond what 'common sense' would acknowledge. It may indeed be that endurantism has common sense on its side in its rejection of talk of temporal parts, but that doesn't mean that endurantism must be entirely bound by all the constraints of common sense. Nor will it do for the perdurantist to object that endurantism is committed to a plethora of spatially coinciding 3D objects, for this only corresponds exactly to the perdurantist's own plethora of temporally overlapping 4D objects. The proper conclusion would seem to be that as far as these rival theories of persistence are concerned, the problem of vagueness in persistence is incapable of favouring either side, since each side has a solution to that problem that is inter-translatable with that of the other side.

It is worth pointing out, finally, that the endurantist can happily allow, as a limiting case, that for any sum of subatomic particles S and moment of time t, there is a 'persisting' object O that is constituted by S at t and which exists *only* at t. This object O is indistinguishable from the perdurantist's momentary temporal stage M = <*S*, *t*>. But, for the endurantist, objects like O are *not* momentary temporal parts of the persisting objects that genuinely *persist* and so exist at *more than one* moment of time. Rather, such persisting objects are momentarily *co-constituted* with objects like *O*, and the latter play no role at all in the endurantist's account of *how* persisting objects persist. So it is remains true to say that the perdurantist and the endurantist offer different accounts of *persistence*. But it seems that they do so without necessarily differing over any fundamental fact of ontology. That is why neither side is entitled to claim victory in the dispute between them concerning vagueness in persistence. Nor will it do for the perdurantist to protest that we have reached this conclusion only because the form of endurantism that we have discussed is just *perdurantism* by any other name. In a sense, so it is. But then, in that same sense, the form of perdurantism that we have discussed, which is widely espoused, is just *endurantism* by any other name. That is precisely the point in calling them 'equivalent' accounts of persistence (For further discussion of the issues raised in this section, see Koslicki, 2003, Lowe, 2005, and Miller, 2005).

2.8 Vague Identity, Vague Existence, and Sorites-Style Reasoning

If, as was suggested earlier in this chapter, there can sometimes be 'no fact of the matter' where *identity* is concerned, it might seem to follow that there can sometimes be 'no fact of the matter' where *existence* is concerned: vague (or indeterminate) identity might seem to imply vague (or indeterminate) existence. And yet the idea of vague existence may seem to make no sense – in which case, if the mooted implication holds, the idea of vague identity can really make no sense either. However, as we shall see, there are reasons to suppose that the mooted implication does *not* hold. There *are* defensible – albeit rather esoteric – examples of vague (or indeterminate) identity, and yet vague existence is not implied by them. Other putative examples of vague identity which do seem to imply vague existence – typically generated in response to Sorites-style reasoning – are very arguably self-undermining, because it seems that what they really serve to show is that certain sortal terms in actual use are conceptually defective and so cannot ever be used to make true (or indeed false) existence claims. Ordinary language appears to contain many such defective sortal terms, such as 'mountain'. It doesn't follow, of course, that we can truly assert that *there are no mountains*. Nor does it follow that common-sense ontology is radically mistaken – just that ordinary language often resorts to *sortal* terms (such as 'mountain') where *mass* terms (such as 'mountainous terrain') would strictly be more appropriate, even though less convenient. So, at least, it will be suggested in the discussion to follow.

We saw in Section 2.5 above that, quite plausibly, there can sometimes be 'no fact of the matter' where questions of identity are concerned. It is a moot point, however, whether this kind of indeterminacy is really best described as being a matter of *vagueness*, such as we find in a classic Sorites paradox. Genuine indeterminacy of identity plausibly only arises in rather arcane cases thrown up by quantum physics, such as when an electron joins another orbiting a helium nucleus and then, later, an electron is ejected from the atom. In this case, we may be inclined to say, there is no fact of the matter as to whether the ejected electron was the electron that was earlier absorbed or the one that was already orbiting the nucleus. However, there is no question here of anything like a Sorites paradox being involved. In particular, there seems to be no basis for seeing any kind of 'tolerance principle' at work in this sort of case. It is not true here, for instance, that there is some succession of small changes affecting one of the electrons concerned, such that each small change seems not to threaten the identity of that electron, but many of them do. Indeed, there is nothing 'gradual' that relevantly affects any of the electrons: there is just a sudden transition from a state in which we have two indisputably distinct and independently identifiable electrons to one in which these two electrons exist in a state of 'superposition', followed by an equally sudden transition to a state in which we once again have two independently identifiable electrons. However, the intervening state of superposition makes it impossible say *which* of the electrons existing at the later time is identical with *which* of the electrons existing at the earlier time – even though it is not disputed that *the same two electrons* existed throughout the whole episode, because there were just two to start with and just two at the end and no electron was created or destroyed throughout the entire process. This sort of case, however, is clearly quite different from a putative case of vague diachronic identity involving the repeated repair of an artefact, such as a car, where we are undecided after many such repairs whether or not to identify the later car with the original car that emerged from the factory.

The example of the car is, of course, similar to that of the electrons at least in one respect: it involves questions of *diachronic* identity. And identity over time is puzzling for all sorts of reasons, quite apart from any that might raise issues of vagueness. So it might be helpful to look instead at some *synchronic* examples, to see if a Sorites-like case of vagueness concerning identity can genuinely arise there. Such examples should be less perplexing and more perspicuous, simply because we have removed time from the picture. Now, in a classic Sorites paradox, we have a *spectrum* of states or conditions with a clear-cut difference between either end and an intermediate borderline area: for example, *bald* at one end and *hirsute* at the other, or *red* at one end and *yellow* at the other – or, indeed, *heap of sand* at one end and *grain of sand* at the other. (It is not really helpful to think of such a spectrum just as having *F* at one end and *non-F* at the other – for instance, *bald* and *non-bald* – because, of course, there are infinitely many different ways of being non-*F*, almost all of which do not lie on a continuum with *F* at the other end.) Bearing this in mind, the following example might seem to be the sort of synchronic case that we are seeking, because it certainly has Sorites-like features.

Suppose we have two mountains, Alpha and Beta, which are separated by a high pass. Then, although the whole terrain involved is mountainous, we find it difficult to say where, in the region of the pass, Alpha gives way to Beta. Perhaps, indeed, we should say that there is 'no fact of the matter' about this. Now, some philosophers might try to exploit this example in order to generate a Sorites-like paradox of mountain identity in the following way, with Alpha at one end of the Sorites 'spectrum' and Beta at the other. If we start on the peak of Alpha and move to a point one centimetre away from that in the direction of Beta, we shall surely still be located on the same mountain as before, *Alpha*. More generally, it may be urged, if we are *anywhere* on Alpha and move to a point one centimetre in the direction of Beta, we shall still be located on the same mountain as before, because such a small movement cannot take us from one mountain to another. But, through repeated applications of this sort of inference-step, the absurd implication seems to be that even when we have moved completely over to the peak of Beta, *we are still on Alpha*, so that Alpha and Beta must in fact be one and the same mountain. In this case the 'tolerance principle' at work is something like this: if you move from one point on a mountain to another point one centimetre away in the direction of another mountain, then you remain on the same mountain. Of course, we must reject this Sorites-style reasoning if we are convinced that Alpha and Beta really are two different mountains. However, it is not at all obvious that rejecting it commits us to the possibility that there can sometimes be 'no fact of the matter' where the identity of mountains is concerned.

Let us expand a little on the latter claim. We conceded a moment ago that there might be 'no fact of the matter' as to where, in the region of the pass, Alpha gives way to Beta. Why doesn't it follow that there might be 'no fact of the matter' as to identity or diversity of Alpha and Beta? Simply for the following reason: the fact, if fact it is, that there is 'no fact of the matter' as to where Alpha gives way to Beta implies only that there can be vagueness or indeterminacy of *constitution* where mountains are concerned – and *constitution is not identity* (see again Section 2.6 above). We are assuming here that mountains, given that they exist as a kind of persisting object, are capable of undergoing changes of material composition, just as things such as tables, cars, and cats are. Mount Everest, for example, doubtless no longer includes amongst its material parts certain bits of rock that have been eroded by weather and climbers over the years. Hence, the mountain is not to be *identified* with the mereological sum or fusion of the various bits of rock that compose it at any one time. Indeed, we want to say that there is 'no fact of the matter' as to *precisely which* bits of rock compose Mount Everest at any given time – because, for example, there is no principled way of deciding whether a certain small bit of rock, loosely attached to others composing the mountain at a given time, counts as being part of the mountain at that time or instead as a piece that has been separated from it by erosion. At any given time, then, there are many numerically distinct, but very largely overlapping, mereological sums of bits of rock that are equally good candidates for being 'the' sum that constitutes Mount Everest at that time. This commits us to vagueness of *constitution* where mountains are concerned. But it doesn't commit us to vagueness of *identity* concerning them, simply because we hold that constitution is not identity. That is to say, we hold that a composite object which, like a mountain, is capable of undergoing *change* of composition, is not to be *identified* with the mereological sum or fusion of its component parts at any time. If we did not hold this – if we held instead that constitution *is* identity – then, of course, we would have to say that there is 'no fact of the matter' as to *which* persisting object is Mount Everest at any given time, because we would have to regard the many numerically distinct, but very largely overlapping, mereological sums of bits of rock in its vicinity as being different but equally good candidates for *being* (that is, being *identical* with) Mount Everest. This would commit us to vagueness of *identity* where mountains are concerned. As it is, however, we can maintain that there is only *one* 'candidate' for *being* Mount Everest at any given time – Mount Everest itself – and that the various different but very largely overlapping mereological sums of bits of rock in its vicinity are merely different candidates for being 'the' sum that constitutes Mount Everest at any given time. (Because we are here considering only questions of *synchronic* identity, we are entitled to ignore, for present purposes, the issues concerning vagueness in persistence that arose in the previous section.)

We can say exactly the same with regard to Alpha and Beta, provided that we distinguish between identity and constitution. We can say, thus, that there is 'no fact of the matter' as to *precisely which* merelogical sums of bits of rock compose Alpha, and equally as to *precisely which* compose Beta, at any given time. However, although many of the mereological sums that are candidates for constituting Alpha will overlap a little with many of the mereological sums that are candidates for constituting Beta at any given time – which is why there is, supposedly, 'no fact of the matter' as to where Alpha gives way to Beta – we clearly should *not* say that any of the mereological sums that are candidates for constituting *Alpha* are *also* candidates for constituting *Beta* at any given time. And that is why we can assert – at this stage of our inquiries, at least – that Alpha and Beta are two distinct mountains, contrary to the absurd conclusion of the fallacious Sorites-style reasoning described earlier. Rejecting that reasoning requires us to acknowledge that there can be vagueness of *constitution* where mountains are concerned, but it does not commit us to acknowledging that there can be vagueness of *identity* concerning them.

We need, however, to consider whether there might be any *other* kind of Sorites-style reasoning that might nevertheless be exploited to sustain, in a case involving mountains, the verdict that there is *no fact of the matter* as to whether 'one' mountain is identical with 'another'. As we shall now see, the answer to this question seems to be positive. The sort of reasoning that we are looking for seems to be provided by a case in which we have some mountainous terrain containing two peaks separated by a dip that is not deep enough to qualify definitely as a high pass between two different mountains nor shallow enough to qualify definitely as a saddle in a single double-peaked mountain. Here it really does look as though we are faced with indeterminacy of *mountain identity*, because it seems to be an open question whether we have in this case just *one* mountain or *two*.

So how, exactly, can Sorites-style reasoning be exploited to support this verdict? In the following way. If we consider all the various different mountain examples which might be constructed along the general lines that we have just been employing, they do seem *collectively* to fall into a Sorites-like series. At one end of this spectrum we seem to have a clear case of two mountains, separated by a deep valley, while at the other we seem to have a clear case of a single mountain, with just one peak. In between we have cases in which there are two peaks, separated by a progressively shallower dip. Our original case of Alpha and Beta seems clearly to fall into the region of this spectrum in which there are definitely two mountains, separated by a pass. Other cases seem clearly to fall into the region of the spectrum in which there is definitely just one saddle-backed mountain. In the middle of the spectrum are the cases in which we don't know whether to say that we have two mountains separated by a high pass or just one double-peaked mountain possessing a deep saddle. Here the tolerance principle at work seems to be something like this: moving from a two-mountain case to another case with only a slightly shallower dip between the peaks always takes us to *another two-mountain case*. The Sorites-style reasoning is still fallacious, of course, but *rejecting* it seems to require us to recognize intermediate cases which are neither definitely two-mountain cases nor definitely one-mountain cases – and that implies that there can sometimes fail to be a fact of the matter about mountain identity. That seems to be the way in which Sorites-type considerations can be exploited to support the view that mountain identity is sometimes indeterminate or vague.

2.9 Does the Notion of Vague Existence Make Any Sense?

There are, however, reasons to be cautious about how we should interpret the conclusion reached at the end of the previous section. We should perhaps agree, for the sort of reasons given there, that there can sometimes fail to be a fact of the matter about synchronic mountain identity – and quite possibly, for that matter, about diachronic car identity too. If that *is* the case where mountains are concerned, however, then perhaps we should take the lesson to be that *mountains* don't really exist at all because what counts as 'one' of them is simply *not well-defined*. (We shall, however, need to qualify this judgement in an important way very shortly.) But that being so, it is just *trivially* true that there can sometimes be 'no fact of the matter' where statements of mountain identity are concerned: trivially true, because it then turns out that there is 'no fact of the matter' where *any* statement putatively about mountains is concerned, such as 'Sir Edmund Hillary and Tenzing Norgay climbed *a mountain* in 1953'. If such a statement contains a term that is not well-defined, then it doesn't express a proposition. As the famous physicist Paul Dirac once said of a theory of which he disapproved, it is *not even false*.

In the light of this verdict, let us now qualify something that was said a moment ago. It was said, in effect, that if there can fail to be a fact of the matter about the identity of *F*s – where '*F*' is a sortal term – then we should assert that *Fs don't really exist*. But this is an infelicitous, if natural, way of making the relevant point. The relevant point is that sortal terms are by definition *count* nouns, so that if '*F*' is a sortal term and yet what *counts* as 'one' *F* is *not well-defined*, then '*F*' is semantically defective: it simply doesn't behave, semantically, in the way that a sortal term is *supposed* to behave (for more on which see Lowe, 1989). Consequently, the sincere use of '*F*' in attempts to make true or false assertions is conceptually confused. *No* literally true or false assertion can be made using such a term, because no sentence containing it even *expresses a proposition*. Hence, if 'mountain' is such a term – which it seemingly is – then the sentence 'There are no mountains' cannot literally be true. Equally, of course, 'There *are* mountains' cannot literally be true either. Even so, there can be a point in saying, to someone who is under the illusion of supposing that 'There are mountains' expresses a literal and obvious truth, 'There aren't *really* any mountains'. This can be said precisely as a way of conveying the fact that 'mountain' is a semantically defective sortal term. But it is a potentially dangerous way of trying to convey that message, because it could easily be confused with a quite different message. There are in fact philosophers who believe that 'mountain', 'car', and the like are not *semantically defective* at all and yet that the actual extension of these terms is empty: they believe, quite literally, that 'There are no mountains' expresses a *truth* (see, for example, van Inwagen, 1990 and Merricks, 2001, both of whom deny the existence of composite objects of most of the sorts posited by common sense, excepting only living beings in the case of van Inwagen and conscious beings in the case of Merricks).

The latter is certainly not the position being recommended here. So, it is probably better for us *not* say 'There aren't *really* any mountains', even if this then invites the confusion that we don't reject, as we now propose to, the literal truth of 'There are mountains'. Since we are proposing that 'mountain' is semantically defective, the safest thing for us to do is never to *use* it, but only to *mention* it, in characterizing our proposed position – tedious and inconvenient though sticking to this regime can be. Of course, this then raises the question of what we *should* say, when we want to convey certain orological facts, given that we think that we should, strictly speaking, abjure any use of the word 'mountain'. We shall come back to this question later. Until then, we shall ignore the foregoing recommendation and continue to say 'There are *really* no *F*s', when strictly what we mean to say is that '*F*' is semantically defective.

Returning from this minor digression to our main theme: it transpires, if what we have said so far is correct, that there can be no *interesting* cases of indeterminacy of identity that arise for the kind of Sorites-style reasons described earlier, because if those reasons are sound, they undermine any case for supposing that objects of the putative sorts concerned *really exist at all.* What is interesting about the *electrons* example, by way of contrast, is that it does not cast any doubt whatever on the existence of electrons. The notion of vague *existence* apparently does not make sense, for reasons to which we shall turn shortly. If there is some sortal term, '*F*', such that there are good grounds for supposing that there can be 'no fact of the matter' as to whether 'There exist exactly *n* *F*s' is true, then that is a good reason to hold that '*F*' is *not well-defined* – that it lacks a determinate meaning and so cannot help to determine a propositional content for any statement containing it, with the consequence that any such statement lacks a truth-value. 'Electron' is apparently not such a term: at least, the example discussed earlier does not imply that it is, since it was never in dispute that there were exactly *two* electrons involved. And yet, as this example seems to show, there sometimes can be 'no fact of the matter' concerning the diachronic *identity* of electrons. The lesson, if we are right, is that vague – or, as we might prefer to describe it, *indeterminate* – identity doesn't necessarily imply vague existence. It seems, however, that any putative example of vague identity that *does* imply vague existence, such as the mountain case described earlier, turns out to be self-undermining, because it impugns the very applicability to the real world of the sortal terms concerned – in this case, 'mountain'.

It may nevertheless seem puzzling to say that vague identity does not necessarily imply vague existence, because it is widely supposed that the concepts of identity and existence are intimately linked in a way that would appear to sustain this implication. It seems safe to say that, currently, the 'default' position concerning the meaning of 'exists' is that associated with Frege, Russell, and Quine, according to which 'exists' is a 'second-level' predicate expressed by means of the so-called existential quantifier. According to this view, in a nutshell, '*a* exists' means 'There is something *x* such that *a* is identical with *x*' or, more formally, 'E!*a*' is logically equivalent to '$(\exists x)\ (x = a)$'. More long-windedly, the view is that what it means to say that *a* exists is just that *the first-level property of being identical with a has at least one instance* – of course, it can't have *more* than one, given the logical properties of the identity relation – so that to make a statement of existence with regard to an object, *a*, is really to predicate a *second-level* property (the property of having at least one instance) of a certain first-level property involving *a*. But suppose that '*a*' is a name for an *electron* and that we are right in maintaining that, in the example discussed earlier, there is 'no fact of the matter' concerning the diachronic identity of the two electrons involved. How, then, given the foregoing doctrine concerning the meaning of 'exists', can we deny that there is any vagueness about the *existence* of these electrons? For, on the standard view, to say that one of these electrons *exists* is just to say that there is something that is *identical* with it – and if there is *indeterminacy* of identity where such electrons are concerned, it would seem to follow that there must be indeterminacy of *existence* too.

Very probably this *does* follow, but we may be inclined to respond simply by saying *so much the worse for that view of existence*. We may just regard this as further evidence against a view that is, in any case, more than a little dubious. We are, of course, by no means alone in querying the Frege–Russell–Quine doctrine of existence (see, for instance, McGinn, 2000, Chapter 2). One fundamental objection to it is that, far from explaining what 'exists' means, it simply presupposes the notion of existence. It should really be obvious that to say that a first-level property 'has at least one instance' is just to say that *some object exists* that instantiates or exemplifies that property. Certainly, it cannot with any plausibility be maintained that the notion of an object's existing is conceptually posterior to that of a first-level property's having at least one instance (compare Lowe, 2003). An alternative view is that the notion of existence is primitive and indefinable, that 'exists' is a *first*-level predicate (that is, a predicate of *objects*, not of first-level properties), but that there is no *property*, in any ontologically robust sense of 'property', that it denotes or expresses. That is to say, 'exists' does not denote a *real universal* (for those who believe in universals), nor are there existence *tropes* (for those who believe in tropes). In other words, the concept of existence is a *formal* concept – which is not at all to imply that facts about existence or non-existence are in any sense conventional or mind-dependent. These are not claims that we have space to defend here in all the detail that they deserve (but see further Lowe, 2006, pp. 193–195). However, it is worth placing them on record to show that, having rejected the Frege–Russell–Quine view of existence, we are not left without anything positive to say about the notion.

More now needs to be said about why we should think that the notion of vague existence *makes no sense*. Various philosophers have claimed this, but they tend to presuppose the Frege–Russell–Quine view of existence. One thing that they say, for instance, is that since existence is what is expressed by the existential quantifier – which is a purely logical expression – and purely logical expressions can harbour no vagueness, we must conclude that the notion of vague existence makes no sense (see, for instance, Lewis, 1986, pp. 212–213 and Sider, 2001, p. 128, as mentioned in Section 2.7 above). This view is usually advanced on the presumption that all vagueness is essentially semantic in origin and that purely logical expressions cannot be the source of semantically-based vagueness. For our own part, we may be happy to concede that purely logical expressions cannot be the source of semantically-based vagueness. There is no inconsistency between our acceptance of this and our proposal that, in a case like that of the electrons, there is indeterminacy of identity: for, although we should be happy enough to classify 'is identical with' as being a purely logical expression, we do not regard the indeterminacy of identity in such a case as being semantical in origin. Rather, we propose to regard this as a case of *ontic* indeterminacy. But to return to the main question at issue – why we should think that the notion of vague existence makes no sense – the most important point seems to be that existence as such is always an *all or nothing* affair. There is simply no room for 'borderline cases' where existence as such is concerned. This, no doubt, is why we find Lewis Carroll's description of the Cheshire Cat in *Alice's Adventures in Wonderland* so amusing: recall that he describes it as gradually fading away until only its grin remained, whereupon that too finally disappeared.

It should be stressed that, according to our own proposals, there are equally no genuine borderline cases where *identity* is concerned – for, as was made clear earlier, none is involved in the example of the two electrons (This is why we might prefer to describe it as a case of *indeterminacy* of identity rather than of *vague* identity). But that then raises the question of why we shouldn't allow that *existence*, likewise, might be indeterminate without being vague. Now, in one qualified sense we should perhaps be prepared to allow this. We should perhaps be prepared to allow that it might be indeterminate when a persisting object *begins* or *ceases* to exist. Indeed, we should perhaps even prepared to allow that this might be *vague*, for reasons given in Section 2.7 above. (In saying this we are not going back on our earlier repudiation of Carroll-style 'fading out of existence', since we are only admitting a temporal analogue of the kind of boundary-indeterminacy that we find in the Alpha and Beta example, which is really at bottom an indeterminacy of *constitution*.) What we very arguably should *not* be prepared to allow is that it could be indeterminate whether or not something exists *simpliciter*. It might be indeterminate or indeed vague, for instance, whether Tibbles the cat *still exists* at a certain time t – although only because it might be indeterminate or vague whether any of various aggregates of feline tissue existing at t still *constitutes* Tibbles at t. But it is hard to see how it could be indeterminate whether Tibbles ever existed *at all*. Admittedly, it is not clear how one could *argue* for this in any way that wouldn't be open to a charge of question-begging. Indeed, we are hampered in this respect if we regard the notion of existence as primitive and indefinable. But, in any case, it is perfectly clear that our example of the electrons does not provide even a *prima facie* instance of indeterminate or vague existence, in the way that it does of indeterminate identity, because in that example *precisely two electrons existed* throughout the period in question in the region of space concerned – for precisely two electrons existed at the beginning, precisely two at the end, and no electron was created or destroyed during the intervening time.

Now we need to return to some more unfinished business, namely, to the question of what we ought to say about certain orological facts that users of ordinary language are apt to attempt to describe by using the (by our account) defective sortal term 'mountain'. As was stressed earlier, although it is tempting to say that, since this term is defective, *there are really no mountains*, this is at best misleading. Above all, it is important not to confuse the view that 'mountain' is a defective sortal term with the sceptical or 'nihilist' view that 'There are no mountains' is strictly and literally true. In fact, taking the view recommended here about the semantic deficiencies of sortal terms such as 'mountain' (and perhaps 'car') has, in itself, no deep ontological implications at all. It doesn't imply that speakers of ordinary language are seriously mistaken about the nature of the extralinguistic reality that they attempt to describe by using it. It just means that they use grammatically inappropriate expressions in making these attempts. What is 'out there' in the world, where they say that there are 'mountains', is just some steeply undulating – or, as we may quite innocently say, *mountainous* – terrain. (There is nothing wrong about talking of 'mountainous terrain', so long as we don't interpret this as simply *meaning* 'terrain *containing mountains*'.) The expression 'mountainous terrain' is, grammatically speaking, a *mass* noun rather than a count noun: we may have *more or less* mountainous terrain here or there, but not some *number* of it, in the way that one can have some number of electrons in a given region of space or some number of people in a room. Crucially, everything *geographically* important that one might want to say, in the language of 'mountains', about some geographical region could equally, if less conveniently, be said in the language of 'mountainous terrain'. For instance, instead of saying that this mountain is higher than that one, we can say that the mountainous terrain over here is higher than the mountainous terrain over there. So it would be quite wrong to say that *mountain scepticism* is a consequence of our recommended view.

Even so, it may be suggested that our recommended view regarding 'mountains' harbours a paradox. The suspected problem is as follows – and for this purpose we shall revert, temporarily, to the reprehensible but convenient practice of characterizing our view as being one according to which *there are really no mountains*. In these terms, then, we have suggested that because 'mountain' is a defective sortal term – in that what counts as 'one mountain' is not well-defined – it follows that *there are really no mountains*. However – and this is the potential problem – 'sortal term' is *itself* a sortal term. Moreover, if our preceding arguments so far are correct, it might appear that it is a *defective* sortal term. Why? Because, it may be contended, what counts as *one (non-defective) sortal term* is not well-defined. How so? Well, we might try to reason, Sorites-style, as follows. On the one hand we have (according to our recommended view) certain definitely *non-defective* sortal terms, such as 'electron', and on the other we have certain definitely *defective* ones, such as 'mountain'. But it might seem that these examples lie at the opposite ends of a Sorites-like spectrum, with borderline cases in between of sortal terms that are neither definitely defective nor definitely non-defective. But in that case, it seems, 'sortal term' is *itself* a defective sortal term, for the same sort of reason that (according to our recommended view) 'mountain' is. Hence, we seem to be committed to saying that *there are really no non-defective sortal terms*, precisely in the way that we are proposing to say that there are really no mountains. But in that case we cannot consistently say, after all, that 'electron' or indeed any other sortal term is non-defective. Hence, it seems, we are committed to saying *there is really nothing at all*, at least in the sense that there are really no *sorts* or *kinds* of thing at all – no *F*s, for any sortal term '*F*' whatsoever. And that looks perilously close to nihilism.

Fortunately, it does not in fact appear that there is a genuine paradox in the making here. First of all, it should be emphasized once again that we don't *literally* want to say that *there are really no mountains*. Our proposed view about 'mountains' has no very deep ontological implications, as was made clear earlier. So there is no general threat of nihilism posed by the foregoing considerations. Even so, it would be worrying if the distinction between defective and non-defective sortal terms turned out not to be a sharp one, for this would indeed seem to imply, by our lights, that 'non-defective sortal term' is defective. But *is there* in fact any good reason to think that the distinction is not a sharp one? It doesn't seem so. A sortal term like 'electron', we want to say, is *non-defective*, because it is well-defined what counts as one electron. And a sortal term like 'mountain', we want to say, is *defective*, because it is *not* well-defined what counts as one mountain. So what would a borderline case of a non-defective sortal term be? Presumably, a sortal term '*F*' such that it is *not well-defined* whether it is well-defined what counts as one *F*. But that seems impossible. Either it *is* well-defined what counts as one *F* or it is *not* well-defined what counts as one *F*. If, *per impossibile*, it were *not well-defined* whether it was well-defined what counts as one *F*, then in fact it would *not* be well-defined what counts as one *F*. Being well-defined, by its very nature, does not seem to admit of borderline cases.

2.10 Concluding Remarks

We may conclude with a brief summary of our findings in this chapter. We have found reason to question the validity of Gareth Evans's famous argument against vague *identity* and to countenance the possibility of genuine *ontic* indeterminacy of identity, but only in rather arcane cases thrown up by quantum physics involving so-called 'entangled' particles. Even there, however, we have found no reason to countenance the possibility of vague *existence*, which is a notion that seems to make no clear sense. As for the possibility of vagueness of *constitution*, *composition*, and *persistence*, we have observed that *semantic* accounts of the source of such vagueness are readily available for cases involving macroscopic material objects, but have also found that such accounts are not the exclusive preserve of any particular metaphysical theory of such objects and their persistence through time, such as the perdurance view with its advocacy of an ontology of temporal parts or stages. We have acknowledged that Sorites-style reasoning, which figures so prominently in the wider philosophical literature on vagueness, has a part to play in the metaphysics of vagueness. We have concluded, however, that rather than sustaining the view that we need to accept vagueness of identity as a ubiquitous feature of common-sense ontology, such reasoning really serves only to show that everyday language is replete with *defective sortal terms*, such as 'mountain', which cannot be used to make assertions that are literally true or false. The lesson, we believe, is not that a radical scepticism or nihilism with regard to common-sense ontology is called for, but merely that everyday language makes over-abundant use of sortal terms – no doubt on account of their pragmatic convenience – where *mass* terms, such as 'mountainous terrain', would strictly speaking be more appropriate. In sum, apart from the interesting case for indeterminate identity at the quantum level, it does not appear that issues to do with vagueness threaten to have any far-reaching impact on questions of fundamental metaphysics and ontology. This is not to say that metaphysicians can safely afford to ignore such issues altogether, but only that there is little reason to suppose that their resolution will settle any longstanding disputes in metaphysics, such as that between perdurantists and endurantists concerning the persistence of material objects through time. That may not be an exciting conclusion, but if correct may at least encourage metaphysicians to look for more fruitful ways of settling their differences than by appeal to considerations concerning vagueness. (For another perspective on the issues discussed in this chapter, see Williamson, 2003.)

References

Cowles, D. (1994), "On van Inwagen's Defense of Vague Identity", *Philosophical Perspectives* 8: 137–158.

Evans, G. (1978), "Can There Be Vague Objects?" *Analysis* 38: 208.

French, S. and Krause, D. (2006), *Identity in Physics: A Historical, Philosophical, and Formal Analysis*, Oxford: Clarendon Press.

Geach, P.T. (1980), *Reference and Generality*, 3rd edn, Ithaca, NY: Cornell University Press.

Hawley, K. (1998), "Indeterminism and Indeterminacy", *Analysis* 58: 101–106.

Hawley, K. (2001), *How Things Persist*, Oxford: Oxford University Press.

Heck, R. (1998), That There Might Be Vague Objects (So Far as Concerns Logic), *The Monist* 81: 274–296.

Hirsch, E. (1999), "The Vagueness of Identity", *Philosophical Topics* 26: 139–158.

Keefe, R. (1995), "Contingent Identity and Vague Identity", *Analysis* 55: 183–190.

Keefe, R. (2000), *Theories of Vagueness*, Cambridge: Cambridge University Press.

Koslicki, K. (2003), "The Crooked Path from Vagueness to Four-Dimensionalism", *Philosophical Studies* 114: 107–134.

Kripke, S.A. (1971), Identity and Necessity, In Munitz, M.K. (ed.), *Identity and Individuation*. New York, NY: New York University Press.

Lewis, D. (1986), *On the Plurality of Worlds*, Oxford: Blackwell.

Lewis, D. (1993), Many, but Almost One, In Bacon, J. Campbell K. and Reinhardt, L. (eds), *Ontology, Causality and Mind: Essays in Honour of D. M. Armstrong*, Cambridge: Cambridge University Press.

Lewis, D.K. (1988), "Vague Identity: Evans Misunderstood", *Analysis* 48: 128–130.

Lowe, E.J. (1982a), "On the Alleged Necessity of True Identity Statements". *Mind* 91: 579–584.
Lowe, E.J. (1982b), "The Paradox of the 1,001 Cats", *Analysis* 42: 27–30.
Lowe, E.J. (1982c), "Reply to Geach", *Analysis* 42: 31.
Lowe, E.J. (1982d), "On Being a Cat", *Analysis* 42: 174–177.
Lowe, E.J. (1989), *Kinds of Being: A Study of Individuation, Identity and the Logic of Sortal Terms*, Oxford: Blackwell.
Lowe, E.J. (1994), "Vague Identity and Quantum Indeterminacy", *Analysis* 54: 110–114.
Lowe, E.J. (1995), "The Problem of the Many and the Vagueness of Constitution", *Analysis* 55: 179–182.
Lowe, E.J. (1997), "Reply to Noonan on Vague Identity", *Analysis* 57: 88–91.
Lowe, E.J. (1998), *The Possibility of Metaphysics: Substance, Identity and Time*, Oxford: Clarendon Press.
Lowe, E.J. (2003), "Identity, Individuality and Unity", *Philosophy* 78: 321–336.
Lowe, E.J. (2005), "Vagueness and Endurance", *Analysis* 65: 104–112.
Lowe, E.J. (2006), *The Four-Category Ontology: A Metaphysical Foundation for Natural Science*, Oxford: Clarendon Press.
McCall, S. and Lowe, E.J. (2003), "3D/4D Equivalence, the Twins Paradox and Absolute Time", *Analysis* 63: 114–123.
McGinn, C. (2000), *Logical Properties: Identity, Existence, Predication, Necessity, Truth*, Oxford: Clarendon Press.
McKinnon, N. (2002), "Supervaluations and the Problem of the Many", *The Philosophical Quarterly* 52: 320–339.
Merricks, T. (2001), *Objects and Persons*, Oxford: Clarendon Press.
Miller, K. (2005), "Blocking the Path from Vagueness to Four-Dimensionalism", *Ratio* 18: 317–31.
Noonan, H.W. (1982), "Vague Objects", *Analysis* 42: 3–6.
Noonan, H.W. (1995), "E. J. Lowe on Vague Identity and Quantum Indeterminacy", *Analysis* 55: 14–19.
Over, D.E. (1989), "Vague Objects and Identity", *Analysis* 49: 97–99.
Parsons, T. (2000), *Indeterminate Identity: Metaphysics and Semantics*, Oxford: Clarendon Press.
Sainsbury, R. M. (1989), "What Is a Vague Object?" *Analysis* 49: 99–103.
Salmon, N. (1982), *Reference and Essence*, Oxford: Blackwell.
Sanford, D. (1993), "The Problem of the Many, Many Composition Questions, and Naïve Mereology", *Noûs* 27: 219–228.
Sider, T. (2001), *Four-Dimensionalism: An Ontology of Persistence and Time*, Oxford: Clarendon Press.
Thomason, R. (1982), "Identity and Vagueness", *Philosophical Studies* 42: 329–332.
Tye, M. (1990), "Vague Objects", *Mind* 99: 535–557.
Unger, P. (1980), "The Problem of the Many", *Midwest Studies in Philosophy* 5: 411–467. Minneapolis: University of Minnesota Press.
van Inwagen, P. (1990), *Material Beings*, Ithaca, NY: Cornell University Press.
Weatherson, B. (2003), "Many Many Problems", *The Philosophical Quarterly* 53: 481–501.
Wiggins, D. (2001), *Sameness and Substance Renewed*, Cambridge: Cambridge University Press.
Williamson, T. (1996), The Necessity and Determinacy of Distinctness, In Lovibond, S. and Williams, S. (eds), *Essays for David Wiggins: Identity, Truth and Value*, Oxford: Blackwell.
Williamson, T. (2002), Vagueness, Identity, and Leibniz's Law, In Giaretta, P. Bottani, A. and Carrara, M. (eds), *Individuals, Essence and Identity: Themes of Analytic Metaphysics*, Dordrecht: Kluwer.
Williamson, T. (2003), Vagueness in Reality, In Loux, M.J. and Zimmerman, D.W. (eds), *The Oxford Handbook of Metaphysics*, Oxford: Oxford University Press.
Zemach, E. (1991), "Vague Objects", *Noûs* 25: 323–340.

Chapter 3
Vagueness and Logic

Stewart Shapiro

3.1 Setting Up

To speak roughly, there are at least two approaches to logic. One of them takes logic to be the (or a) canon of correct *inference*. It thus focuses on the rules of correct reasoning. On this approach, an argument in a formal language is valid if its conclusion can be reached from its premises by invoking the stipulated rules of inference. Nowadays, the rules are typically given by introduction and elimination rules that are supposed to be constitutive of the meaning of the logical terminology.

The other approach to logic is model-theoretic. The logician provides a range of interpretations, or models, of the formal language. An argument is valid if its conclusion is true in every interpretation that makes the premises true.

To illustrate the differences, consider the rule of modus ponens, or arrow elimination, which allows one to infer a conclusion Φ from premises in the form Ψ and $\Psi\rightarrow\Phi$. On the deductive approach, this rule is at least partly constitutive of the meaning of the arrow, or the English phrase "if . . . then". So, on the deductive account, if a logician wants to reject this inference, she will be disputing, or perhaps changing, the meaning of the arrow or of the English phrase, "if . . . then". She might argue that these terms have a different meaning, or that there is nothing that has the supposed meaning, or that the connective or phrase with the supposed meaning is not appropriate in a particular discourse.

On a model-theoretic account, the rule of modus ponens is valid if every interpretation of the language in which sentences in the form Ψ and $\Psi\rightarrow\Phi$ are both true also makes Φ true. A logician who disputes the validity of this inference will claim that there are legitimate interpretations for which this is not so. This, too, seems to turn on the meaning of the arrow or the English phrase, but the dispute concerns a different aspect of this meaning.

I opt for a model-theoretic approach here. The plan of this survey is to discuss the sort of model-theory that is suggested (or demanded) by the main, rival accounts of

S. Shapiro (✉)
The Ohio State University, Columbus, OH, USA; The University of St. Andrews, St. Andrews, UK
e-mail: shapiro.4@osu.edu

G. Ronzitti (ed.), *Vagueness: A Guide*, Logic, Epistemology, and the Unity of Science 19, DOI 10.1007/978-94-007-0375-9_3,

vagueness, and to thereby delineate the logic of each. To be precise, I will try to indicate, in each case, what the logic would be if the account in question were correct.

Since the main logical problem facing vagueness is the sorites paradox, the present survey will assess what each account has to say about typical sorites arguments. To fix an example, consider a series of one billion people. The first is 1 second old, and each person in the series, after the first, is 1 second older than the one just before. For convenience, use the first billion natural numbers, starting with 1, as names of the people in the list. So, for each $n \leq 1{,}000{,}000{,}000$, person n is exactly n seconds old. Let Cx say that x is a child (in the everyday, non-legal sense). Clearly, $C1$ and $\neg C10^9$ (since 10^9 seconds is a bit over 31 years). One version of the sorites argument has a billion premises:

$$\begin{array}{l} C1 \\ C1 \rightarrow C2 \\ C2 \rightarrow C3 \\ \ldots \\ C999{,}999{,}999 \rightarrow C1{,}000{,}000{,}000 \\ \hline C1{,}000{,}000{,}000 \end{array}$$

The conclusion follows from the premises by 999,999,999 instances of modus ponens. Another version of the argument introduces notation for the natural numbers. It has only two premises:

$$\begin{array}{l} C1 \\ \forall x < 1{,}000{,}000{,}000(Cx \rightarrow C(x+1)) \\ \hline C1{,}000{,}000{,}000 \end{array}$$

The second line of this argument is sometimes called the *inductive premise*. The conclusion follows from the two premises, together with some uncontroversial principles about the natural numbers.

In both arguments, the first premise is clearly true and the conclusion clearly false. So, to show what has gone wrong – if, indeed, something has – one must either show that modus ponens fails, at least when it is applied that many times in succession, or else show that at least one of the conditionals in the first argument and the inductive premise in the second argument fail to be true. Of course, the different accounts of vagueness do this in different ways. These ways are reflected in the model theories.

In the cases at hand, the conditionals and the inductive premise are plausible. How can a single second mark the transition from being a child to being in a state which incompatible with childhood? Maturity, and adulthood, are gradual transitions, not accomplished in a moment. In any standard model-theoretic interpretation, however, if $C1$ is true and $C10^9$ is false, then the inductive premise $\forall x(Cx \rightarrow C(x{+}1))$ is also false, as is at least one of the conditionals in the first argument. This is because in standard interpretations, the extension of each predicate is a set, which has sharp boundaries. For each set s and each object o in the domain of the interpretation, either $o \in s$ or $o \notin s$. So if, in a given interpretation of the language, the object denoted by 1 is in the extension of C and if the object denoted by 10^9 is not in the extension of C, then there must be a natural number $n < 10^9$ such that the object denoted by n is in the extension of C, but the object denoted by $n + 1$ is not in the extension of C, in that same interpretation. Such is number theory (and set theory).

As a first shot at our problem, then, it seems that the practice of assigning a subset of the domain of discourse to each predicate of the language is in conflict with the intuitive thought that sanctions the inductive premise of the second argument and the myriad (or, to be more precise, the 100,000-fold myriad) of material conditionals in the first.

Model theory has enjoyed considerable success in logic, linguistics, and philosophy – intuitionism notwithstanding. So one would be loath to give it up. In addition, there are some pragmatic reasons to maintain classical logic. The underlying set theory is well-understood and the framework has nice meta-theoretic properties, including a complete and tractable deductive system. Moreover, model theory is familiar to just about everyone working in philosophy. It is common for theorists to tout the acceptability of classical logic – if not full model theory – as a virtue of their views. That is, the familiarity of the proposed logic is sometimes taken as a plus, to be weighed against any defects the theory may have, with respect to rival proposals that demand a non-classical logic.

One should note, however, that model theory was developed, originally, to shed light on the logic of (classical) *mathematical* languages, and those, it seems, do not exhibit vagueness. In logic, then, the main tool we have, and are keen to employ, was not designed to accommodate vagueness, and it may be too much of a stretch to demand, or even hope, that it do so. The familiarity of model-theoretic semantics is not an argument that it is appropriate outside of mathematics.

Note also that although the foregoing argument relies on the law of excluded middle and the classical notion of set, in the meta-theory, it would not help to switch to an intuitionistic background. The only substantial inference invoked, in the object language, is modus ponens, which is acceptable to the intuitionist. Moreover, for the intuitionist and the classicist alike, if, in a given interpretation of the language, the object denoted by 1 is in the extension of C and the object denoted by 10^9 is not in the extension of C, then it is not the case that for every natural number $n < 10^9$, if n is in the extension of C, then so is $n + 1$. And it is not the case that every conditional in the first argument is true if the first premise is and the conclusion is false (see Read and Wright, 1985; Chambers, 1998, responses to Putnam, 1983).

3.2 The Ordinary Model Theory Will Do

There are at least two views on offer that do not demand any changes to standard model-theoretic semantics, or at least none motivated by the vagueness of ordinary discourse. One is a sort of nihilistic position. In a nutshell, the argument begins with the intuitions that support the conditionals in the first argument form and the inductive premise of the second argument form. A single second does not and cannot mark any kind of transition out of childhood; a single hair cannot take a man from being bald to not being bald, etc. Vague predicates seem to be tolerant in this way, and, on this view, they are as they seem. According to the view in question, the proper conclusion to draw from the sorites arguments is that vague language is ultimately incoherent. If there were coherent vague predicates, we would have to hold that people 10^9s old are still children, that a stack of millions of grains of sand is not a heap, and that a man with 30,000 hairs is bald. Some versions of this view come with pragmatic advice on how to deploy vague predicates, but, strictly speaking, there can be no sound *logic* for them (see, for example, Dummett, 1975; Horgan, 1994). Logic, properly so-called, only makes sense on sharply defined predicates.

In a sense, the so-called "epistemic" account of vagueness is the polar opposite of nihilism. The epistemicist holds that once contextual and indexical elements are taken into account, all legitimate predicates, including vague ones, have sharply delineated boundaries. So there is a single nanosecond upon which a given person stops being a child and assumes a status incompatible with childhood. There is a single number of hairs (and an arrangement thereof) that marks the end of baldness and the beginning of its complement, and there is a single nanosecond that marks the very last time a person can show up and have it be "around noon". The epistemicist typically argues that with vague predicates, the exact boundaries are not known, nor are they knowable—thus the name "epistemicism". The slogan is that vagueness is a purely epistemic matter. As far as model theory, and logic, go, however, the ordinary, classical framework is the correct one. Standard model theory gives the proper semantics for vague discourse (Sorenson, 2001; Williamson, 1994).

Of course, there is a lot to be said for and against those views, and the literature on them is extensive. But we need not dwell on them in a survey on the logic of vagueness. On both views, the model theory, and thus the logic, is the familiar one from our logic classes.

3.3 Partial Interpretations, and Sharpenings Thereof

Something in the neighborhood of epistemicism is a straightforward consequence of imposing ordinary model-theoretic semantics, in a classical meta-theory, on a language with vague predicates. The practice of assigning sets (with sharp boundaries) to predicates seems to deny the very phenomena of vagueness, at anything but an epistemic level. So if we are to embrace something other than a nihilistic or epistemicist view, we will need to modify the model theory.

Intuitively, some people are clearly children, at least the first 300,000,000 people in our sorites series, and some people are clearly not children, at least the last 300,000,000. Somewhere in the middle of the series, there are borderline cases, which are neither clearly children nor clearly non-children. To accommodate this intuition, we introduce the notion of a *partial interpretation*. This is a pair $M = <d,I>$, where d is a non-empty set – the domain of discourse—and I is a function which provides interpretations of the non-logical terminology. Let R be an n-place relation letter. In the partial interpretation $M = <d,I>$, IR is a pair $<p,q>$ of sets such that $p \subseteq d^n$, $q \subseteq d^n$, and p is disjoint from q. The set p is the *extension* of R in the partial interpretation, the n-tuples of objects to which the relation applies in the interpretation M, and q is the *anti-extension* of R, the n-tuples of objects to which the relation fails to apply in M. If $IR = <p,q>$, then define $IR^+ = p$ and $IR^- = q$. Any n-tuples from the domain of discourse d that are in neither IR^+ nor IR^- are *borderline cases* of R in the partial interpretation M.

If $IR^+ \cup IR^- = d^n$, then R has no borderline cases in M, in which case we say that R is *sharp* in M. A partial interpretation M is *completely sharp* if every relation in the language is sharp in M. A completely sharp interpretation corresponds to a classical interpretation since, in that case, the anti-extension of each predicate is just the complement of the extension.

We introduce a "three-valued" semantics on partial interpretations. The "values" are **t** (truth), **f** (falsehood), and **i** (indeterminate). For some purposes, it is convenient to not think of **i** as a truth-value on a par with truth and falsehood. Think of **i** as indicating the lack of a standard truth-value in the given partial interpretation.

The atomic cases are straightforward:

> Let $M = <d,I>$ be a partial interpretation and s an assignment of a member of d to every variable. Let R be an n-place predicate letter, and $t_1, \ldots t_n$ terms. For each i, let m_i be the denotation of t_i under M,s. Then $Rt_1 \ldots t_n$ is true in M,s if $<m_1, \ldots, m_n>$ is in IR^+; $Rt_1 \ldots t_n$ is false in M,s if $<m_1, \ldots, m_n>$ is in IR^-; and $Rt_1 \ldots t_n$ is indeterminate in M,s otherwise.

There are a number of different options for the connectives. Here, we use the strong, internal choice negation. Its truth table is the following:

Φ	$\neg\Phi$
t	**f**
f	**t**
i	**i**

For the other connectives, we employ the strong-Kleene truth tables. The main idea is that if we have enough information to give a compound a standard truth-value (truth or falsehood), we do so:

$\Phi\&\Psi$	**t**	**f**	**i**
t	**t**	**f**	**i**
f	**f**	**f**	**f**
i	**i**	**f**	**i**

$\Phi\vee\Psi$	**t**	**f**	**i**
t	**t**	**f**	**i**
f	**f**	**f**	**f**
i	**i**	**f**	**i**

$\Phi\rightarrow\Psi$	**t**	**f**	**i**
t	**t**	**f**	**i**
f	**t**	**t**	**t**
i	**t**	**i**	**i**

One important feature of the system, as developed so far, is that the language is truth-functional, in the sense that the truth-value (or lack thereof) of a compound is a function of the truth-values (or lack thereof) of the parts. Second, if the parts of a compound have standard truth-values, truth or falsehood, then the compound gets the truth-value it would have in a classical interpretation. So the model theory agrees with the classical one on completely sharp interpretations.

The quantifiers are also interpreted in line with the strong Kleene truth tables:

$\forall x\Phi$ is true in M,s if and only if Φ is true in M,s' for every assignment s' that agrees with s at every variable except possibly x; $\forall x\Phi$ is false in M,s if and only if there is an assignment s' that agrees with s except possibly at x such that Φ is false in M,s'; $\forall x\Phi$ is indeterminate in M,s otherwise.

$\exists x\Phi$ is true in M,s if and only if there is an assignment s' that agrees with s except possibly at x such that Φ is true in M,s'; $\exists x\Phi$ is false in M,s if and only if Φ is false in M,s' for every assignment s' that agrees with s at every variable except possibly x; $\exists x\Phi$ is indeterminate in M,s otherwise.

So far, we do not have a plausible model for a semantics of vagueness. The aforementioned truth-functionality is problematic. Suppose, for example, that a certain person t is a borderline case of a child. To express this in the semantics, we would make the statement Ct indeterminate. So $\neg Ct$ would also be indeterminate. But then both $(Ct\&\neg Ct)$ and $\neg(Ct\&\neg Ct)$ would also be indeterminate. This seems wrong. Even if it is indeterminate that person an child, it surely true that she is not both a child and not a child. Nothing can be a child and a non-child at the same time, and in the same respect.

For a second example, consider a pair of people, s, t. Both are borderline children, but suppose that s is a bit older than t. A partial interpretation that reflects this situation would have Cs and Ct both indeterminate, and so $Cs\rightarrow Ct$ is indeterminate. But surely the conditional should come out true, and not indeterminate. Even if s is a borderline child, it is still true that *if* she is a child, then so is t, since t is even younger.

The framework of supervaluation is intended to remedy this defect of the simple three-valued system, and head us toward a more plausible account of vagueness. Let $M_1 = <d_1,I_1>$ and $M_2 = <d_2,I_2>$ be partial interpretations. Say that $M_1 \leq M_2$ if:

(1) $d_1 = d_2$;
(2) the interpretation functions I_1 and I_2 agree on each constant and function letter; and
(3) for each relation letter R, $I_1{}^+R \subseteq I_2{}^+R$ and $I_1{}^-R \subseteq I_2{}^-R$.

The idea is that if $M_1 \leq M_2$ then the two interpretations agree on the clear (non-borderline) cases of M_1. But M_2 may give a standard truth-value, truth or falsehood, to atomic sentences that are indeterminate in M_1. If $M_1 \leq M_2$, say that M_2 *sharpens* M_1. Kit Fine, (1975) calls M_2 a "precisification" of M_1. Since $M_1 \leq M_1$, we say that each M_1 sharpens itself, conceding the abuse of ordinary language.

A straightforward induction on the complexity of formulas shows that the semantics is *monotone*: Suppose that $M_1 \leq M_2$, and let s be an assignment to the variables (over the common domain). If a formula Φ is true (resp. false) under s in M_1, then Φ is true (resp. false) under s in M_2. In other words, as we sharpen, we do not change the truth-values of formulas that have standard truth-values; we can only give truth-values to formulas that previously lacked them.

This result depends on the particular logical terminology in the object language, as defined by the above truth-tables. The following connective is sometimes called a weak, or external, or exclusion negation:

Φ	**∼Φ**
t	**f**
f	**t**
i	**t**

And here is an operator for a kind of determinacy:

Φ	**DΦ**
t	**t**
f	**f**
i	**f**

Both of these operators are what we may call "sharpeners", since they only take the standard truth-values as values. If our language had either of these operators, montonicty would fail. Suppose that a constant a denotes a borderline case of a predicate P in an interpretation M. Then since, in M, Pa is **i**, $\sim Pa$ is true and DPa is false. Let M_1 be a sharpening of M in which the object denoted by a is in the extension of P. Then $\sim Pa$ is false in M_1 and DPa is true in M_1.

Returning to the main theme, notice that not every sharpening is legitimate, or true to the meanings of the terms being modeled. Recall the above pair of people, s, t, where s is a bit older than t, but both are borderline cases of children. A sharpening that puts s in the extension and t in the anti-extension of the predicate C is not true to the meaning of the English word "child". Similarly, a sharpening that declares a man bald and declares a man with less hair (arranged similarly) to be not bald is likewise unacceptable.

Fine (1975) uses the term "penumbral connection" for relations that turn on the meaning of the vague terms. An example of a penumbral connection is that if someone is a child, then anyone younger is also a child. Another penumbral connection is that if someone is not wealthy, then neither is someone with less money (other things equal). Another is that nothing is both completely red and completely orange.

In giving an account of vagueness, we are only interested in the sharpenings that do not violate penumbral connections. Of course, formal languages do not have such penumbral connections; the non-logical predicate letters and constants have no pre-theoretic meaning at all. To reflect the underlying notion, we add another layer to the framework, along the lines of Kripke-structures for intuitionistic logic, but with provisions for anti-extensions.

Define a *frame* F to be a pair <W,M> in which W is a collection of partial interpretations, $M \in W$, and for every partial interpretation N in W, $M \leq N$ (so that all of the partial interpretations in W have the same domain). The designated partial interpretation M is the *base* of the frame F.

A frame is what Fine (1975) calls a "specification space", with each N in W being a "specification point". Burgess and Humberstone (1987) invoke a similar notion, but without a designated base.

The sentences that are true in the base M of a frame F = <W,M> represent *determinate* truths, and the sentences false at the base represent determinate falsehoods. The other sentences are indeterminate in that frame. Each sharpening in the frame represents one way that some indeterminacies can turn out, consistent with the meaning of the predicates, the non-linguistic facts, and any other contextual factors, such as the comparison class or paradigm cases of vague predicates.

A number of different, and competing, philosophical accounts of vagueness use a framework like this one. They differ in how they define the various logical notions, such as logical consequence, validity, and even truth, in terms of partial interpretations within frames. Let us turn to some of these views.

3.3.1 Supervaluation

Among philosophers, supervaluationism may well be the most popular view on vagueness. The main philosophical thesis is that a sentence Φ that contains vague terminology is considered true if it comes out true on all *acceptable sharpenings* of the language. And a sharpening is acceptable only if it respects penumbral connections and gets the clear, or determinate, cases right.

Fine's (1975) original articulation and defense of supervaluationism proposes a *completability requirement*, a thesis that every acceptable partial interpretation has an acceptable, *completely* sharp sharpening. Rosanna Keefe's (2000) more philosophical defense of supervaluation also presupposes completability. With this requirement in place, the main thesis of supervaluationism is that a sentence Φ is true if it comes out true on every acceptable, completely sharp sharpening of the language.

Formulating this in the present, formal context is straightforward. Say that a frame F = <W,M> is *complete* if, for each partial interpretation $N \in W$, there is a completely sharp $N' \in M$ such that $N \leq N'$. In words, a frame is complete if each partial interpretation in the frame has a completely sharp sharpening in the frame. The supervaluationist restricts attention to complete frames.

Let F be a complete frame and let Φ be a sentence in the formal language. Say that Φ is *super-true* in F if Φ is true in every completely sharp interpretation in F. The idea, again, is that Φ is super-true in the frame just in case Φ comes out true no matter how the vague predicates are sharpened in the frame. The mantra of supervaluationism is that truth is super-truth. So all of the semantic and logical notions are defined in terms of super-truth.

Along similar lines, define Φ to be *super-false* in F if Φ is false in every completely sharp interpretation in F. And Φ is *indeterminate* in F if it is neither super-true nor super-false. In other words, Φ is indeterminate in a complete frame just in case is comes out true on some completely sharp interpretations in the frame and false on others. In a sense, if Φ is indeterminate, then it can go either way. This is a richer notion than that of a sentence being indeterminate in a partial interpretation.

Notice that, in this setup, the only partial interpretations that matter are the base and the completely sharp ones. So the supervaluationist might as well just define a frame to be a base and a set of completely sharp sharpenings of it. Moreover, there is no need to evaluate formulas at the base. All of the action takes place in the completely sharp interpretations in the frame, and those are all classical. So the three-valued semantics sketched above does no work for the supervaluationist. We will maintain the general definition, however, so we can use it later to deal with other accounts of vagueness.

Let us characterize a complete frame F that models our foregoing sorites series. The domain of each partial interpretation in F is the set consisting of the billion people in the series. In the base of F, the extension of C consists of all of the people labeled with the numbers from 1 to, say, 400,000,000. The oldest person in that list is not quite 13 years old. The anti-extension of C at the base contains those labeled 700,000,000 and greater; the youngest of those is almost 23. The only penumbral connections we will consider are that if a person is a child, then anyone younger is also a child, and if a person is not a child, then anyone older is also not a child. So for each pair of numbers m,n, such that $400{,}000{,}000 < m \leq n < 700{,}000{,}000$, there is a partial interpretation N_{mn} in F in which the extension of C consists of the folks in the domain whose label is less than or equal to m and the anti-extension of C is the folks whose label is greater than n. Notice that F is complete. A completely sharp interpretation N_{mm} puts the border of childhood right at m: in N_{mm}, m is a child, and $m+1$ is not. And a sentence Φ is super-true in F just in case Φ is true in every interpretation of the form N_{mm}.

To labor the obvious, $C120$ is super-true. A person who is two minutes old is a child. Similarly, $C1{,}000{,}000{,}000$ is super-false, and, on this model, $C500{,}000{,}000$ is indeterminate. The latter is true on some completely sharp sharpenings in F and false on others.

Now consider the conditionals in the first sorites argument. For any $n < 1{,}000{,}000{,}000$, the sentence $Cn \rightarrow Cn+1$ is true in a partial interpretation N_{mm} in our frame if and only if $n \neq m$. So each completely sharp interpretation in F makes (exactly) one of the premises of the first argument false. This is enough to make it the case that some of the premises of the argument are not super-true. Indeed, $Cn \rightarrow Cn+1$ fails to be super-true for each n between 400,000,000 and 700,000,000.

Next recall the inductive premise of the second argument, $\forall x(Cx \rightarrow C(x+1))$. This is super-false, i.e., false on *every* completely sharp sharpening in our frame F. Once again, for the supervaluationist, for sentences with vague terms, truth is super-truth. So, according to the supervaluationist, neither of the sorites arguments is sound. Although the first one has no premises that are super-false, many of the premises fail to be super-true. The second argument has a super-false premise.

The (super-)falsity of the inductive premise illustrates a much discussed feature of the supervaluationist framework. Consider a (classical) contradictory to the inductive premise: $\exists x(Cx\&\neg Cx{+}1)$. This sentence is super-true in the frame F: every completely sharp interpretation in F does have a person in the extension of C where the next person, who is 1s older, is in the anti-extension of C. So our supervaluationist holds that (it is (super-)true that) there is a sharp boundary separating children from non-children. But, if n is any number in the given range, it is emphatically not the case that $Cn\&\neg Cn{+}1$ is super-true. Indeed, for each such n, the sentence in question is false in all but one of the 300 million completely sharp interpretations in F. In light of the slogan, our supervaluationist countenances existential statements that are true, but have no true instances. Burgess and Humberstone (1987, p. 226) put the criticism rather sharply:

> It is disconcerting to be told that while it is true that something is Φ, there is nothing of which it is true that that thing is Φ ... The usual reaction to this is to say that if we are told that for some n, [Φ (n)], then we are entitled to ask "Which n?". The reply, "Oh, for no particular n" appears sophistical.

Along similar lines, consider the instance of excluded middle,

$$C500{,}000{,}000 \vee \neg C500{,}000{,}000.$$

For every completely sharp interpretation in F, either 500,000,000 in the extension of C, or 500,000,000 is in the anti-extension of C. Such are completely sharp interpretations. So the disjunction is super-true. But neither C500,000,000 nor $\neg C$500,000,000 is super-true. So our supervaluationist countenances true disjunctions, neither of whose disjuncts is true.

Intuitively, validity is the necessary preservation of truth. In model-theoretic systems, an argument is valid if its conclusion is true under every interpretation of the language on which its premises are true. In the present framework, "interpretations" of the language are complete frames, and, again, the slogan of super-valuationism is that truth is super-truth. So validity is the necessary preservation of super-truth. The super-valuationist thus adopts what we may call an *external* notion of logical consequence:

> Let Γ be a set of sentences Φ a sentence in the formal language. Then $\Gamma \models_e \Phi$ if, for each complete frame F, if every member of Γ is super-true in F, then Φ is super-true in F.

It is straightforward to verify that $\Gamma \models_e \Phi$ if and only if Φ is a classical consequence of Γ. The crucial observation is that for every classical interpretation M of the language, there is a complete frame $\langle\{M\},M\rangle$ whose only interpretation is M. It follows that both of our sorites arguments are externally valid, but, as above, neither is sound. Each has at least one premise that fails to be super-true.

Most supervaluationists list it as a strength of their view that it sanctions classical logic. All and only classical logical truths are logically true for the supervaluationist;

and all and only classically valid arguments are externally valid. But this depends on maintaining the usual collection of logical terminology. It is natural for an advocate of the present framework to add an operator **T**, for determinate truth (a.k.a. super-truth). This is just to include the crucial item of the theory in the object language.

So let F be a frame, N a partial interpretation in F, and Φ a sentence in the language. Consider the following definition:

$\mathbf{T}\Phi$ is true at N if Φ is super-true in F.

In the three-valued background, we should also give falsehood (and indeterminacy) conditions for **T**. We can either say that $\mathbf{T}\Phi$ is false if Φ is not super-true, or that $\mathbf{T}\Phi$ is false if Φ is super-false (and indeterminate otherwise).

With this piece of terminology in the object language, some classical (and intuitionistic) inference patterns are no longer externally valid. Notice, for example, that $\Phi \models_e \mathbf{T}\Phi$. That is, for any frame Φ, if Φ is super-true in F, then $\mathbf{T}\Phi$ is true in every partial interpretation in F. So if Φ is super-true, then so is $\mathbf{T}\Phi$. But we do not have $\models_e(\Phi\rightarrow\mathbf{T}\Phi)$. Consider, for example, the frame that goes with our sorites series. Let N be any completely sharp interpretation in that frame in which the person labeled 500,000,000 is in the extension of C (i.e., is a child). In that interpretation $C500,000,000$ is true, but $\mathbf{T}C500,000,000$ is not. So $(C500,000,000 \rightarrow \mathbf{T}C500,000,000)$ is not true at that interpretation, and so is not super-true in the frame. So, with an operator for determinacy (or super-truth), the simple rule of arrow-introduction is not valid. The following inference, however, is valid:

$$\text{If } \Gamma \cup \{\Psi\} \models_e \Phi, \text{then } \Gamma \models (\mathrm{T}\Psi \rightarrow \Phi)\,.$$

Some philosophers who advocate the supervaluationist perspective do not fully endorse the slogan that truth is super-truth. Vann McGee and Brain McLaughlin (1994), for example, suggest that, when it comes to vague predicates and related linguistic phenomena, there are two different notions of truth at work. One, which they call *definite truth*, corresponds to the philosophical view that truth is correspondence with reality. To say that a sentence is definitely true is to say that the language fixes conditions for the application of the terminology in the sentence, and that those conditions are met.

Because of truth-value gaps, involving vague predicates and the like, definite truth does not fully obey the Tarskian scheme: that S is true if and only if p, where S the name of a sentence, and p expresses that same sentence. In McGee and McLaughlin's supervaluationist semantics, definite truth comes to super-truth, as seems plausible. Their other notion of truth is more deflationary, obeying the ordinary Tarskian rules, but carrying no substantial notion of correspondence.

McGee and McLaughlin argue that both notions of truth are legitimate, and have a role to play in semantics and, presumably, logic. Thus, I would think that they would favor a supervaluationist-style model theory, but one with two different notions of truth. Possibly, then, there would be two different notions of logical consequence, one being the necessary preservation of definite truth/super-truth, as above, and the other being the necessary preservation of deflationary truth. It is not clear how this would play itself out in the three-valued framework.

3.3.2 Open-Texture

I take the liberty of including a brief account of the model theory that goes with my own account of vagueness (Shapiro, (2006)). The key philosophical thesis is that, in some contexts, a competent speaker can go either way with a borderline case of a vague predicate, without compromising her competence, contravening the "facts", etc. The view thus invokes the supervaluationist notion of an acceptable sharpening of the language. For me, each acceptable sharpening represents a way that vague predicates can be deployed, consistent with the meaning of the terms, the non-linguistic facts, and the like. Although one can define super-truth, as above, this notion does not play a major role in the semantics. Truth is not super-truth. Suppose, for example, that in the course of a conversation, a competent speaker says that a person 500,000,000 s old is a child, and this assertion goes unchallenged in the conversation. Then, in that context, person 500,000,000 *is* a child, and it is true that she is a child. The statement to that effect goes on the conversational record (following the lead of Lewis, (1979)).

The view has no special need for *completely* sharp interpretations of the language. In the course of everyday conversation, predicates do get sharpened – borderline cases are put in the extension or the anti-extension of vague predicates – but it is rare for vague predicates to be *completely* sharpened, to the point that there are no indeterminacies in the range of applicability of the predicate. Some philosophers have gone so far as to argue that completely sharp interpretations are not consistent with the meaning of at least some vague predicates. In terms of Fine (1975), the claim is that something in the neighborhood of the inductive premise of a sorites argument is a penumbral connection. If so, then there are no acceptable, completely sharp interpretations of the language. My own view does not go that far. There are conversational situations in which speakers competently impose a sharp boundary on a vague predicate. But normal situations do enforce some sort of tolerance on the vague predicates: small differences do not mark changes in status, although large differences do. So Fine's completability requirement is rejected, and the model theory does not demand that frames be complete.

I take that one purpose of our philosophical enterprise is to model the kinematics and logic of conversations in which extensions and anti-extensions of the predicates are in flux. For present purposes, then, the background framework of super-valuation carries over, but the semantic and logical notions are defined differently. A partial interpretation in a frame represents a possible stage in a conversation; sharpenings of the partial interpretation represent possible futures in which nothing is "taken back". They represent ways that the predicates can be further sharpened, without any "unsharpening".

The strong Kleene semantics gives us a notion of truth-in-a-partial-interpretation, as above. As with supervaluationism, however, this is not the central notion in the model theory. The key logical notions are defined in terms of all of the interpretations in a frame.

Let $F = <W,M>$ be a frame, with $N \in W$, and let Φ be a sentence in the object language. Say that Φ is *weakly forced* at N if there is no sharpening of N in W in which Φ is false. In other words, Φ is weakly forced at N if Φ is true in every N' in W such that $N \leq N'$ and Φ has a truth-value (truth or falsehood) in N' (see Tappenden, (1993), where this notion is prominent). It is easy to see that every classical logical truth is weakly forced at every partial interpretation in every frame. Weak forcing is perhaps a loose analogue of truth, but as we shall soon see, I'd insist on emphasizing the word "loose".

Let us turn to a sample frame G, in which the domain consists of one billion people, of various ages, as above, and we have a predicate C, for being a child. This time, we do not require the frame to be complete. The base of the frame is as before: the extension of C at the base consists of all of the people labeled with the numbers from 1 to 400,000,000, and the anti- extension of C at the base contains those labeled 700,000,000 and greater. The other partial interpretations in G represent possible extensions and anti-extensions of the predicate, consistent with its meaning, non-linguistic facts, etc. Assume that our frame G has *no* completely sharp interpretations. In particular, assume that there is no partial interpretation in G such that a number n is in the extension of C and $n+1$ is in the anti-extension. We are modeling conversations in which participants sharpen the predicate, but do not completely sharpen it.

In these terms, the main penumbral connection is that if $j < i$, then $Ci \rightarrow Cj$ and $\neg Cj \rightarrow \neg Ci$ are both weakly forced in G. Moreover, since G has no completely sharp partial interpretations, the conditionals in our first sorites argument, $Cn \rightarrow Cn{+}1$, and the inductive premise of the second, $\forall x(Cx \rightarrow C(x{+}1))$, are all weakly forced. This registers intuitions that support these intuitions.

However, weak forcing is much too weak to serve as a close analogue of truth. For one thing, weak forcing does not preserve modus ponens: there are frames F and sentences Φ, Ψ, such that Φ and $\Phi \rightarrow \Psi$ are both weakly forced in F, but Ψ is not. Indeed, the sample frame sketched just now is one such. The premises of both sorites arguments are all weakly forced, but its conclusion is false in *every* partial interpretation in the frame.

The central notion in the semantics is what I call *forcing*. It is a sort of local version of super-truth. Let $F = <W,M>$ be a frame and let $N \in W$ be a partial interpretation in F. Let Φ be a sentence in the object language.

> Say that Φ is *forced* at N if for each sharpening N_1 of N in W, there is a sharpening N_2 of N_1 in W such that Φ is true in N_2.

Burgess and Humberstone (1987) invoke a similar notion. Notice that, in light of monotonicity, if a sentence Φ is true in N, ala the strong Kleene semantics, then Φ is forced at N in F. And if Φ is forced, then Φ is weakly forced. The converses can fail.

The idea is that a sentence is forced at a partial interpretation in a frame if it is "eventually" true in the frame: if every sharpening of the frame itself has a sharpening in the frame in which the sentence is true. If a sentence Φ is forced at a sharpening in a frame, then no matter how things turn out concerning borderline cases (according to the frame), there is always a further sharpening in which Φ is true. If an indeterminate sentence Φ is forced at a partial interpretation in a frame, then the frame and partial interpretation *guarantee* that Φ will become true.

It is straightforward to verify that forcing preserves modus ponens. Consequently, some (indeed, most) of the conditionals in the first sorites argument are not forced, nor is the inductive premise of the second.

If my view had a snappy slogan, it would not be that truth is super-truth. Rather, truth is something like truth-in-a-conversation. It is a local notion, sensitive to whatever competent calls have been made concerning borderline cases of vague predicates. Since forcing is a close analogue of this notion, it is used to define the central logical notions. Validity is the necessary preservation of forcing:

> Let Γ be a set of sentences and let Φ be a single sentence in the language. Say that $\Gamma \models_i \Phi$ if Φ is forced at every partial interpretation in every frame in which each member of Γ is forced.

The framework of partial interpretations, and the like, allows us to define alternate connectives and quantifiers. These plausibly represent different ways that connectives and quantifiers are used in ordinary language, especially when vague terms are deployed. I'll close this sub-section with a small sample.

Hans Kamp (1981, p. 245) presents an account of vagueness that is similar to mine in many respects, at least on the philosophical front. He argues that the contextual deployment of vague terms requires a "non-standard account of the conditional". As Kamp puts it, a "conditional 'if ϕ then ψ' is true in a context c iff, provided the evaluation of ϕ in c is positive the evaluation of ψ *in the context modified by this evaluation* is positive too" (p. 247, emphasis mine). The idea is to evaluate the consequent of a conditional in sharpenings in which the antecedent is true. This suggests a treatment along the lines of how the conditional is defined in Kripke semantics for intuitionistic languages:

> Let $F = \langle W,M \rangle$ be a frame with $N \in W$. Say that $(\Phi \Rightarrow \Psi)$ is true at N in F if for any N' in W such that $N \leq N'$, if Φ is true in N', then Ψ is true at N'.

In words, $(\Phi \Rightarrow \Psi)$ holds in a partial interpretation just in case Ψ comes out true once we sharpen things such that Φ becomes true.

This allows us to express penumbral connections in the object language. In our sample frame above, if $i<j$, then $Cj \Rightarrow Ci$ and $\neg Ci \Rightarrow \neg Cj$ both hold in every partial interpretation in the frame. In words, once we sharpen to make a given person a child, then everyone younger is also a child.

We can also add a second negation operator, to mirror the defined operator in intuitionism:

Let $F = \langle W,M \rangle$ be a frame, with $N \in W$. Say that $-\Phi$ is true at N under s in F if for any N' in W such that $N \leq N'$, it is not the case that Φ is true at N' under s.

The two negations correspond to rather different concepts in the logic of vague predicates. An atomic sentence in the form $\neg Pa$ is true in a partial interpretation if the object denoted by a is in the *anti*-extension of P in that partial interpretation. This is a strong statement, amounting to a positive judgment that Pa is false. In contrast, $-Pa$ is true in a partial interpretation in a frame if the object denoted by a is not in the extension of P in any sharpening of the given partial interpretation in the frame. In a sense, $-Pa$ says that Pa cannot be true, consistent with the meaning of the predicate and the borderline cases that have been called thus far. This is a relatively weak statement that Pa is never judged to be true (in any further sharpening). A plausible principle of tolerance is that if a' is only marginally different from a, then $Pa \Rightarrow - \neg Pa'$. In words, if we sharpen to put a in the extension of P, then we cannot put a' into the anti-extension.

It would take us too far afield to go into definitions of other connectives and quantifiers, and to check the logic of each. It will have to suffice to note that, for any set Γ of sentences and any sentence Φ, if $\Gamma \models_i \Phi$, then Φ is a classical consequence of Γ. There is a sort of converse to this. The standard intuitionistic elimination rules are sound for all of the connectives of our language – old and new – and the introduction rules are sound for everything but the material conditional "$\rightarrow$", the original negation "$\neg$", and the universal quantifier "$\forall$". And the rule of double negation elimination is sound for both negations. Thus, if Γ is a set of sentences and Φ a sentence in our language, none of which contain a material conditional, the original, strong negation, and the original universal quantifier, then if Φ is a classical consequence of Γ, then $\Gamma \models_i \Phi$. Unlike supervaluationism, this holds even if a (reasonable) determinacy operator is added. So classical reasoning is good after all, provided that we are careful how the logical terminology is interpreted. See Shapiro (2006, Chapters 3–4) for details.

3.3.3 Inconsistency Again

There are some other accounts of vagueness whose model theory could also make use of a framework of sharpenings, partial interpretations, and frames. As noted in §2 above, some philosophers argue that vague predicates are, in some sense, inconsistent. The claim is that the predicates come with rules of application – purported analytic truths, perhaps – that, if followed, lead to contradiction. For example, the rules for our sample predicate "child" would entail that, say, newborns are children, and that those over 21 years old are not children. And the rules support something in the neighborhood of the induction premise of the second sorites argument: if a person is a child, then so is someone one second older. Above, we briefly considered some thinkers who conclude from this that vague predicates cannot be deployed in a coherent way. This pessimistic result seems inevitable when the inconsistency is combined with some standard views on meaning.

Matti Eklund (2002, 2005) agrees with the other inconsistency theorists that one cannot coherently deploy vague predicates in accordance with all of their rules of use. He sketches a program in which such predicates can nevertheless be deployed in a coherent manner, remaining useful for the daily needs of communication. The idea is that competent speakers do their best to minimize the violation of the rules of application. Typically, there is no one way to deploy the terms that is "best" – that does the least damage to the rules of use. This is because there is no single measure to place on the attempts to minimize violations: some uses seem to be as good as others. Semantic theorists – us philosophers – are to consider the range of ways that vague terms can be deployed, minimizing the violations to the rules of application.

Presumably, it would do too much damage to the rules to declare that all humans are children, or that no humans are children, or that everyone is bald, or that there are no heaps. Predicates like these would be useless. So it seems that the acceptable ways to minimize violations, and maintain classical logic, involve giving up principles like the inductive premise of the second sorites argument. So, for Eklund, acceptable ways to deploy the predicate are what the supervaluationist calls acceptable, complete sharpenings – at least in this simple case involving a single, vague predicate. A sentence is determinately true if it comes out true on all ways of consistently deploying it, minimizing violations of the rules of application.

Although Eklund does not develop a model theory, or discuss the logic extensively, his perspective suggests a framework that is structurally similar to the supervaluationist model theory sketched above, at least on the simple examples. A frame or perhaps a complete frame, represents various ways that a predicate can be deployed while doing minimal damage to its rules of use. The underlying philosophy is very different from that of supervaluationism, however. For the supervaluationist, ordinary practice leaves the borderline cases undetermined. If *a* is a borderline case of a child, then the rules of use, and the non-linguistic world, do not determine a verdict. In a sense, the rules of use give out, leaving that case open. According to the supervaluationist, a speaker is not pulled in either direction, and she works with the different ways of filling in the gaps. Thus the notion of supertruth. For inconsistency theorists, the rules of use determine too much. The speaker is pulled in *both* directions, toward asserting and denying childhood of the same individual. Eklund has the theorist consider the different ways of cutting down, to maintain consistency. Despite this crucial philosophical difference, as far as I can see, the model theories, and thus the logic, are the same, or at least very similar.

To conclude this section, a small, but dedicated group of philosophers propose turning the supervaluationist perspective upside down, accepting the truth of some contradictions. Suppose, for example, that *a* is a borderline child. For the supervaluationist, the sentence *Ca* is neither true, nor false. For the sub-valuationist, *Ca* is *both* true and false. The model theory is a sort of dual to that of the supervaluationist one. An "extra-interpretation" is the dual to a partial interpretation, consisting of a pair, $<d,I>$, where d is a non-empty set, the domain of the interpretation. For each predicate R in the language, IR is a pair $<p,q>$ where, again, p is the extension of R and q is the anti-extension. Here, however, there is no requirement that p and q be disjoint. Instead, the *sub-valuationist* insists that p and q together exhaust the domain: $p \cup q = d$. Any objects in the intersection of p and q are the borderline cases of the predicate. The sub-valuationist then develops a three-valued semantics, usually with two designated values, and then lessons for the logic are drawn. See, for example, Hyde (1997).

In the history of technical philosophy, especially the philosophy of mathematics, it often happens that a formal program developed in support of a philosophical orientation survives its original motivation, and finds use by those who do not hold the original orientation. Apparently, the supervaluationist framework is a case at hand.

3.3.4 Addendum: Running Up the Orders

Higher-order vagueness is vagueness concerning borderline cases of vague predicates or, perhaps equivalently, vagueness concerning determinacy. Consider our running sorites series consisting of 1 billion people of various ages. The theories of vagueness try to make sense of the intuitive thought that there is no sharp boundary between the (determinate) children at the start and the (determinate) non-children at the end. It also seems that there is no sharp boundary between the determinate children and the borderline children in the middle, nor is there a boundary between the borderline children and the determinate non-children at the end of the series.

By definition, a *second-order borderline case* of "child" is a borderline case of "borderline child". Equivalently, a second-order borderline case of "bald" is a borderline case of either "determinately a child" or "determinately not a child". Call such a person a *borderline-borderline* child. Say that a person is *determinately-determinately* a child if she is determinately a child and (determinately) not a borderline-borderline child. Presumably, the first few kids in our list are determinately-determinately children. After all, they are only a few seconds old.

Higher-order vagueness need not stop at this second level. Is there a sharp boundary between the determinately-determinate children and the borderline-borderline children? We have, or seem to have, borderline-borderline-borderline children. And on it goes. One of the motivations for running up the series of higher-order vagueness is an intuitive belief that there should be *no* relevant sharp borders anywhere in the series. There simply is no sharp line separating the children from those of any property that is incompatible with childhood and has something to do with how old a person is. Crispin Wright (1976, §1) registers the intuition that "no sharp distinction may be drawn between cases where it is definitely correct to apply [a vague] predicate and cases of *any* other sort".

On the surface, the model theory that underlies the views canvassed in this section does not allow for even second-order vagueness. At the base of each frame, each predicate *P* is assigned two sets, its extension and its anti-extension. The former are the determinate cases of the predicate and the latter are the determinate cases of its complement. And, of course, sets have no indeterminacy concerning their members, at least as the notions are employed in standard set theory. So for each object *a* in the domain and each predicate *P* in the language, either *a* is determinately *P* in the frame, *a* is determinately not-*P* in the frame, or *a* is borderline in the frame. There is no provision for an object to be borderline-determinately *P*, or borderline-borderline *P*.

So an advocate of one of the views canvassed in this section must either argue that there is no higher-order vagueness or else complicate the system to accommodate it. There is no need to discuss the former option in this survey of model theories. I will briefly sketch a version of the treatment of higher-order vagueness in the supervaluationist framework of Fine (1975, §5). It is adaptable to all of the philosophical accounts of this section.

The key notion in the accounts is that of an *acceptable* partial interpretation. To be sure, there is disagreement among advocates of the various accounts over what makes a partial interpretation acceptable, and how the notion of acceptable sharpening relates to the natural language analogues of the various terminology. Nevertheless, on all of these accounts, the key to understanding higher-order vagueness – if there is any – is to take "acceptable" to be a vague predicate of partial interpretations.

As developed so far, a frame is what we may call the "unit" of the present model theories. It is what corresponds to an interpretation in ordinary, classical model theory. Sentences get truth values at the base and in the partial interpretations in frames, and validity is defined in terms of what holds in all frames. To accommodate second-order vagueness, one might take the "unit" to be a *set* Θ of frames, all with the same language, and all involving the same universe of discourse. Let $F = \langle W, M \rangle$ be a frame in Θ. The base M of F represents *one* acceptable way to fix the extensions of predicates like "determinately a child", and the other partial interpretations in F represent possible extensions of that one acceptable way. The frames in the set Θ thus represent the various ways that the extensions of predicates like "determinately a child" and "acceptable sharpening" can be fixed, consistent with the meaning of the terms and the non-linguistic facts.

Return to our sorites series, and its formalization. As above, a person a is determinately a child in a frame F in the set Θ if a is in the extension of the predicate C at the base of F. And a is determinately-determinately a child if a is in the extension of C in *every* partial interpretation in Θ; a is borderline-determinately a child if a is the extension of C in some but not all of the frames in Θ.

The procedure here iterates. To accommodate third-order vagueness, we would take the "unit" to be a set of sets of frames. Each set of frames in the unit would represent one acceptable range of ways of indicating what the range of acceptable sharpenings is. The procedure generalizes in a straightforward, if tedious, manner. We can carry it out as far as we want. Fine (1975, §5) briefly presents an ingenious system that accommodates all of the (finite) iterations at once. For Fine, a "borderline" is a sequence $c_0, c_1, c_2 \ldots$, where c_0 is a complete sharpening, c_1 is a set of complete sharpenings, c_2 is a set of sets of complete sharpenings, etc.

3.4 Many-Values

Let us return to ordinary, or so-called "first-order" vagueness. Another major approach insists that three truth-values are not enough. Consider two color patches, p, q, both of which are about midway between blue and green, with q being a bit closer to a pure green than p. And let G be a predicate for "green". Then on the foregoing accounts, the two sentences Gp and Gq come out indeterminate, since neither is quite true nor quite false. But there is a sense in which Gq is *more* true than Gp, or that Gq is *closer* to truth than Gp is. Thoughts like this motivate the many-valued, or "fuzzy", approach to vagueness.

The fuzzy-theorist begins with a set $\boldsymbol{T}$ of truth-values. In each interpretation, sentences in the language are assigned members of $\boldsymbol{T}$, presumably in a systematic manner. If Φ is a sentence, then let $[\![\Phi]\!]$ be its truth-value.

The most common choice for the set $\boldsymbol{T}$ of truth-values, by far, is the closed interval [0,1], whose members are the real numbers between 0 and 1, inclusive. A sentence with truth-value 1 is completely true, and a sentence with truth-value 0 is utterly false. The values in between represent partial truths. In the situation with the color patches, for example, one might say that $[\![Gp]\!] = 0.4$ and $[\![Gq]\!] = 0.6$.

On views like this, an interpretation of the language is, as usual, a pair $<d,I>$ where d is a set, the domain of discourse, and the interpretation function I gives the extensions of the non-logical terminology. If R is an n-place relation letter, then IR is a function from d^n to $\boldsymbol{T}$, the set of truth- values. This fixes truth-values for the atomic formulas in the straightforward manner: in the interpretation, $[\![Rt_1, \ldots, t_n]\!] = IR<m_1, \ldots, m_n>$ where, for each i, m_i is the denotation, in the interpretation, of t_i.

3.4.1 Truth-Functionality

The first issue for the theorist who opts for an account like this is whether the semantics is to be truth-functional. That is, should the truth-value of a compound formula be a function of the truth-values of its components? For purposes of exposition, and familiarity, the truth-functional approach is certainly the most convenient. After all, the ordinary, two-valued classical semantics is truth-functional, and it is only a matter of extending that feature to the vague language. But, to be sure, being technically convenient and familiar is not the same as being correct or even best. Still, we start here with the truth-functional approach. As with the three-valued approaches, one desideratum is that the model theory agree with the standard one on the truth-values 0 and 1. In other words, if all of the parts of a compound are assigned standard truth-values, 0 or 1, then the compound itself should receive the same truth-value it would have with that assignment on a classical interpretation.

Even if we stay truth-functional, and enforce the above desideratum, there are several options available for each connective and quantifier. The most common account of negation is this:

$$[\![\neg\Phi]\!] = 1 - [\![\Phi]\!] .$$

So if the truth-value of Gq is 0.6, as above, then the truth-value of $\neg Gq$ is 0.4. This is a rough analogue of the strong, internal, choice negation employed above. The negation of a sentence is a measure of how "far" the sentence is from truth. An utterly false sentence is all the way – distance 1 – from truth, while a 0.6 is 0.4 from truth.

One can also define an analogue of the weak, external, exclusion negation: $[\![\sim\Phi]\!] = 1$ if $[\![\Phi]\!]<1$, and $[\![\sim\Phi]\!] = 0$ otherwise. In effect, $\sim\Phi$ says that Φ is something other than completely true. In line with the weak negation above, this is what we may call a "sharpener", since its output is always either 1 or 0, full truth or utter falsehood.

The most common definitions for conjunction and disjunction are perhaps the simplest. The truth-value of a conjunction is the smallest among the truth-values of the conjuncts, and the truth-value of a disjunction is the greatest among the truth-values of the disjuncts:

$$\begin{aligned}[\![\Phi\&\Psi]\!] &= \min\{[\![\Phi]\!], [\![\Psi]\!]\},\\ [\![\Phi\vee\Psi]\!] &= \max\{[\![\Phi]\!], [\![\Psi]\!]\}.\end{aligned}$$

See Machina (1976). These are not the only options deployed, however. Another possibility is to define $[\![\Phi\&\Psi]\!]$ to be $[\![\Phi]\!]\cdot[\![\Psi]\!]$. In our example above, about the two color patches, the truth-value of $Gp\&Gq$ would be 0.24. When we conjoin our two approximately half-truths, we end up with about a quarter-truth.

The most popular option for the material conditional is this one:

$$[\![\Phi \rightarrow \Psi]\!] = \min\{1, 1 - ([\![\Phi]\!] - [\![\Psi]\!])\}.$$

In words, if Ψ is at least as true as Φ (i.e., if $[\![\Phi]\!]\leq[\![\Psi]\!]$), then $\Phi\rightarrow\Psi$ is completely true. Otherwise, the truth-value of $\Phi\rightarrow\Psi$ is the difference between complete truth and the difference in the truth-values of the components. In the latter case, the conditional measures the "drop" in truth-value from antecedent to consequent. Recall that in our running example, the truth-value of Gq is 0.6 and the truth-value of Gp is 0.4. So the truth-value of $Gp\rightarrow Gq$ is 1. Since q is a bit greener than p, then, surely, it is completely true that *if* p is green, then so is q. The truth-value of the converse, $Gq\rightarrow Gp$ is 0.8. This is because the truth-value drops 0.2 between antecedent and consequent.

It is common to interpret the quantifiers along the lines of conjunction and disjunction. In particular, the truth-value $[\![(\forall x)\Phi(x)]\!]$ of a universally quantified formula is the greatest lower-bound of the truth-values of its instances $[\![\Phi(x)]\!]$, and the truth-value $[\![(\exists x)\Phi(x)]\!]$ of an existentially quantified formula is the least-upper-bound of the truth-values of its instances $[\![\Phi(x)]\!]$. An alternative is to define $[\![(\forall x)\Phi(x)]\!]$ to be the (possibly infinite) product of the instances: $\Pi[\![\Phi(i)]\!]$.

Let us examine a typical sorites argument, one a bit simpler than our previous example with a billion people. Suppose we have a series of 200 colored patches. Use the numbers from 1 to 200 as names of the patches. The first, #1, is a pure blue and the last, #200, is a pure green, and suppose that the transition from card to card is uniform. As above, let G be a predicate for being green. Say that the first fifty cards are clearly non-green and the last fifty are clearly green. The other 100 have intermediate values, distributed evenly. So $[\![Gn]\!] = 0$ if $n \leq 50$, $[\![Gn]\!] = 1$ if $n \geq 151$, $[\![G51]\!] = 0.99$, $[\![G73]\!] = 0.87$, etc.

One type of sorites argument is this:

$$\begin{array}{l} G1 \\ G1 \rightarrow G2 \\ G2 \rightarrow G3 \\ \ldots \\ \underline{G199 \rightarrow G200} \\ G200 \end{array}$$

On the foregoing sketch, the first fifty premises and the last fifty premises are completely true. Each of the others has a truth-value of 0.99. Yet the conclusion is utterly false, truth-value 0.

As above, another sort of sorites argument has only two premises:

$$\begin{array}{l} G1 \\ \underline{\forall x < 200\,(Gx \rightarrow G\,(x+1))} \\ G200 \end{array}$$

The first premise is completely true, and the conclusion is completely false. On the common accounts, the second has truth-value 0.99, since that is the lowest among the truth-values of the conditionals. On the "product" interpretation of the universal quantifier, the truth-value of the second premise is about 0.366.

So both arguments consist of premises which are either completely true or nearly true (or, on one reading, at least a third true) and whose conclusions are completely false. Whether the arguments are valid depends on the definition of validity, and so we turn to that.

Once again, the underlying theme is that validity is the necessary preservation of truth. But there is an ambiguity in this. What is it that should be "preserved" from premises to conclusion? What do we mean by "truth" in this many-valued context? One notion, which we may call "sharp validity", is that complete truth (and only complete truth) needs to be preserved. Let Γ be a set of sentences and Φ a sentence. Then $\Gamma \models_s \Phi$ if every interpretation that gives the truth-value 1 to every member of Γ also gives truth-value 1 to Φ. On the present sketch, it is easy to see that $\Gamma \models_s \Phi$ if and only if Φ is a classical consequence of Γ. This is a consequence of the fact that the present model theory agrees with the classical one on interpretations that only assign the truth-values 0,1 to formulas. So our two sorites arguments are valid. Neither is sound, however, since each has at least one premise that is not completely true, remembering that even 0.99 is short of complete truth.

Arguably, this notion of sharp validity is not appropriate for reasoning with vague predicates. We sometimes deal with premises that are not completely true – and not on the assumption that these premises are completely true. One may think, for example, that 0.99 is enough to count as truth for the purpose of reasoning. On what we may call "fuzzy validity", what should be preserved from premises to conclusion (so to speak) is the truth-value of the least true premise (if there is one). Say that $\Gamma \models_f \Phi$ if on every interpretation, the truth-value of the conclusion is greater than or equal to the greatest lower bound of the truth-values of the premises. On all readings of the connectives canvassed so far, our two sorites arguments are fuzzy invalid. The one that comes "closest", so to speak, is the second argument, if we invoke the product interpretation of the universal quantifier. Even in that case, the premises are at least 0.366 true and the conclusion is completely false.

Notice that modus ponens is not fuzzy valid. Suppose, for example, that $[\![\Phi]\!] = 0.9$ and $[\![\Psi]\!] = 0.8$. Then $[\![\Phi \rightarrow \Psi]\!] = 0.9$. So the conclusion of this instance of modus ponens is less true than both premises. The "problem", if that is what it is, is that each premise "drops" 0.1 from truth; when combined via this inference, the conclusion "drops" the sum of those, 0.2.

Another natural definition of validity is proposed by Dorothy Edgington (1997). Define the "untruth" of a formula Φ, under an interpretation (and assignment) to be $1 - [\![\Phi]\!]$. That is, the untruth of Φ is the "distance" from Φ to complete truth. And define the "maximal untruth" of a set Γ to be the minimum of 1 and the sum of the untruths of the members of Γ:

$$\max\left\{1, \sum \{1 - [\![\Phi]\!] : \Phi \in \Gamma\}\right\}.$$

The maximal untruth of a set is something like the worse case scenario; it is a measure of how far from truth the members of the set, taken together, can be.

Now say that $\Gamma \models_e \Phi$ if the untruth of Φ is not larger than the maximal untruth of Γ. The idea here is that what should be preserved, from premises to conclusion, is the sum of the "distances" from truth. The conclusion should not drop further from truth than the sum of the drops of the premises. Modus ponens is valid, in this sense. So is the first sorties argument above. Each of the premises is, of course, almost completely true, but since there are so many such premises, their untruths add up to 1.

On the present sketch, the second sorites argument remains invalid. The maximal untruth of the two premises is 0.1 (or about 0.634 on the product interpretation of the universal quantifier), while the completely false conclusion has an untruth of 1. But that may be due to our having a poor choice for how to interpret the universal quantifier. If one is to maintain the truth-functional approach with this conception of validity, then perhaps one should define conjunction and disjunction accordingly. The untruth of $\Phi\&\Psi$, for example, would be the sum of the untruths of Φ and Ψ, or 1, whichever is less. So $[\![\Phi\&\Psi]\!]$ would be the minimum of 0 and $[\![\Phi]\!]+[\![\Psi]\!]-1$. And the untruth of $(\forall x)\Phi(x)$ would be the (possibly infinite) sum of the untruths of the instances (or 1, whichever is less). Then the truth-value of the inductive premise would be 0: the untruths of the instances add up to 1. And that argument is valid as well.

3.4.2 Non-truth-Functionality

Edgington (1997) herself argues against a truth-functional approach for the logic of vagueness. Consider, for example, a ball b that is both borderline orange O and borderline round R. Say that $[\![Ob]\!] = 0.5$ and $[\![Rb]\!] = 0.5$. Then, of course, $[\![Ob]\!]$,

$[\![Rb]\!]$, $[\![\neg Ob]\!]$, and $[\![\neg Rb]\!]$ all have the same truth-value (at least on the usual account for negation). Intuitively, one would think that $[\![Ob\&Ob]\!]$ should also be 0.5. Surely *Ob* is equivalent to *Ob*&*Ob*. It says the same thing. What of $[\![Ob\&\neg Ob]\!]$? Should that also be 0.5 (or 0.25)? And what of $[\![Ob\&Rb]\!]$? Surely, the borderline status of *Rb* should detract from the truth-value of the conjunction. Similarly, let *B* be a predicate for "is a ball", and let $[\![Bb]\!] = 1$, since by hypothesis, *b* is definitely a ball. Then, on all accounts for conjunction, $[\![Ob\&Bb]\!] = 0.5$, and, intuitively, that seems correct. A conjunction of a half-truth with a full truth is a half-truth. On the standard truth-functional account of conjunction, however, $[\![Ob\&Rb]\!]$ is also 0.5. But, surely, the latter is less true than the former, for it is a conjunction of two half-truths. The product interpretation of conjunction gets this one right, intuitively: $[\![Ob\&Rb]\!]$ is 0.25. But, since it is truth-functional, we also have that $[\![Ob\&Ob]\!]$ is 0.25.

To be sure, a non-truth-functional model theory is more complex than the more standard truth-functional systems. The crucial difference is that for each *formula* (atomic or otherwise) with n free variables, the interpretation function I assigns a function from d^n to the set $\boldsymbol{T}$ of truth-values. So if $\Phi(x_1 \ldots x_n)$ is a formula, all of whose free variables are indicated, then $[\![\Phi(t_1 \ldots t_n)]\!] = I\Phi{<}m_1, \ldots, m_n{>}$ where, for each i, m_i is the denotation, in the interpretation, of t_i. There will be some structural constraints on the assignments of compound formulas, corresponding, roughly, to the truth-functional rules. Suppose, for example, that Φ and Ψ are sentences and that $[\![\Phi]\!] = r$ and $[\![\Psi]\!] = s$. Then, intuitively, the *highest* $[\![\Phi\&\Psi]\!]$ can be is $\max\{r,s\}$. That is, a conjunction cannot be more true than its truest conjunct. Also, $[\![\Phi\&\Psi]\!]$ cannot be *lower* than $1 - ([\![\Phi]\!] + [\![\Psi]\!])$. A conjunction cannot be further from truth and the sum of the distances from truth of the conjunctions. Also, the truth-value of a conjunction cannot be lower than 0, of course. So the model theoretic semantics would have a rule that the truth-value assigned to the conjunction must lie in the closed interval $[\max\{0,([\![\Phi]\!] + [\![\Psi]\!])-1\}, \min\{[\![\Phi]\!],[\![\Psi]\!]\}]$. I forego details here.

3.4.3 Having Our Cake and Eating It, Too

Some of the aforementioned problems with truth-functional systems can be traced to the use of the set of real numbers [0,1] as the truth- values, rather than with truth-functionality itself. Suppose, instead, that we use the members of a Boolean lattice as the set of truth-values. A bonus of this approach (for those who think it such) is that classical logic is maintained.

To fix on an example, let the set $\boldsymbol{T}$ of truth-values be the subsets of a circle C whose area is 1 square unit. Any Boolean lattice will do, but on this one we can talk about size or measure of at least some truth-values.

On this model, the entire circle C represents complete truth, and the empty set ϕ represents utter falsehood. The other subsets of C represent partial truths. The key feature of this approach is that there are different ways a proposition can be, say, half true, one for each subset of C whose measure is 0.5. This allows us to maintain truth-functionality while sanctioning the above intuitions that undermine some standard many-valued, truth-functional accounts.

An interpretation is, as usual, a pair $<d,I>$. For each n-place predicate R, IR is a function from d^n to $\boldsymbol{T}$. Atomic formulas are interpreted in the straightforward manner: $[\![R(t_1 \ldots t_n)]\!] = IR<m_1, \ldots, m_n>$ where, for each i, m_i is the denotation, in the interpretation, of t_i. The connectives are interpreted as follows:

$[\![\neg\Phi]\!] = C - [\![\Phi]\!]$, the complement of $[\![\Phi]\!]$ in the circle C.
$[\![\Phi \& \Psi]\!] = [\![\Phi]\!] \cap [\![\Psi]\!]$, the intersection of $[\![\Phi]\!]$ and $[\![\Psi]\!]$.
$[\![\Phi \vee \Psi]\!] = [\![\Phi]\!] \cup [\![\Psi]\!]$, the union of $[\![\Phi]\!]$ and $[\![\Psi]\!]$.
$[\![\Phi \rightarrow \Psi]\!] = (C - [\![\Phi]\!]) \cup [\![\Psi]\!]$, the union of the complement of $[\![\Phi]\!]$ with $[\![\Psi]\!]$.

The quantifiers are interpreted similarly: $[\![\forall x \Phi(x)]\!]$ is the intersection of the truth-values of the instances $[\![\Phi(x)]\!]$, and $[\![\exists x \Phi(x)]\!]$ is the union of the truth-values of the instances $[\![\Phi(x)]\!]$.

Let us return to our ball b that is both borderline orange O and borderline round R. Assume that b is about halfway between orange and red, and assume that it is what we may call half-round as well. Let $[\![Ob]\!]$ be the upper semi-circle, whose boundary is a horizontal line, and let $[\![Rb]\!]$ be the left semi-circle whose boundary is a vertical line. Then, of course, $[\![Ob]\!]$, $[\![Rb]\!]$, $[\![\neg Ob]\!]$, and $[\![\neg Rb]\!]$ are all half-truths, but each has a different truth-value. Notice, first, that $[\![Ob \& Ob]\!]$ is just $[\![Ob]\!]$, as expected, but $[\![Ob \& \neg Ob]\!]$ is the empty set ϕ. And $[\![Ob \& Rb]\!]$ is the upper-left quadrant of the circle C, and is thus a quarter-truth. That is, the borderline status of Rb does detract from the truth-value of the conjunction, as expected. Similarly, let B be a predicate for "is a ball", and let $[\![Bb]\!]$ be the entire circle C (since by hypothesis, b is definitely a ball). Then $[\![Ob \& Bb]\!]$ is the upper semi-circle, a half-truth. As with the real-valued accounts, a conjunction of a half-truth with a full truth is a half-truth.

To repeat the familiar slogan, one more time, validity is the necessary preservation of truth. In the present context, we get different notions of validity, depending on what, exactly, is to be preserved. As above, "sharp validity" is the preservation of complete truth. Let Γ be a set of sentences and Φ a sentence. Then $\Gamma \models_s \Phi$ if every interpretation that assigns the entire circle C to every member of Γ also assigns the entire circle to Φ.

Recall that on what we call "fuzzy validity", what is preserved from premises to conclusion is the truth-value of the least true premise (if there is one). In the present, Boolean context, this breaks into two notions, corresponding to two different notions of "less true". One can say, first, that Φ is less true than Ψ, in a given interpretation M, if $[\![\Phi]\!] \subseteq [\![\Psi]\!]$ in M. This is a partial order, and not a linear order. Or else one can say that Φ is less true than Ψ if the measure of Φ is smaller than the measure of Ψ. This, of course, is a linear order on the *measurable* subsets of the circle C.

Notice that $[\![\Phi]\!]$ can be a proper subset of $[\![\Psi]\!]$ even if the measure of $[\![\Phi]\!]$ is identical to the measure of $[\![\Psi]\!]$ (if the difference has measure zero). For example, a sentence can have the same measure as a complete truth without itself being a complete truth. Readers who find this unpalatable can either eschew one of these notions of "less true" or else use a finite, Boolean lattice with an additive measure as the collection of truth-values, instead of the subsets of our circle. Or she can simply drop the notion of the "measure" of a truth-value.

As noted, our different notions of "less true" give us different notions of validity. Let us call one of them *Boolean validity*: $\Gamma \models_b \Phi$ if on every interpretation, the intersection of the truth-values of the premises is a subset of the truth-value of the conclusion. The idea is that no chunk of truth (i.e., no subset of the circle C) is "lost" in going from premises to conclusion in a valid argument. If a subset of C is contained in every premise, then it is contained in the conclusion.

We also define *fuzzy validity*: $\Gamma \models_f \Phi$ if on every interpretation, the measure of the truth-value of the conclusion is greater than or equal to greatest lower bound of the measure of the truth-values of the premises. For this notion to be of use, we might insist that only measurable subsets of C be assigned as truth-values.

The resolution of the sorites series is similar to that broached above, on the real-valued approach. I forego details. Notice that modus ponens is not fuzzy-valid. To see this, suppose that $[\![\Phi]\!]$ is the left semi-circle and that $[\![\Psi]\!]$ is the upper-right quadrant. Then $[\![\Phi \rightarrow \Psi]\!]$ is the right semi-circle. So the premises of this instance of modus ponens are each half-true and the conclusion is a quarter-true.

In this example, the intersection of the truth-values of the premises is the empty set, which, of course, is a subset of the truth-value of the conclusion. In general, modus ponens is Boolean valid. Indeed, it is straightforward to verify that sharp validity and Boolean validity are both classical: $\Gamma \models_s \Phi$ if and only if $\Gamma \models_b \Phi$ if and only if Φ is a classical consequence of Γ. So those who find the preservation of classical validity to be a plus, and are otherwise attracted to the many-valued approach, have something to work with. See Weatherson (2005) for a rich and subtle variation on this theme.

3.4.4 Addendum: Running Up the Orders Again

It seems to me that higher-order vagueness, if such there be, is harder to accommodate on the many-valued approach. The reason, in short, is that unlike the supervaluationist-type frameworks, the key notions deployed in the various model theories do not readily iterate.

From the many-valued point of view, an object a is determinately C if the sentence Ca is completely true; a is determinately non-C if Ca is utterly false; and a is borderline C otherwise – if the truth value of Ca lies strictly between complete true and complete falsehood. The object a would be borderline-determinately C if it is not quite a complete truth and not quite less than fully true. It is hard to figure out what that would be. The phrase "not quite a complete truth" sounds synonymous with "not quite less than fully true". The formal semantics leaves no room for a distinction. In any interpretation of the sorites series, for example, there will be a first sentence in the series that fails to be completely true. Since it fails to be completely true, how can it be borderline between complete truth and less than complete truth? What would its truth-value be? If it is 1, or the full circle C, or the top of the Boolean lattice, then the sentence is completely true, and it is borderline if it gets any other assignment.

Second-order vagueness of a predicate C is vagueness in "determinately C" and/or vagueness in "borderline C". If an account of vagueness to be comprehensive, and if there is second-order vagueness, then the account should account for it the same way it accounts for any vagueness. It is not clear that this makes sense on the many-valued approaches. Let us stick to the mainstream accounts that use the real numbers between 0 and 1 as truth-values. A statement that Ca is determinate comes to "'Ca' has truth value 1". What would it be for *that* sentence to be borderline? Presumably, the many-valued theorist would try to apply her account here, at the meta-linguistic level. So she would end up saying things like "'"Ca" has truth value 1' has truth value 0.8". And perhaps also, for the same target sentence, "'"Ca" has truth value 0.99' has truth value 0.2". I suppose that this would make Ca borderline determinate. But it is not obvious that this iterated framework even makes sense. And higher-order vagueness does not stop at this level.

There are, of course, other mathematical structures and concepts one might try. Perhaps the theorist can assign an uncountable set of values, together with something like a probability measure on the set, to each sentence. Or maybe the problem is with using a model-theoretic semantics, formulated in standard set theory, at all. Mathematics and vagueness do not mix. If this is right, then, thankfully, we have reached the limits of this survey.

In any case, the present section does little more than scratch the surface of fuzzy or many-valued logic, even restricted to its application to vagueness. There is a rich industry of exploring different many-valued systems, various conceptions of the connectives and quantifiers, and applications. The interested reader can consult the overviews Novák (2006) and Hájek (2006), and the wealth of references cited there.

References

Burgess, J.A. and Humberstone I.L. (1987), "Natural deduction rules for a logic of vagueness", *Erkenntnis* 27: 197–229.

Chambers, T. (1998) "On vagueness, sorites, and Putnam's 'Intuitionistic Strategy'", *Monist* 81: 343–8.

Dummett, M. (1975), "Wang's paradox", *Synthese* 30: 301–324; reprinted in Keefe and Smith (1997), 99–118.

Edgington, D. (1997), "Vagueness by degrees", in Keefe and Smith (1997), 294–316.

Eklund, M. (2002), "Inconsistent languages", *Philosophy and Phenomenological Research* 64: 251–275.

Eklund, M. (2005), "What vagueness consists in", *Philosophical Studies* 125: 27–60.

Fine, K. (1975), "Vagueness, truth and logic", *Synthese* 30: 265–300; reprinted in Keefe and Smith (1979), 119–150.

Hájek, P. (2006), "What is mathematical fuzzy logic?", *Fuzzy Sets and Systems* 157: 597–603.

Horgan, T. (1994), "Transvaluationism: a Dionysian approach to vagueness", *The Southern Journal of Philosophy* 33(supplement): 97–126.

Hyde, D. (1997), "From heaps and gaps to heaps of gluts", *Mind* 106: 641–660.

Kamp, H. (1981), "The paradox of the heap", in *Aspects of philosophical logic*, edited by U. Mönnich, Dordrecht, Holland, D. Reidel, 225–277.

Keefe, R. (2000), *Theories of Vagueness*, Cambridge: Cambridge University Press.

Keefe, R. and P. Smith (1997), *Vagueness: A Reader*, Cambridge, MA: MIT Press.

Lewis, D. (1979), "Scorekeeping in a Language Game", *Journal of Philosophical Logic* 8: 339–359.
Machina, K.F. (1976), "Truth, Belief and Vagueness", *Journal of Philosophical Logic* 5: 47–78; reprinted in Keefe and Smith (1997), 174–203.
McGee, V. and McLaughlin B. (1994), "Distinctions Without a Difference", *Southern Journal of Philosophy* 33(supplement): 203–251.
Novák, V. (2006), "Which Logic Is the Real Fuzzy Logic?", *Fuzzy Sets and Systems* 157: 635–641.
Putnam, H. (1983), "Vagueness and Alternate Logic", *Realism and reason*, Cambridge: Cambridge University Press, 271–286.
Read, S. and Wright C. (1985), "Harrier than Putnam Thought", *Analysis* 45: 56–58.
Shapiro, S. (2006), *Vagueness in Context*, Oxford: Oxford University Press.
Sorenson, R. (2001), *Vagueness and Contradiction*, Oxford: Oxford University Press.
Tappenden, J. (1993), "The Liar and Sorites Paradoxes: Toward a Unified Treatment", *Journal of Philosophy* 90: 551–577.
Weatherson, B. (2005), "True, Truer, Truest", *Philosophical Studies* 123: 47–80.
Williamson, T. (1994), *Vagueness*, London and New York, NY: Routledge Publishing Company.
Wright, C. (1976), "Language Mastery and the Sorites Paradox", in G. Evans and J. McDowell, editors, *Truth and Meaning: Essays in Semantics*, Oxford: Oxford University Press, 223–247.

Chapter 4
Vagueness and Meaning

Roy T. Cook

4.1 Introduction

At first glance, it is natural to conclude that vagueness is a phenomenon intimately tied to meaning. After all, it is expressions, such as vague predicates (or vague terms, or vague quantifiers, etc.[1]), to which we attribute vagueness,[2] and most of the philosophically important characteristics that linguistic expressions have are tied to their meanings or, at least, tied to conundrums or other phenomenon involving the meanings of the expressions in question.

This conclusion is not, however, unavoidable. Broadly speaking, there are three ways in which one might attempt to explain the vagueness of a predicate such as 'bald':

The semantic view: Vagueness is a phenomenon that arises in language.
The *in rebus* view: Vagueness is a phenomenon that arises in the world.
The epistemic view: Vagueness is a phenomenon that arises in our knowledge.[3]

R.T. Cook (✉)
Department of Philosophy, University of Minnesota, Minneapolis, MN, USA
e-mail: Cookx432@umn.edu

[1]For the remainder of this chapter we shall simplify our discussion by restricting our attention to vague predicates. The reader should keep in mind, however, that the considerations below can be generalized to all vague expressions.

[2]Of course, there is also a large literature on the issue of vague objects and metaphysical vagueness more generally – that is, so-called ontic vagueness (see, e.g Evans (1978), Parsons (2000)). While the issues tied up with the existence, or not, of vague objects are interesting and important, they are rather orthogonal to the present topic.

[3]In point of fact, the epistemic conception of vagueness can be thought of as a particularly sophisticated variant of the semantic view: By epistemicist lights, vagueness is a phenomenon that occurs in language, but it occurs in a different portion of language than we might have originally thought (in particular, the indeterminacy occurs not in simple predications of a vague predicate (e.g. "Bob is bald"), but in epistemic claims about such predications (e.g. "We can know that Bob is bald"). For our purposes here, however, it will prove more convenient to treat the epistemic view as a separate position.

G. Ronzitti (ed.), *Vagueness: A Guide*, Logic, Epistemology, and the Unity of Science 19, DOI 10.1007/978-94-007-0375-9_4,

This trichotomy of views can be fleshed out in a bit more detail: To start with, vagueness seems to involve some sort of indeterminacy – for example, it is indeterminate of some men whether or not the predicate 'bald' applies to them. The three sorts of view can then be distinguished in terms of where each view locates the source of this indeterminacy.

The semantic view finds the root of this indeterminacy in some shortcoming of our language – for example, vague predicates might be meaningful while nevertheless failing to determine precisely to which (precise, sharply delineated) objects they apply. The *in rebus* view, on the other hand, finds no indeterminacy in our language – instead, it is the world that is 'fuzzy', and as a result there are objects (or other 'stuff') of which it is indeterminate whether they meet the precise satisfaction conditions of our predicates. The epistemic view, finally, finds the root of this indeterminacy in neither our language nor the world, but instead locates the 'problem' in our epistemological powers – in other words, according to the epistemic account there is a precise fit between our language and the world (and thus, for example, a determinate fact of the matter regarding, of each man, whether he is bald) and our intuitions to the contrary are explained in terms of our in-principle inability to determine what the extensions of vague predicates actually are. Put bluntly, on the epistemic view vague predicates have precise meanings, and are differentiated from non-vague expressions solely in terms of their epistemology.

In this chapter we shall focus on the semantic and the epistemological views of vagueness. The reason for this is that our purpose here is to examine the connection between the vagueness of an expression and the meaning of that expression. Both the semantic and epistemic views of vagueness allow one to draw tight connections between vagueness of expressions and the meaning of those expressions: If one is convinced that vagueness is attributable to some sort indeterminacy of the meanings of our expressions – that is, if one accepts the semantic conception – then one of the central tasks in accounting for vague predicates and the puzzles and paradoxes that seem to arise from them will be to provide a meaning theory for vague language. Furthermore, if one thinks that vagueness is attributable to some sort of epistemic failing – that is, if one accepts the epistemic view – then, since our ability to know particular claims is intimately tied to our understanding of those claims, it is also not hard to see that one of the main tasks will be to explore how the vagueness of expressions is tied to their meanings. The *in rebus* approach to vagueness, on the other hand, makes vagueness more of a metaphysical, and less of a language-oriented, phenomenon – one can imagine a possible world whose objects, properties, etc. were not in any way indeterminate, and, on the *in rebus* view, presumably our expressions would have the same meanings in this imagined possible world as they have in the actual world, yet be completely precise.

Thus, we shall here be examining how proponents of the semantic and epistemic conceptions of vagueness account for the meaning of vague expressions and the contribution that meaning makes to those expressions being vague.

The next task is, of course, to ask what a theory of meaning should provide us in general, as well as how a theory of meaning will be particularly relevant to addressing various issues that arise due to vagueness. A theory of meaning can serve a number of interconnected explanatory roles, including:

(a) Providing an account of the connection between a linguistic expression and its meaning. In other words, a theory of meaning should provide explanatory statements of the form:

 'Φ means X'

(b) Providing an account of the manner in which the meaning of an expression plays a role in how that expression refers to or otherwise represents some potential or actual features of the world. In other words, a meaning theory should provide an account of how the meanings of expressions contribute to their having the reference (or other semantic values) that they in fact have.
(c) Providing an account of the manner in which the meanings of expressions impose normative constraints on how we ought to use those expressions. In other words, a meaning theory should explain how the meanings of expressions are tied up with not only how we actually use those expressions, but how we *ought* to use those expressions.[4]
(d) Providing an account of the manner in which the meanings of expressions are (in light of (c) above) nevertheless largely a function of how we use those expressions.

The natural way in which to survey the various theories of meaning proposed for languages involving vagueness would be to just that: briefly explain and critique each of the meaning theories in question. The problem with this approach, however, is that there are very few such well-worked out theories of meaning – in other words, very few theorists have explicitly addressed (a) above, much less (b) through (d). Instead of providing an (informal, philosophical) account of the meaning of vague terms, or even discussing how they obtain their meanings in any detail, most theorists make some preliminary comments regarding meaning and then move on to providing a formal semantics.[5] As John Burgess points out, at the beginning of 'Vagueness, Epistemicism, and Response-Dependence':

> It is a noteworthy, if unfortunate, feature of most... accounts of vagueness that they provide, in answering... [questions about the meaning of vague expressions]... a formal semantic explication... (2001, p. 516)

While few will doubt that there is a clear connection between theories of meaning and formal semantics (we shall return to this connection in the final section of the

---

[4]If the target of this chapter was 'solving' the Sorites paradoxs and similar puzzles that arise due to vagueness, then (c) would undoubtably play the most prominent role in our discussion.

[5]Of course, if the theorist in question holds a Davidsonian-like view that equates a theory of meaning with a (possibly formal) account of the truth conditions of statements (see, e.g. Davidson (1967)), then this complaint is unfounded (Sainsbury (1990) suggests (with some reservations) such a Davidsonian approach to the meaning of vague expressions).

chapter), a formal semantics does not provide, on its own, a philosophically illuminating account of meaning. Thus, lacking well-worked out philosophical accounts of the meaning of vague expressions, we need another approach.

The approach we shall take is a problem-oriented one. There are three main puzzles regarding meaning that have arisen in the literature on vagueness. Although each was raised as a problem for a particular account of vagueness, in their general form they promise to plague any account that draws a strong connection between the vagueness of an expression and the meaning of that expression. Thus, for each of these puzzles, we shall strive to formulate it in its most general form, and then examine how various accounts of vagueness have responded to the problem (or, in some cases, we shall carefully guess how a particular account should, could, or will respond).

Two of these problems find their earliest or best expression in the writings of Crispin Wright, who is amongst the few philosophers working on vagueness who has clearly and continually kept his eye on philosophical issues having to do with meaning, and in particular, on how the meaning of vague expressions is connected to the use that we make of them. The third problem is due to John Burgess, and also involves connections between the meaning and our use of vague expressions. As a result, much of our discussion will connect most closely to tasks (c) and (d) above – that is, on how our use of vague predicates is both constitutive of, yet governed by, the meaning of those predicates – and how these tasks connect to (b), the manner in which the meaning of vague predicates determines which objects are, and are not, instances of those predicates.

Before moving on to the first such puzzle, one last methodological note is in order: In the discussion of each problem below we shall further subdivide the semantic approach to vagueness into two camps: indeterminist theories, and contextualist theories. These two subdivisions of the semantic conception of vagueness, plus the epistemic approach, cover most, if not all, of the extant approaches to dealing with vague expressions and the paradoxes that arise from them (other than *in rebus* approaches, which we have already ruled out of our discussion here). Thus, a bit more should be said about what falls under each of these headings.

An indeterminist theory is any theory that explains vagueness in terms of there being cases – so called borderline cases – that receive some value other than standard true or false as their semantic value. Indeterminist theories include supervaluational approaches (where borderline cases fail to receive a truth value, and are consistent with either truth value in precisifications, see e.g. Fine (1975)), subvaluational approaches (where borderline cases receive both truth values, and are consistent with either truth value in precisifications, see e.g. Hyde (1997)) degree-theoretic approaches (where borderline cases receive degrees of truth, or verities, strictly between truth and falsity, see e.g. Machina (1976), Edgington (1997)), three-valued logics, including but not limited to dialethic logics (where borderline cases receive some third value other than truth or falsity, see, e.g. Priest (2003)), etc. Put a bit loosely, an account of vagueness is an indeterminist theory if and only if it involves the use of a non-standard logic – one that allows for sentences to receive semantic values other than the traditional values (simply) true and (simply) false.[6] No doubt there are many important philosophical differences between these disparate views. For our purposes here, however, we can (for the most part) lump them all together into one category, since the three puzzles that we shall consider below will, for the most part, affect them equally. The crucial issue, in terms of meaning, is that indeterminate value theories involve the claim that the meaning of a vague expression is 'incomplete' in some sense, insofar as certain applications of the vague expression will receive values other than the traditional two, truth and falsity.

Contextualist approaches, on the other hand, involve the idea that every application of a vague predicate to an object will be either true or false,[7] but the truth value of particular applications will depend not only on the predicate and object in question, but on the context in which these applications occur. Thus, one and the same object can be bald in one context and not bald in another, without any intrinsic change in the object itself. As a result, we can retain classical logic (in a sense), since in any context all claims, including claims involving vague expressions, will be either true or false What is crucial, on the contextualist approach, is that there is no context in which we are 'looking' at the location where the sharp boundary between instances and non-instances of the vague expression. As Jason Stanley puts it:

> . . . when we look for the boundary of the extension of a vague expression in its penumbra, our very looking has the effect of changing the interpretation of the vague expression so that the boundary is not where we are looking. This accounts for the persuasive force of Sorites arguments. (2003, p. 269)

Thus, the contextualist approach is, in essence, a way of accepting that vague predicates impose sharp boundaries between their instances and their non-instances, while explaining the intuition that they do not (and cannot) impose such boundaries (see Raffman (1995), Graff (2000), or Shapiro (2006) for more details).

Once we have surveyed our three problems relating to philosophical accounts of the meanings of vague expressions, and determined what possible responses might be available to epistemicist, contextualists, and indeterminists in turn, we shall address one final issue – an analogue of the first problem – that plagues not only philosophical accounts of meaning but the formal semantics we often use in developing such an account.

---

[6]The qualifier "simply" is required here in order to handle dialethic accounts, which do not allow for any semantic values other than truth and falsity, but which do allow statements to be both. In addition, we shall assume that accounts which allow statements to fail to receive a value (so-called 'gappy' logics) to count as indeterminist accounts, interpreting the lack of a semantic value as a third semantic 'status'.

[7]This is a bit of a simplification, since some contextualist views (e.g. Tappenden (1993), Soames (1999), Shapiro (2006), involve a context imposing a sharp, tripartite division between the true, the false, and the other. We will avoid such complications in what follows, however.

4.2 The Governing View

The first problem, which we shall here call the governing view problem, begins with Crispin Wright's characterization of a vague predicate as a predicate that is tolerant (relevant to some underlying characteristics). In 'Language-mastery and the Sorites Paradox' he writes that:

> What is involved in...[a predicate's being vague]... is a certain *tolerance*... a notion of degree of change too small to make any difference, as it were.... More exactly, suppose Φ to be a concept related to a predicate, F, as follows: that any object which F characterizes may be changed into one which it does not simply by sufficient change in respect of Φ.... Then F is *tolerant* with respect to Φ if there is also some positive degree of change in respect of Φ insufficient ever to affect the justice with which F applies to a particular case. (1976, pp. 156–157)

The intuitive idea here is clear: A predicate F is vague (i.e. tolerant) if, and only if, sufficiently small changes in the relevant underlying concept Φ do not correspond to any change in the appropriateness (or correctness) of applications of F. Thus, 'bald' is tolerant with respect to the number of hairs on a subject's head since very small changes in this number (e.g. one hair more or less) never result in a difference in the justice with which one can apply (or not apply) the predicate 'bald'. Crucially, Wright's characterization of vagueness in terms of tolerance requires not only that there be no sharp boundary between the clear cases of F and the clear cases of ~ F, but additionally requires that there be no sharp boundary between any two distinct applications of 'F-ness'.[8]

The characterization of vagueness in terms of tolerance is perfectly aligned with the present investigation into the role of meaning, and meaning theories, in vagueness: Wright characterizes predicates as tolerant (and thus vague) in terms of the justice with which we can apply the predicate to particular instances. Presumably, a competent user of the vague predicate in question would (modulo standard *ceteris paribus* clauses) apply the predicate exactly in accord with the justice with which he *can* apply the predicate (i.e. he will use it as he should). Thus, a predicate is tolerant if and only if competent users of the predicate will apply that predicate in particular ways – in particular, if he will not apply it differently in cases that differ by some sufficiently marginal amount. Since a competent user of a predicate is (minimally) one who understands the meaning of the predicate, and applies that predicate accordingly, we can conclude that a predicate's being vague is a consequence of the predicate in question having a particular sort of meaning.

So far, so good. Wright, however, goes on to describes what he calls the 'governing view' – a general characterization of how our expressions obtain their meaning, and how we can come to understand the meaning our expressions have:

> ...we may legitimately approach our use of language from within, i.e. reflectively as self-conscious masters of it, rather than externally, equipped only with behavioural notions. Thus

[8]Characterizations of vagueness in terms similar to Wright's have since been proposed by Sainsbury (1990, p.260) and Soames (1999, p. 215).

it is legitimate to appeal to our conception of what justifies the application of a particular expression; to our conception of what we should count as an adequate explanation of the sense of a particular expression; to the limitations imposed by our senses and memories on the kind of instruction which we can actually carry out in practice; and to the kind of consequence which we associate with the application of a particular predicate, to what we think of as the point or interest of the distinction which the predicate implements. The primary concern of this paper is with the idea, henceforward referred to as the *governing view*, that from such considerations can be derived a reflective awareness of how we understand expressions in our language, and so of the nature of the rules which determine their correct use. The governing view, then is a conjunction of two claims: that our use of language is rightly seen, like a game, as a practice in which the admissibility of a move is determined by a rule, and that general properties of the rules may be discovered by means of the sorts of consideration just described. (1976, p. 153)

Wright argues that, at least for the case of vague predicates, the governing view is incoherent.

The reasons for this incoherence are worth going over in a little detail. The first conjunct of the governing view states that the meanings of expressions are codified by rules that determine the correct usage of those expressions. We can summarize this principle as:

[Rule Governed] The meanings of expressions (including vague expressions) are determined by the rules governing their correct, or competent, use.

The second thesis merely states that we can, through reflection, theorizing, and the like, discover what those rules are, which we can summarize as:

[Transparency] We are able, through reflection, to discover what rules govern correct, or competent, usage of expressions (including vague expressions).

The problem, of course, as Wright takes pains to carefully point out, is that the rules which we arrive at by introspection, investigation, etc. for vague predicates seem to involve, in an essential manner, the idea that these predicates are tolerant (in exactly the sense described above). After examining a number of examples of vague predicates in detail, Wright concludes that we are forced:

... to concede that the vagueness of these examples is a phenomenon of semantic depth – that it is sacrificed at much more than the cost of the intellectual labour of the stipulation – and that it is a structurally incoherent feature. (1976, p. 159)

In other words, vague predicates are tolerant predicates, tolerant predicates legitimate the reasoning underlying the Sorites paradox, and thus the rules we arrive at through reflection and theorizing are essentially incoherent.

We are faced, as a result, with four choices: The first is to accept the conclusion of the argument: vague predicates are, indeed, incoherent, and thus any attempt to provide a coherent meaning theory for languages involving them is doomed from the start. Although this option has been embraced by some (e.g. Dummett (1975) and Eklund (2005)), it is of little interest for our purposes here, since our goal is to investigate what meaning theories for vague predicates might look like, and not to deny the very coherence of such theories from the outset. The second option is to give up the idea that correct theorizing about the meanings of vague expressions involves determining the rules that govern correct usage of these expressions – in other words, to give up [rule-governed] above. Again, this option is a non-starter from the perspective of this chapter, since (like the first option) it amounts to abandoning the attempt to provide a meaning theory for vague expressions (and it is extremely unattractive on independent grounds) – after all, if an account of the meaning of vague expressions cannot be provided in terms of the rules for correct application, understanding 'rule' rather broadly to include truth conditions, inference rules, and the like, then what other form could such a theory take? The third option is to give up the principle of [transparency], accepting that the rules that govern correct usage of vague predicates are not accessible to us through, or constrained by, reflection or similar a priori philosophical theorizing. Since it is through our acceptance of [transparency] that we conclude that vague predicates are tolerant, this option allows us to avoid the conclusion that vague expressions are incoherent. This is the route taken by Wright in (1976) (although he backs off of this position somewhat in later writings, see (1987, 2001)). He writes:

> The methodological approach... must be more purely behavioristic and anti-reflective, if a general theory of meaning is to be possible at all. (1976, p. 173)

The fourth option is attractive for much the same reasons as the third. Here, we retain the governing view, but reject Wright's claim that reflection shows that vague predicates are tolerant. Instead, on this option we would deny that careful reflection on and consideration of our usage dictates that vague predicates are truly tolerant. The success of such an approach hinges on an additional explanation for why vague predicates might appear, at first glance, to be tolerant – that is, one who adopts this strategy needs to provide some account of why tolerance *seems* to be such a central feature of vague predicates and how such a view does not, contrary to Wright, involve more intellectual labor than the view is worth.

This fourth option is the one adopted by all of the views about the meaning of vague expressions under consideration here. Nevertheless, the move is made quite differently in the three different types of view under consideration. Thus, it will behoove us to look at each in turn, determining in each case how tolerance is denied and, more critically, what explanation can be given for the attractiveness of the thought that vague predicates are tolerant.

4.2.1 The Governing View and Epistemicist Theories

The epistemicist is perhaps the most straightforward in his denial of tolerance, since the epistemicist claims that there is a sharp boundary between those objects to which a vague predicate applies and those to which it doesn't. Unlike the indeterminist theorist, he does not 'pad' the change from true applications to false applications with applications that receive some other semantic value, nor does he suggest that the sharp boundary in question moves around from context to context. What the epistemicist does have in common with the contextualist, however, is the thought that our temptation to think tolerance true is a result of an epistemological inadequacy of some sort. The contextualist thinks that we can never find the boundary between, say, bald and non-bald objects, since that boundary is always somewhere other than where we are looking. The epistemicist, on the other hand, makes a much stronger claim regarding our epistemic limitations: if we are looking at two sufficiently similar cases, then we might not be able to tell that one is bald and the other is not – in other words, we cannot tell where the boundary between true and false applications of a vague predicate lies, even if we are looking right at it. Williamson mobilizes what he calls margin-for-error principles in order to defend this idea. A margin for error principle holds for a predicate F if and only if, for any a and b such that a and b differ (with respect to the characteristics relevant to F) by a marginal amount, knowledge of Fa implies the truth of Fb (see Williamson (1994), pp. 230–237 for details). Given the factivity of knowledge, this implies that we can never know, of any a and b that differ by a sufficiently marginal amount, that Fa and not Fb. Given the formal similarity between the margin-for error principle (small changes cannot take us from a knowably true case to a false case) and tolerance (small changes cannot take us from a true case to a false case), the epistemicist can both explain the attractiveness of tolerance and argue for its failure.

4.2.2 The Governing View and Contextualist Theories

The denial of tolerance, and the accompanying explanation of the intuition underlying one's temptation to think vague predicates are tolerant, is a bit subtler and more complex on the contextualist approach. On the one hand, the contextualist thinks that there is, in any context, an exact boundary between those objects of which the vague predicate is true and those objects of which the vague predicate is false. The intuition underlying tolerance is explained, however, by the fact that one can never identify such a boundary (or any boundary constituting a change of any sort in the applicability of the predicate). Given a particular context, and the boundary between 'bald' and 'not bald' within that context, if one could immediately look to where the boundary 'is' in that context, this would amount to a change in the context, so that the boundary would now be somewhere else. As Delia Graff puts it, the task is 'to explain *why* vague predicates seem tolerant to us, even though Sorites reasoning shows us that they cannot be' (2000, p. 54), and her answer is that:

> We cannot find the boundary of the extension of a vague predicate in a Sorites series for that predicate, because the boundary can never be where we are looking. It shifts around. ... we may say that it is no wonder that we were so inclined in the first place to regard the universal generalization as true, given that any instance of it we consider is in fact true at the time we consider it. (2000, p. 59)

As a result, we are tempted to think that there are changes small enough such that they never affect the justice with which we can apply the vague predicate merely because, in any particular context, no counterexamples are apparent to us (and attempts to find such counterexamples always result in the counterexamples being somewhere other than where we are looking). In other words, the contextualist accepts that the tolerance principle holds 'within' a context, since sufficiently small differences between a and b entail that a and b cannot be judged differently in the same context, but tolerance fails globally, since extremely similar objects, and even a single, obviously self-identical object, can be judged differently in different contexts.

4.2.3 The Governing View and Indeterminist Theories

In indeterminist theories, applications of a vague predicate to borderline cases receive a semantic value other than the traditional truth or falsity (whether this semantic value is 'both', 'neither', some degree of truth between truth and falsity, etc.). On this sort of account, tolerance is rejected, since for any small change in the relevant underlying characteristics we will be able to find to possible objects for which applications of the vague predicate receive different semantic values. For example, on the degree-theoretic approach there will be some number of hairs n such that the application of 'bald' to anyone with more n hairs on his head receives 1 as semantic value, while application of 'bald' to anyone with n or fewer hairs on his head will receive a value less than 1. Nevertheless, the indeterminist can explain the intuition underlying tolerance as follows: Sufficiently small changes can never take one from a case where application of the predicate in question receives truth as its semantic value to a case where the application of the predicate receives false as its semantic value.

4.3 The Relation of Meaning to Use

The next problem facing meaning theories for vague predicates is more closely tied to the connection between the meaning of a vague expression and the use that we make of that expression. One natural thought about this connection, one which is seldom challenged in the literature on meaning in general, and the meanings of vague expressions in particular, is that the meanings of our expressions, vague and non-vague alike, is a function of our use of those terms (or, more carefully, of our use of those terms in cases judged to be correct, or competent). Stephen Shiffer, in *The Things We Mean* (2003), makes this point quite directly:

> ... meaning simply is not a use-independent property. What an expression means for someone is determined by how that expression is used, if the expression is simple, or, if it's semantically complex, by how the expressions and structures composing it are used. If anything is a datum in these muddy waters, that is. (2003, p. 185)

Now, if the meaning of a vague predicate is determined by its use, and the extension of that predicate (or its semantic value more generally, in theories of vagueness that do not assign a straightforward extension to vague predicates) is determined by the meaning of the predicate, then facts about which objects are and are not instances of the predicate in question, and in particular, facts about the existence and location of boundaries, if there are such, should be explainable in terms of the use we make of vague predicates. Brian Weatherson, in 'Epistemicism, Parasites and Vague Names' (and paraphrasing an argument due to Burgess (2001)), puts it as follows:

> Here are some platitudes about the metaphysics of content that are very widely accepted... If a word t has content c, this must be in virtue of some more primitive fact obtaining. Facts about content, such as this, are not among the fundamental constituents of reality. Roughly, facts about linguistic content must obtain in virtue of facts about use. But there are simply not enough facts about use to determine a precise meaning for paradigmatically vague terms like 'rich'. Any theory that holds that 'rich' does have a precise meaning must meet this objection, by either identifying the relevant facts, or showing why the widely accepted philosophical platitudes about the metaphysics of content are not actually true. (2003, p. 276)

Both Burgess's original discussion, and Weatherson's summary of it, have epistemicism as their main target, which is natural given that the single sharp boundary imposed by vague predicates is an obvious target for this style of objection. But the point can be formulated much more generally: whatever content is ascribed to a vague predicate by some account of vagueness, that content had better arise in virtue of the use we make of the predicate in question.

4.3.1 Meaning, Use, and Epistemicist Theories

As already noted, the main target of Burgess and Weatherson in formulating this challenge is epistemicism, and both theorists conclude that epistemicism fails – that is, there is nothing in our use of vague predicates that could underlie their having a single, precise borderline between those applications that receive truth as semantic value, and those that receive falsity.[9] Their conclusions are, however, tentative at best, and there are good reasons for this: It follows from epistemicism that, if the meaning of a vague predicate (and thus, the precise boundary between instances and non-instances of that predicate) is determined by our use of that predicate (an assumption that epistemicists accept), then the manner in which our use of a predicate determines the extension of that predicate cannot, in a certain sense, be accessible to us. In 'Vagueness, Indeterminacy, and Social Meaning' Williamson writes:

> The epistemicist can consistently maintain that meaning is a function of use. What the epistemicist should deny is that meaning is a transparent function of use – that is, a function that enables us simply to deduce the cut-off point for a vague term from some canonical description of the use. For we have no idea how to make any such deduction. But we have grounds independent of vagueness for denying that meaning is a transparent function of use. (2001, pp. 71–72)

[9] In fact, the challenge to the epistemicist is even more serious, since (at least on Williamson's development of the view) there will potentially be infinitely many different boundaries that must be accounted for – not just the boundary between instances of the predicate and non-instances, but between knowable instances (i.e. those instances that can be known to be instances) and non-knowable instances, between knowable non-knowable instances and non-knowable non-knowable instances, etc.

The point is quite simple: The epistemicist, on Williamson's view, must agree with Burgess and Weatherson's platitudes regarding the dependence of meaning on use, and thus, in the present instance, of the dependence of the sharp boundary between, for example, bald and non-bald men on our use of the predicate bald. Williamson also agrees with his critics that there is no obvious explanation of the location of the sharp boundary that follows from the actual facts about how we use the term 'bald'. But on his view, this is exactly as it should be – it is one thing to answer Weatherson's challenge by 'identifying the relevant facts' upon which the epistemicist's precise meanings and borderlines depend, and quite another to provide, in addition, an explanation of *how* those facts determine the meaning and extension of vague terms. Williamson believes he has done the former, but he is right to object that the latter is, on his view, impossible – after all, if he could determine in detail exactly how the relevant facts determined the boundary, then this would in effect amount to locating the boundary itself – an impossibility, on the epistemicist view.

4.3.2 Meaning, Use, and Contextualist Theories

The situation with regard to the connection between meaning and use is even worse for the contextualist, at first glance, than it is for the epistemicist – after all, the epistemicist is faced with explaining how our usage of a vague predicate such as 'bald' can secure a single precise boundary between instances of the predicate and non-instances of the predicate, but the contextualist is faced with the more daunting task of explaining how that same usage can provide a multitude of distinct sharp borders, one for each context (although, of course, some distinct contexts might have the same boundary for 'bald', the view depends on there being at least some contexts with distinct borderlines). The flip-side of this, however, is that the contextualist can adopt the same solution to the problem as that suggested by the epistemicist – that is, accept that the extension of a vague predicate (within a context) can, on the contextualist's account, be determined by our use of that predicate without accepting the stronger claim that such determination must be transparent. In other words, the contextualist can claim that use determining meaning, and thus determining the location of sharp cut-offs in particular contexts, is consistent with our inability to explain exactly how use determines these cut-offs. After all, if we could provide a complete account of how our usage determines meaning and reference of vague predicates, then we could presumably determine exactly where these sharp borderlines lay. And this is impossible, from the perspective of the contextualist, since the view entails that although sharp borders exist, they are always undetectable by us (i.e. they never lie where we are looking).

4.3.3 Meaning, Use, and Indeterminist Theories

It might seem that the indeterminist theorist, unlike the epistemicist or the contextualist, has little problem here, since indeterminist theories are motivated by the need to do away with sharp borders between instances where a vague predicate clearly applies and instances where that same vague predicate clearly does not apply – thus, the indeterminist denies that there is an exact number of hairs that determines the sharp borderline between men whom are bald and men who are not bald. Instead, on indeterminist theories there are intermediate cases that receive something other than the traditional values true or false. As a result, the indeterminist can answer the objection by pointing out her view does not require us to explain how our use of vague predicates determines sharp borders between true applications of those predicates and false applications of those predicates.

The problem for indeterminist theories comes when we realize that such a theory has replaced a sharp boundary between the true and the false with at least two sharp borders: that between the true and the indeterminate value or values, and that between the false and the indeterminate value or values (in some cases, such as degree-theoretic accounts, we will have up to continuum many sharp borders). R. M. Sainsbury explains the problem nicely in his 'Concepts without Boundaries':

> . . . you do not improve upon a bad idea by iterating it. In more detail, suppose we have a finished account of a predicate, associating it with some possibly infinite number of boundaries, and some possibly infinite number of sets. Given the aims of the description, we must be able to organize the sets in the following threefold way: one of them is the set supposedly corresponding to the things of which the predicate is absolutely definitely and unimpugnably true, the things to which the predicate's application is untainted by the shadow of vagueness; one of them is the set supposedly corresponding to the things of which the predicate is absolutely definitely and unimpugnably false, the things to which the predicate's non-application is untainted by the shadow of vagueness; the union of the remaining sets would correspond to one or another kind of borderline case. So the old problem re-emerges: no sharp cut-off to the shadow of vagueness is marked in our linguistic practice, so to attribute it to the predicate is to misdescribe it. (1990, p. 255)

Thus, the indeterminist is faced with a version of the same problem as the epistemicist and the contextualist: The meanings of vague predicates (plus external factors) must somehow determine the locations of these boundaries. Since the meanings of our expressions are determined by the use we make of them, and there seems to be nothing in our use that could impose strict boundaries between the true instances and the intermediate instances, or between the intermediate instances and the false instances, this would seem to be a serious problem.

In addition, the strategy for dealing with this issue adopted by epistemicists (and suggested above for contextualists as well) does not seem open to indeterminists. The indeterminist typically is motivated by the rejection of sharp boundaries between true and false applications of a vague predicate, and in fact the rejection of sharp borders of any sort associated with vagueness. Thus, to be forced into a position where we now must explain the existence of some other set of sharp borders seems against the spirit, if not the letter, of the indeterminist theory approach (although, to be fair, different variants of the indeterminist theory might have different things to say here). Thus, some other approach is warranted.

There are a number of approaches that the indeterminist might take. Perhaps the most common is to suggest that the new set of boundaries is itself vague. Thus, we reapply our semantics, not to the supposed line between truth and falsity, but to the boundary between true and indeterminate, and the boundary between indeterminate and false (and further, to any borders between distinct indeterminate states). As a result, given a particular vague predicate, we now have the instances where it is true that application of the predicate results in truth, and instances where it is false that application of the predicate results in truth (since the instance in question is clearly indeterminate) and instances where it is indeterminate whether application of the predicate results in truth (these typically are also cases where it is indeterminate whether application of the predicate results in indeterminacy). Of course, this only replaces one sharp boundary (that between true and intermediate) with two more, so we apply the process again, iterating *ad infinitum.*

As Sainbury's remark about not improving 'a bad idea by iterating it' suggests, there is some temptation to think that this response does not address the problem at hand, since in the end, we have replaced one sharp boundary between truth and falsity with an infinite collection of borders between all of the different ways in which a vague claim might be indeterminate. Thus, an alternative strategy for dealing with this problem has arisen: formulate one's meaning theory within a vague metalanguage. The first variation of this idea is due to Sainsbury, who suggests that we adopt a homophonic semantics:

> I would urge an idea of Donald Davidson's. A semantic theory can quite legitimately be *homophonic*, that is, can reuse in the metalanguage the very expressions whose object-language behaviour it is attempting to characterize. Asked how a boundaryless predicate like 'red' works, my first response would be: 'red' is true of something iff that thing is red. (p. 260)

Thus, for Sainsbury, an adequate meaning theory for vague expressions such as 'is red' will consist of (or at least be based on) homophonic meaning-principles of the form:

> 'a is red' is true iff a is red.

which will contribute to a Davidsonian-style meaning-theory-as-truth-theory account. Michael Tye, in 'Sorites Paradoxes and the Semantics of Vagueness' develops an alternative version of this approach utilizing a vague set theory based on an underlying three-valued (or 'gappy'[10]) logic. He characterizes the vague sets populating the universe of his theory as follows:

> ... I classify a set S as vague (in the ordinary robust sense in which the set of tall men is vague) if, and only if, (a) it has borderline members and (b) there is no determinate fact of the matter about whether there are objects that are neither members, borderline members, nor non-members. (1994b, p. 284)

[10]It should be noted that Tye takes pains to stress that his logic is not, in fact, three-valued, but is instead a gappy logic, where statements take at most one of true and false, but might receive neither. From the technical perspective at issue here, however, the distinction between such gappy logics and three-valued logics makes no difference.

The obvious drawback to either way of fleshing out the vague metatheory approach, however, is that we lose the power of non-vague metatheories for proving powerful results about our theory of meaning (for example, no set theoretic principle is completely true in Tye's approach). This issue is closely related to the problem of inappropriate precision, which we shall turn to in Section 4.5.

4.4 Open Texture

The third puzzle plaguing attempts to formulate an adequate theory of meaning for languages containing vague predicates is raised by Crispin Wright in 'On Being in a Quandary: Relativism, Vagueness, Logical Revisionism' (2001). Wright examines the sort of indeterminacy involved in borderline cases of vague predicates, and concludes that:

> It is quite unsatisfactory in general to represent *in*determinacy as any kind of determinate truth-status – any kind of middle situation, contrasting with both the poles (truth and falsity) – since one cannot thereby do justice to the absolutely basic datum that in general borderline cases come across as hard cases: as cases where we are baffled to choose between conflicting verdicts about which polar verdict applies, rather than as cases which we recognize as enjoying a status inconsistent with both. Sure sometimes people may non-interactively agree – that is, agree without any sociological evidence about other verdicts – that a shade of colour, say, is indeterminate (though I do not think it is clear what is the *content* of such an agreement); but more often – and more basically – the indeterminacy will be initially manifest not in (relatively confident) verdicts of indeterminacy but in (hesitant) differences of opinion (either between subjects at a given time or within a single subject's opinions at different times) about a polar verdict, which we have no idea how to settle, and which, therefore, we do not recognize as wrong. (p. 70)

To put it simply: Imagine a line of 100,000 men, ranging from Yul Brynner to Jerry Garcia, where each man in the line has one more hair than the man that preceded him.[11] Some of these men (such as Mr. Brynner) will be clear cases where application of the predicate 'bald' results in a true claim, and some of them (such as Mr. Garcia) will be clear cases where application of the predicate 'bald' results in a false claim. Wright's observation is simply this: the cases in the middle – the 'hard cases' as Wright puts it – are not cases where neither verdict is appropriate, but are instead cases where both verdicts seem appropriate, acceptable, etc (of course, the idea here is that, in borderline cases we seem free to adopt either verdict, not that we are free to simultaneously adopt both).

Stewart Shapiro shares the same intuitions about our freedom to make either judgement when confronted with borderline cases, calling this the open texture thesis[12]:

> Suppose . . . that a is a borderline case of P. I take it as another premise that, in some situations, a speaker is free to assert Pa and free to assert ¬Pa, without offending against the

[11] I am cheerfully borrowing Stewart Shapiro's favorite example here.

[12] The term is originally due to Friedrich Weismann (1968), where he suggested the term for expressions whose meanings do not provide for, or determine, every possible instance of application.

> meanings of the terms, or against any other rule of language use. Unsettled entails open. The rules of language use, as they are fixed by what we say and do, allow someone to go either way in the borderline region. Let us call this the open-texture thesis. (2003, p. 43)

If borderline cases of vagueness are cases where either verdict is acceptable, then our theory of meaning should explain this. In other words, if Wright is right, then the indeterminacy of the sort found in vague predicates should not be explained by some additional third status, but should instead involve somehow the idea that such borderline cases are compatible with either verdict.[13]

4.4.1 Open Texture and Epistemicist Theories

The epistemicist seems to have a straightforward answer to this worry. On her view, of course, borderline cases are not cases where application of the vague predicate in question is compatible with either a verdict of 'true', or a verdict of 'false', at least not if we understand compatibility in terms of correctness. The epistemicist can explain Wright's observation that both verdicts are acceptable, however, by pointing out that they are both consistent with everything that we know (and everything that we can know). Thus, on the epistemicist view, the fact that it seems like we can judge borderline cases either way can be explained by the fact that either judgment is compatible with our epistemic situation, since for the epistemicist borderline cases just are those cases where we cannot know, of the vague predicate, whether it holds or not. In other words, borderline cases appear, on the epistemicist's account, to be instances of open texture because either verdict is consistent with everything we know and can know, although at least one verdict will be incompatible with the (unknowable) facts.

4.4.2 Open Texture and Contextualist Theories

The contextualist would seem to have an equally easy time of explaining away Wright's and Shapiro's worry here (in fact, the open texture thesis is one of four guiding principles behind Shapiro's (2006) variant of contextualism). On the contextualist view, claims involving a vague predicate are only true or false relative to a context, and borderline cases are cases where application of the vague predicate results in a true statement in some contexts and a false statement in others. As a result, borderline cases are 'hard cases' because, even if true in one context, they might have been false in another, and our uncertainty is compounded because we might, in certain contexts, not have enough information to determine whether the case at hand is one in which the particular predication at hand is true or false (since, on the contextualist view, we can never know, of a particular context, exactly where the boundary for our vague predicate lies, even though we can be sure that

[13] It should be noted that other theorists – notably Paul Horwich (see (1997)) – have characterized borderline cases of a vague predicate as cases where neither verdict is appropriate. Williamson (1997) contains a convincing refutation of this sort of view, however.

it lies somewhere). Thus, for the contextualist, the appearance of open texture with regard to vague predicates is explained in virtue of each borderline instance being one for which there is some context in which application of the vague predicate in question is appropriate, and there is some other context in which its application is inappropriate.

4.4.3 Open Texture and Indeterminist Theories

The problem of open texture arose, in Wright's paper, from consideration of indeterminist theories, and it is indeterminist theories that would seem to have the most trouble here. The point of indeterminist theories is to have an intermediate semantic value (whether 'neither', or degrees of truth, or something else) that separates the instances where application of the predicate is (simply) true from instances where application of the predicate is (simply) false. As a result, a borderline case is, on the indeterminist view, one that is neither true nor false, and, as a result, the theory of meaning associated with such views will entail that borderline cases are cases where applications of the vague predicate in question result in a semantic status incompatible with either truth or falsity. In addition, there seems no clear way, on the indeterminist approach, to explain away Wright's requirement that borderline cases are cases where either verdict is appropriate as merely apparent, as is done by the contextualist or the epistemicist.

There are two particular versions of the indeterminist approach that might look immune to these worries, however, although in one of these cases the resistance is only apparent. First, one might think that the supervaluational approach can account for Wright's observation, since borderline cases are, on supervaluational accountss, exactly those cases that are true in some precisifications and false in others. As a result, we can account for the acceptability of either verdict in borderline cases, since our vague predicate is compatible both with precisifications of it that make the application of the vague predicate to this case true, and precisifications that make application of the predicate to this case false. This, however, would be to miss the point (either of Wright's worry, or of supervaluational semantics). On the supervaluational account a statement involving vagueness is, properly understood, not true in a particular precisification (although this unfortunate terminology is typically used). Instead, a statement is true (properly speaking – the term 'supertrue' is often misleadingly used here) if and only if it is true on every relevant precisification. As a result, since borderline cases, relative to a vague predicate, are those that result in verdicts of true on some precisifications and false in others, it follows that borderline cases are neither true nor false – they receive a third value (or, more carefully, they fail to receive a semantic value at all) and, as a result, borderline cases are incompatible with either a verdict of 'true' or a verdict of 'false'.

Dialethic approaches, however (such as that found in Priest (2003)), do seem to handle Wright's point adequately. On the dialethic approach a borderline case is one where application of the vague predicate results in a statement that is both true and false. As a result, there is little need to explain the apparent acceptability of both a 'true' verdict and a 'false' verdict, since either verdict is literally correct (even if, on its own, incomplete).

4.5 The Problem of Inappropriate Precision

The final problem we shall look at in our examination of vagueness and meaning theories is a bit different, addressing not philosophical accounts of the meaning of vague predicates directly, but rather the formal semantics that are often used as tools in studying the meaning of vague expressions and that (often) are critical parts of one's meaning theory. While one can debate exactly what role formalisms are to play in the development of an account of the meaning of vague terms, there is no doubt that formal logics and formal semantics do play a substantial role in theorizing about vague expressions (hence the obvious importance of such work, even if at the end of the day some feel that important questions, such as the three discussed above, are left somewhat unaddressed by formalism). Thus, the first part of the present puzzle consists of the following very natural thought:

> [Pro-Precision] : A meaning theory (in particular, a meaning theory for vagueness) requires (as a significant ingredient, at least) the use of a precise mathematical structure.

This thought is a formal analogue of what we called [rule-governed] in our discussion of the governing view in Section 4.2 above and, in a certain sense, can be seen as following from it. Our theory of meaning for a class of expressions will consist, on the governing view, of a set of rules that determine correct usage of those expressions. If this is right, then the tools of formal logic and semantics ought to play a central role in the construction of a meaning theory, since it is through the use of such tools that we will be able to formulate clear, precise codifications of the relevant rules governing use.

The utility of formal semantics in theorizing about natural languages is not hard to explain: natural languages are the messy result of centuries of evolution. As a result, we can often learn much more about a linguistic phenomenon by studying a formal model of the language in question instead being forced to deal with the (possibly irrelevant) complexities and messiness involved in studying the natural language itself. As a result, it is not surprising that the last few decades have seen an immense amount of time and energy devoted to providing formal semantics for vague languages. A quick survey of the literature turns up super-valuational semantics (Fine (1975)), sub-valuational semantics (Hyde (1997)), degree-theoretic semantics (Machina (1976), Edgington (1997)), and a host of other options. Not surprisingly, these systems are fascinating from both a philosophical and mathematical perspective. So what could be the problem (other than deciding which of these various systems to choose)?

The problem, of course, stems from a second, equally natural line of thought. If Wright's characterization of vagueness as tolerance is correct, then vagueness is caused by a deep and fundamental antipathy to sharp boundaries of any sort. Formal semantics, however, are so useful precisely because they impose sharp boundaries. As a result, any formal semantics, in virtue of its precision, will amount to a misdescription of the phenomenon in question.

The problem is nicely outlined by Michael Tye in 'Vagueness: Welcome to the Quicksand' (although his comments are aimed at degree-theoretic semantics in particular, it is clear that the objection can be applied more generally, to any semantics based on precise mathematical constructions):

> One serious objection to [degree-theoretic semantics] is that it really replaces vagueness with the most refined and incredible precision. Set membership, as viewed by the degrees of truth theorist, comes in precise degrees, as does predicate application and truth. The result is a commitment to precise dividing lines that is not only unbelievable but also thoroughly contrary to what I ... [call] 'robust' or 'resilient' vagueness. For ... it seems an essential part of the resilient vagueness of ordinary terms such as 'bald', 'tall', and 'overweight' that in Sorites sequences ... there is indeterminacy with respect to the conditionals that have the value 1, and those that have the next highest value, whatever it might be. It is this central feature of vagueness which the degrees of truth approach, in its standard form, fails to accommodate, regardless of how many truth-values it introduces. (1994a, p. 14)[14]

Simply put, Tye's worry is this: No sharp boundaries are present in our actual linguistic usage of vague predicates, and this is not an accident, or a consequence of some sort of linguistic laziness in not fully specifying the extensions of vague predicates. Instead, this lack of a precise dividing line between cases where a vague predicate clearly applies and cases where it does not (or between any other sorts of case) is an essential aspect of that predicate – that is, the lack of sharp boundaries of any sort follows from the meaning of the predicate. As a result, any semantics built upon a precise mathematical structure (i.e. set theory or anything equivalent) will, in virtue of that precision, provide us with, at best, a misdescription of at least some of the fundamental semantic features of that predicate. In short: we have our second line of thought:

> [Anti-Precision] : An adequate meaning theory for vagueness cannot be based on a precise mathematical structure, since precise mathematical constructions will misrepresent the (border-free) phenomenon of vagueness.

Unsurprisingly, this principle is a formal analogue of the principle of [transparency] from the discussion above (or, more carefully, is a formal analogue of the claim that vagueness is, essentially, a matter of tolerance, which follows, so the story goes, from transparency).

The problem of inappropriate precision, in a nutshell, is nothing more than the (apparent) conflict between [pro-precision] and [anti-precision] – in other words, how can we successfully use a tool (formal semantics) whose defining characteristic, and principle advantage, is precision to successfully study and explain a phenomenon (vagueness) whose defining characteristic is exactly the lack of such precision?[15]

---

[14] The reader should also consider R. M. Sainsbury's comments, quoted in Section 4.3.3, in light of this problem.

[15] It is worth noting that a move to non-standard mathematical theories, such as constructive or intuitionistic mathematics, does not seem to help here, since although the structures studied in such non-standard mathematical settings are less determinate in the sense of, for example, failing to satisfy bivalence, they are nevertheless still mathematically precise in the relevant sense.

4.5.1 The Problem of Inappropriate Precision and Epistemicist Theories

The epistemicist, who denies that there is any imprecision in the extension of a vague predicate, can be interpreted as being motivated by, at least in part, the problem of inappropriate precision. Williams, in his 'Imagination, Stipulation, and Vagueness' writes that:

> The initial case for the epistemic view is powerful. Nevertheless, many philosophers regard the view as too counterintuitive to be taken seriously. Is epistemicism about vagueness therefore like David Lewis's modal realism and Graham Priest's dialetheism – hard to refute, hard to believe, the victim of the of the incredulous stare? One crucial difference is that modal realism and dialetheism, unlike epistemicism, are revisionary in logic... Epistemicism employs a different methodology: one holds one's logic fixed, to discipline one's philosophical thinking. It is its opponents who reject the discipline. The epistemicist's hunch is that in the long run the results of the discipline will be more satisfying from a philosophical as well as from a logical point of view. (1997, pp. 217–218)

For Williamson, the retention of classical semantics is a fundamental methodological maxim. As a result, it is not difficult to interpret (some of) Williamson's arguments for epistemicism as explicitly addressing this apparent mismatch between the precision of formal (in particular, classical) semantics and the imprecision of vague expressions. If we must reject one or the other, as the problem of inappropriate precision suggests, then Williamson thinks that it is the extremely successful formal systems of classical logic that we should retain, and not the intuition that vagueness involves a complete lack of precision.

The worry here, however, is that the problem of inappropriate precision might reappear in a new guise. After all, the epistemicist explains the intuition that vague predicates are tolerant by invoking the margin-for-error principles discussed in Section 4.2.1 above. If, however, the lack of precision that we thought was present in the application of vague predicates is explained away in terms of knowledge claims involving vague predicates, then the natural thought is that these epistemic claims will involve imprecision in an essential manner (since if they do not, then it is not clear how invoking them could explain the apparent lack of precision in applications of the vague predicate itself). But if this is right, then we should wonder about the lack of fit between the precision of formal semantics for classical epistemic logic (in Williamson's case, the modal logic KT – see the appendix to (1994)) and the lack of precision in epistemic claims involving vague predicates.

4.5.2 The Problem of Inappropriate Precision and Contextualist Theories

The contextualist would, at first glance, seem to have the least worries here, since her position amounts to the idea that vague predicates, within a particular context, are completely precise and can thus be formalized unproblematically using precise semantics understood as codifying truth conditions, etc., within a particular context. Things are not, however, quite as simple as they seem: The contextualist also owes an account of the semantic status of claims as we shift from one context to another, and this requires a formal semantics that is trans-contextual. Since, for the contextualist, it is in the relations between contexts that the essential imprecision of vague expressions is to be found, the problem clearly reappears.

Stewart Shapiro has developed has developed a sophisticated formal semantics for his preferred variant of contextualism in his (2006). Before doing so, however, he notes that 'any account of vagueness that employs classical set theory as its metalanguage will encounter sharp boundaries in unwanted places' (2006, p. 57). Such a boundary will occur, for example, between the men who are bald in all contexts, and the men who fail to be bald in some context. Shapiro concludes that a novel attitude must be taken towards the formal semantics, one which he (following Cook (2002)) he calls the logic-as-modeling approach to formal semantics. Since this is also the most promising solution to the problem of inappropriate precision for the proponent of an indeterminacy theory as well, we shall move on to a discussion of those accounts.

4.5.3 The Problem of Inappropriate Precision and Indeterminacy Theories

The problem of inappropriate precision is clearly a serious problem for the defender of an indeterminacy theory. After all, it is the indeterminacy theorist who attempts to take the apparent lack of precise borders between true instances of a predicate, false instances, etc. as close as possible to a face value reading. Thus, the indeterminacy theorist is saddled with explaining how her adherence to the idea that vague expressions really do involve imprecision and lack of borders in an essential way is consistent with her use of precise formal semantics.

There are two main approaches to dealing with this difficulty. The first, already mentioned earlier, is to abandon the precision of classical formal semantics, opting instead for an imprecise, vague metatheory – and, in the case at hand, formulating formal semantics that are vague in the requisite manner. Michael Tye adopts this approach, formulating a vague set theory based on an underlying three-valued logic, and describes the benefits of his approach as follows:

> I conclude that sorites paradoxes present no real difficulty for my semantics. This is, I maintain, largely because, unlike other prominent semantics, it concedes that the world is, in certain respects, intrinsically, robustly vague; and it avoids, *at all levels*, a commitment to sharp dividing lines. This position is, I suggest, consonant with both our ordinary common-sense view of what there is and our pre-theoretical intuitions about vagueness. (1994b, p. 293)

While this approach, which we might dub the 'imprecisionist' approach to formal semantics, is internally coherent, it is not clear that it actually helps with the present problem. The reason for this is that it throws out the benefits of precise, formal semantics along with the unwanted precision. After all, it is precisely the clarity and tractability of precise formal semantics built up out of standard set-theoretic constructions that makes them so useful, since this clarity and tractability allow us to study these systems, proving theorems within and about them and in general advancing our understanding of the phenomenon in question. Formal systems constructed within such 'imprecisionist', vague metatheories, on the other hand, eliminate the utility of formal semantics when they eliminate the precision of formal semantics: As Tye happily admits, within his system no set theoretic claim come out completely true – at best they receive the third, intermediate value (pp. 285–286). One is left wondering how one is to develop and study an account of vague expressions if the mathematics underlying the account contains no actual truths with which we can begin!

The other approach to the problem of inappropriate precision was already mentioned in the previous subsection, in our discussion of contextualism (and, in particular, Shapiro's (2006) work on contextualism). This approach, called logic-as-modeling, treats the formal semantics, not as a completely accurate description of the linguistic phenomenon being codified, but instead as a fruitful mathematical model of the phenomenon, which gets some, but not all, aspects of the phenomenon right. In defending her version of the degree-theoretic approach, Dorothy Edgington describes the position this way[16]:

> The numbers serve a useful purpose as a theoretical tool, even if there is no perfect mapping between them and the phenomenon; they give us a way of representing significant and insignificant differences, and the logical structure and combination of these... The result may still be approximately correct. (1997, p. 297)

Shapiro gives a more detailed, and more general, formulation of the idea as follows:

> The present claim is that a formal language is a mathematical model of a natural language, in roughly the same sense as, say, a Turing machine is a model of calculation, a collection of point masses is a model of a system of physical objects, and the Bohr construction is a model of an atom. In other words, a formal language displays certain features of natural languages, or idealizations thereof, while simplifying other features ... with mathematical models generally, there is typically no question of 'getting it exactly right'. For a given purpose, there may be bad models – models that are clearly incorrect – and there may be good models, but it is unlikely that one can speak of the one and only correct model. There is almost always a gap between a model and what it is a model of. (Shapiro, 2006, p. 50)

Shapiro calls those aspects of the model that fail to 'match up' with aspects of the phenomenon being modeled in the appropriate manner artifacts, and aspects that do appropriately 'match up' representors (see also Shapiro (1998)). Thus, the solution to the problem of inappropriate precision, on the present approach, is to claim that the precision of formal semantics is merely an artifact of the model, not representing anything actually present in vague discourse.[17]

---

[16]It should be noted that Edgington did not herself use the term 'logic-as-modeling' – the term arose in later writings by Cook (e.g. (2002)) and Shapiro (e.g. (2006)) that attempted to further flesh out the import of her comments (and those of other writers) on this topic. The view finds it earliest substantial developments in Corcoran (1973).

[17]The logic-as-modeling approach has been criticized (notably, by Keefe (2000)) for merely hypothesizing an artifact/representor distinction without failing to adequately account for where, exactly, the line between artifact and representor lies, although Cook (2002) goes some ways towards assuaging this worry.

4.6 Conclusion

In the previous sections we surveyed four difficulties facing any account of the meaning of vague predicates – three that directly address such a meaning theory, and a fourth that plagues the formal semantics often used to illuminate such accounts of meaning. In each case, we saw that the problem in question was a difficulty for most, if not all, of the popular approaches to dealing with vague language: the epistemicist approach, the contextualist approach, and the various versions of imprecisionist approach. While in some cases we noted promising avenues for dealing with these problems, there is little doubt that much more work needs to be done on the problem of accounting for the meaning of vague expressions.

References

Beall, J. (2003), *Liars and Heaps*, Oxford: Oxford University Press.

Bunge, M. (ed.) (1973), *The Methodological Unity of Science*, Dordrecht: D. Reidel.

Burgess, J. (2001), "Vagueness, Epistemicism, and Response-Dependence", *Australasian Journal of Philosophy* 79: 507–524.

Cook, R. (2002), "Vagueness and Mathematical Precision", *Mind* 111: 225–247.

Corcoran, J. (1973), "Gaps Between Logical Theory and Mathematical practice", in Bunge (1973): 23–50.

Davidson, D. (1967), "Truth and Meaning", in Davidson (1984): 17–36. Originally published in *Synthese*17: 304–323.

Davidson, D. (1984), *Inquiries into Truth and Interpretation*, Clarendon Press, Oxford.

Dummett, M (1975), "Wang's Paradox", Synthese 30: 301–324, reprinted in Keefe and Smith (1997): 99–118.

Edgington, D. (1997), "Vagueness by Degrees", in Keefe and Smith (1997): 294–316.

Eklund, M. (2005), "What Vagueness Consists In" *Philosophical Studies*125 (2005): 27–60.

Evans, G. (1978), "Can There Be Vague Objects?", *Analysis* 38: 208.

Evans, G. and McDowell, J. (1976), *Truth and Meaning, Essays in Semantics*, Oxford: Clarendon Press.

Fine, K. (1975), "Vagueness, Truth, and Logic", in Keefe and Smith (1997): 119–150. Originally published in *Synthese*30: 265–300.

Flew, A. (ed.) (1951), *Logic and Language*, Oxford: Basil Blackwell.

Graff, D. (2000) "Shifting Sands: An Interest-relative Theory of Vagueness", *Philosophical Topics* 28: 45–81.

Horwich, P. (1997), "The Nature of Vagueness" *Philosophy and Phenomenological Research* 62: 929–935.

Hyde, D. (1997), "From Heaps of Gaps to Heaps of Gluts", *Mind*106: 641–660.

Keefe, R. and P. Smith (eds.) (1997), *Vagueness: A Reader*, Cambridge, MA: MIT Press.

Keefe, R. (2000), *Theories of Vagueness*, Cambridge: Cambridge University Press.

Machina, K. (1976), "Truth, Belief, and Vagueness", in Keefe and Smith (1997): 174–203. Originally published in *Journal of Philosophical Logic*5: 47–78.

Moruzzi, S. and Sereni, A. (eds.) (2005), *Issues on Vagueness*, Padua: Poligrafo.

Parsons, T. (2000), *Indeterminate Identity – Metaphysics and Semantics*, Oxford: Clarendon Press.

Priest, G. (2003), "A Site For Sorites", in Beall (2003): 9–23.

Raffman, D. (1996), "Vagueness and Context-Sensitivity", *Philosophical Studies* 81: 175–192.

Sainsbury, R. (1990), "Concepts Without Boundaries", in Keefe and Smith (1997), 251–264. Originally published as *Inaugural Lecture* by the King's College London Department of Philosophy.

Schirn, M. (ed.) (1998), *Philosophy of Mathematics Today: Proceedings of an International Congress in Munich*, Oxford: Oxford University Press.
Shapiro, S. (1998), "Logical Consequence: Models and Modality", in Schirn (1998): 131–156.
Shapiro, S. (2006), *Vagueness in Context*, Oxford: Clarendon Press.
Shiffer, S. (2003), *The Things We Mean*, Oxford: Oxford University Press.
Soames, S. (1999), *Understanding Truth*, Oxford: Oxford University Press.
Stanley, J. (2003) "Context, Interest-Relativity, and the Sorites", *Analysis* 63: 269–280.
Tappenden, J. 1993. "The Liar and Sorites Paradoxes: Towards a Unified Treatment", *Journal of Philosophy* 90: 551–77.
Tomberlin, J. (1994), *Philosophical Perspectives 8: Logic and Language*, Atascedero, CA: Ridgeview Publishing.
Tye, M. (1994a), "Vagueness: Welcome to the Quicksand", *Southern Journal of Philosophy*33(supplement): 1–22.
Tye, M. (1994b), "Sorites Paradox and the Semantics of Vagueness", in Keefe and Smith (1997): 281–293. Originally published in Tomberlin (1994): 189–206.
Villanueva, E. (ed.) (1997), *Philosophical Issues 8: Truth*, Atascedero, CA: Ridgeview.
Waismann, F. (1951), "Verifiability", in Flew (1968): 119–123.
Weatherson, B. (2003), "Epistemicism, Parasites and Vague Names", *Australasian Journal of Philosophy*81: 276-9.
Williamson, T. (1994), *Vagueness*, London: Routledge.
Williamson, T. (1997), "Imagination, Stipulation, and Vagueness", in Villanueva (1997): 215–228.
Williamson, T. (2001), "Vagueness, Indeterminacy, and Social Meaning", *Critical Studies* 16: 61–76.
Wright, C. (1976), "Language Mastery and the Sorites Paradox", in Keefe and Smith (1997): 151–173. Originally published in Evans and McDowell (1976): 223–247.
Wright, C. (2001), "On Being in a Quandary: Relativism, Vagueness, Logical Revisionism" *Mind* 110: 45–98.

Chapter 5
Vagueness and Observationality

Diana Raffman

Of the many families of words that are thought to be vague, so-called observational predicates may be both the most fascinating and the most confounding. Roughly, observational predicates are terms that apply to objects on the basis of how those objects appear to us perceptually. 'Red', 'loud', 'sweet', 'acrid', and 'smooth' are good examples. Delia Graff explains that a "predicate is *observational* just in case its applicability to an object (given a fixed context of evaluation) depends only on the way that object appears" (2001: 3). By the same token, observational predicates are, as Crispin Wright observes, terms "whose senses are taught entirely by ostension" (1976).

Like other vague predicates, observational words appear to generate sorites paradoxes. Consider for example a series of 20 colored patches progressing from a clearly red one to a clearly orange one, so ordered that each patch is just noticeably different in hue from the one before. The following argument then seems forced upon us:

(1) Patch #1 is red.
(2) Any patch that differs only slightly in hue from a red patch is itself red.
(3) Therefore patch #20 is red.

Premise (2) expresses what Wright has called the *tolerance* of 'red': the application of the predicate tolerates small changes in a decisive parameter (here, hue). Of course, most vague predicates, hence most versions of the sorites, are not observational. For instance, given a series of ages progressing by increments of a single day from a clearly old age, say 80 years old, to a clearly not-old age, say 10 years old, the same puzzle arises for the vague predicate 'old':

D. Raffman (✉)
Department of Philosophy, University of Toronto, 170 St. George Street, Toronto, Ontario M5R 2M8, Canada
e-mail: diana.raffman@utoronto.ca

G. Ronzitti (ed.), *Vagueness: A Guide*, Logic, Epistemology, and the Unity of Science 19, DOI 10.1007/978-94-007-0375-9_5,

(1) 80 years is old.
(2) Any age that is one day less old than an old age is itself old.
(3) Therefore 10 years is old.

However, observational terms and their associated sorites paradoxes are thought to pose special difficulties for theories of vagueness and theories of perception generally. I want to examine two of these difficulties to see whether they really are as bad, or as special, as is commonly supposed.

5.1 The Two Difficulties

What are the two difficulties? First, observational predicates are thought to generate the most intractable form of the sorites. They do this by permitting the construction of sorites series in which neighboring items are indiscriminable, not just slightly different, on the relevant dimension. For example, we can construct a sorites series for the predicate 'red' containing colored patches so ordered that each is indiscriminable (indistinguishable, indiscernible) in hue from its neighbors. And while it is at least non-incredible that neighboring, slightly different patches in a sorites series are category-different (one red and the other not), the idea that indiscriminable items could be category-different seems beyond the pale. Should you have any doubts about 'red' in this regard, consider that a sorites paradox is spawned equally by the "hyper-observational" vague predicate 'looks red'. How could two indiscriminable items be such that one looks red but the other does not?

Second, the indiscriminability relation obtaining between neighboring items in a series of indiscriminables appears to be *non-transitive*: each item is indiscriminable from the next but the first and last are discriminably, indeed category-, different. Timothy Williamson writes:

> Two stimuli whose difference is below the threshold cannot be discriminated. Since many indiscriminable differences can add up to a discriminable difference, one can have a series of stimuli each indiscriminable from its successor, of which the first member is discriminable from the last. Indiscriminability is a non-transitive relation (1994: 69).

(For convenience, let us call a series of indiscriminable items an 'indiscriminability sorites series' or 'I-series' for short.) This feature, non-transitivity, is not peculiar to a series of indiscriminables. The relation *slightly older* is non-transitive too, as the paradox for 'old' reveals. Indeed a non-transitive relation of indiscriminability or slight difference is supposed to be required for any sorites series. But the non-transitivity of the indiscriminability relation is thought to give rise to at least two distinctive problems. (i) The existence (even the possibility) of I-series seems to call into question the coherence of the commonsensical idea of maximally determinate observational qualities – determinate shades, loudness levels, pitches, etc. (e.g., Dummett 1975). It seems natural to say that objects have the same determinate observational quality just in case they are indiscriminable on the relevant dimension: objects have the same shade just in case they are indiscriminable on the dimension of hue, and sounds have the same determinate loudness level just in case they are indiscriminable on the dimension of loudness. But the sameness or identity relation, unlike indiscriminability, is transitive; so this natural way of individuating determinate qualities is not available. Christopher Peacocke writes:

> [I]t is pretheoretically tempting to suppose that. . .perceived shades s and s′ are identical if and only if s is not discriminably different from s′. The non-transitivity of nondiscriminable difference ("matching") entails that there is no way of dividing the spectrum into shades that meets that condition. Take an example in which, in respect of color, x matches y, y matches z, but x does not match z. To conform to the above principle about shades, the shade of y would have to be identical with shades that are distinct from one another (1992: 83).[1]

Peacocke and Nelson Goodman (1951) among others have proposed alternative ways to individuate determinate qualities, but each is counterintuitive in one way or another. (ii) Worse yet, the existence of I-series seems to call into question the coherence of our perceptual experience. Lynda Burns warns:

> If patch *a* appears to an observer to be some particular shade of color, and patch *b* appears to be indistinguishable from it. . .then we might say that *b* appears to be the same shade of color. But then the next member, *c*, is indiscernible in shade from *b*, and so must be the same shade also. Yet *c* is just discernibly different in shade from *a*.. . .Denying the existence of phenomenal properties or the coherence of observational language still leaves us with a puzzle of making sense of our visual experience (1994: 37).

These then are two reputedly serious and distinctive problems associated with observational predicates – their specially lethal soriticality, and the threat, posed by the non-transitivity of indiscriminability, to the coherence of determinate observational qualities and of perceptual experience itself. Let's look at them more closely.

5.2 Indiscriminability and the Sorites

Consider a sorites paradox for 'red' using a red/orange I-series of 20 patches:

(1) Patch #1 is red.
(2) Any patch indiscriminable in color from a red patch is itself red.
(3) Therefore patch #20 is red.

I know of only one family of proposed solutions to the paradox that are specific to the I-series version. These accounts contend that there are no (humanly) indiscriminable stimuli, and so an I-series, and its attendant paradox, cannot be constructed. Are they right?

To answer this question we need first to get clear just what is meant by 'indiscriminable' in the philosophical literature. Philosophers often seem to conceive of

[1] The term 'match' is used in various ways in the literature. Nelson Goodman, whose use of it is perhaps most familiar, seems to conceive of matching as an invariant relation of appearing (e.g., looking) the same that holds between two stimuli or objects. Peacocke appears to follow suit. Since I don't believe that such a relation can be instantiated in human perceptual experience, I will not use the term here. See pp. 9–10 above.

indiscriminability as a relationship obtaining between two items (objects, stimuli), for or relative to a perceiver, when it is impossible for the perceiver to detect any difference between them, i.e., impossible to tell them apart.[2] In other words, philosophers seem to understand indiscriminability as an invariant relation: under fixed, optimal conditions, stimuli that are indiscriminable by a given perceiver always look the same to him, i.e., he would invariably judge them the same in a same/different task, while discriminable stimuli always look different.[3] (The perceiver is assumed to be linguistically competent, visually normal, sincere, constant in his standards or "criteria" across time, and so forth. I will tie all of this together and call such a perceiver 'competent'.) For example, David Armstrong seems to have such a conception in mind when he makes these remarks about a so-called Armstrong triad:

> Suppose that we have three samples of cloth, *A, B,* and *C,* which are exactly alike except that they differ very slightly in colour. Suppose further, however, that *A* and *B* are *perceptually completely indistinguishable* in respect of colour, and *B* and *C* are *perceptually completely indistinguishable* in respect of colour. Suppose, however, that *A* and *C* can be perceptually distinguished from each other in this respect [emphasis added].... (1968: 218).

As C. L. Hardin remarks, it is "plain that Armstrong takes indistinguishability to be an all-or-nothing affair" (1988: 179). Hardin notes that

> [w]hen philosophers write about whether or not one homogeneously colored patch is discriminable in color from another, it is easy to get the impression that one could decide whether or not one had a match rather easily, just by giving a good straight look. If a difference between the patches falls above the threshold of discriminability and the conditions of seeing are optimal, the straight look will reveal that difference, but if the difference falls below the threshold, neither that look nor any succeeding look will uncover the discrepancy, and the samples will match perfectly. [This conception assumes] the existence of a fixed, sharp discrimination threshold (op.cit., 214).

The philosophers' invariant conception of indiscriminability has at least two shortcomings – one easily remedied, the other more serious. First, the fact is that given enough trials, any perceiver will eventually produce false alarms (responses of 'different' to stimuli that are physically identical in the relevant respect, e.g., colored lights of the same wavelength). That is to say, there are no stimuli that always appear the same, even to a competent perceiver under optimal conditions. This problem is easily fixed, however, because the psychologists have a way of weeding out the

---

[2]Philosophers (not psychologists) have also taken indiscriminability to be a relation holding between phenomenal properties of stimuli (e.g., Peacocke, 1992), between qualia (e.g., Goodman, 1951), and between experiential "characters" (Williamson, 1990); but we can skim over these variations here.

[3]For present purposes I am going to use the terms 'appears Φ' (e.g., 'looks Φ') and 'is judged Φ' interchangeably. In particular, I will speak indifferently of objects appearing the same or different and objects being judged the same or different in a same/different task. In talking this way I am of course ignoring many important questions about the relationships among experience, judgment, and verbal report; but I think we can safely set those questions aside here. See Raffman, 2000 for discussion.

false alarms to yield a true picture of a perceiver's ability to detect stimulus difference. They use an analytical technique called 'signal detection theory' that in effect subtracts the false alarms from the hits (correct detections of stimulus difference).[4]

A more serious problem remains, however. For even after the false alarms are weeded out, there probably are no physically different stimuli that always appear the same to a competent perceiver under optimal conditions. In other words, there probably is no absolute perceptual discrimination threshold, no increment of physical difference so small as to be absolutely undetectable by the human visual system.[5] Following a famous paper by the psychophysicist Swets (1964), Hardin observes that in all likelihood we can discriminate any two different stimuli, no matter how small the difference. (In the following passage from Hardin, the 'signal' is a stimulus difference, e.g., a difference in wavelength, between two simultaneously presented stimuli. Where stimuli are identical, the signal is absent. Subjects' task is to say whether the signal is present or absent, i.e., whether the presented stimuli appear the same or different.)

> [Perceptual] sensitivity has no fixed lower limit. In the ideal case,. . .any two repeatedly presented signals above the noise level may be distinguished from one another by the difference in their proportions of hits to false alarms. All that is required is that the number of trials be large enough to distinguish those two proportions. (In actual cases, things are not so simple, since the receiver′s sensitivity is apt to change with time.)(217). . ..Over a series of trials, the presence of a. . .wavelength difference. . .will manifest itself in a statistical difference in the ratio of hits to false alarms. The smaller the difference, the greater the number of trials required to uncover it. . .. Let us return now to the situation which is commonly described as one in which sample x is indistinguishable in color from y, and y from z, but x is distinguishable in color from **z.** We have seen how, in such a circumstance, y could in fact be distinguished from both x and z, given a sufficiently large number of [same/different] trials. The data represent nothing beyond comparisons of the appearances of objects, but no given pair of comparisons is sufficient to decide the distinguishability or indistinguishability of x and y, or of y and z (218).

The psychophysicists I have queried concur with Swets, and explain that discrimination thresholds are really just "for relevant purposes" or "for all practical purposes". Hardin makes this point too:

> [It may be that] there is no compelling reason to suppose that there is such an absolute discrimination limit in principle, but every reason to regard many physically distinct stimuli as indistinguishable in practice. This is because one rapidly reaches the point in which the number of trials which is required to make a discrimination exceeds the ability of the observer and the experimenter to maintain constancy in the experimental situation.

---

[4] More precisely, signal detection theory computes the ratio of hits to false alarms.

[5] Philosophers may find this surprising. Wright speaks for many when he considers the possibility that

> between [any] pair of [stimuli] discriminable in respect of Φ lies a stage discriminable from them both and from any stage outside the region which they flank. We have to suppose that we have in this sense infinite powers of discrimination. . ., that we can always directly discern some distinction more minute than any discerned so far. . ..[We may naturally suppose] that this is not so (1976, 346).

> Boredom sets in, the organism's sensitivity changes, the alignment of the apparatus shifts, etcetera, etcetera. Over the long run – the very long run – these perturbing factors distribute themselves in a statistically normal fashion. But in the shorter, humanly possible run, they bias the experimental results. The signal gets buried in the noise (220).[6]

Hardin's conclusion is that if indiscriminability is taken to be an invariant relation, as I-series sorites mongers appear to do, then as a matter of psychological possibility there can be no I-series. And if there can be no I-series, there can be no I-series paradox.

Perhaps the sorites monger will reply that an absolute threshold is at least nomologically possible, and that that is enough to get an I-series paradox up and running. But the sorites is supposed to be a paradox about human natural language; so it's not obvious what that mere nomological possibility would show. Alternatively, he might try to reconstruct his paradox using a statistical threshold of the sort employed in psychophysics. In that case stimuli are discriminable by a subject just in case she detects the difference between them on a certain percentage of same/different trials; and indiscriminable otherwise. Depending on the operative task demands, the criterial percentage might be set at 75%, or at 60%, or at 90%, among others. Can the I-series sorites monger get his paradox going using a statistical conception of indiscriminability? Well, he can of course construct a series of physically different stimuli whose difference is detected no more than, say, 5% of the time – in other words, a series in which neighboring stimuli are judged the same on at least 95% of trials. And we may reasonably suppose that an observational predicate would be tolerant with respect to this relation: for example, if a given patch is red, then any patch that looks the same in hue as that patch at least 95% of the time is also red. So he can construct a paradox. However, again it isn't clear to me whether this would be the specially lethal kind of paradox that has been associated with observational vague words. Do items that appear the same 95% of the time, even 99% or 99.999...% of the time, appear the same in the strong way that is supposed to render intuitively incredible the idea that a category difference could obtain between them? I don't know the answer.

A more promising response by the sorites monger might be to employ an "occasional" version of his invariant indiscriminability relation. In that case the paradox would originate not in a series of indiscriminable items, but in a series in which neighboring items *appear the same*, where appearing (e.g., looking, sounding) the same or different is a relation that obtains between stimuli *at a given time*, e.g., in a given trial. For clarity let's call this kind of series an 'appear-same' ('look-same', 'sound-same') series. In contrast, discriminability and indiscriminability or match are standing relations that depend upon the frequency with which stimuli appear the

---

[6]Hellie (2005) claims that "noise is a central source of the non-transitivity of perceptual indiscriminability even under optimal, normal circumstances. Noise blurs subtle differences; for sufficiently similar colors, this yields uncertainty whether they are distinct. If all signals were clean, perhaps only identical colors would be perceptually indiscriminable" (2005, 506). The idea seems to be that in the absence of noise, we might be indefinitely sensitive discriminators even "in the short run". This hypothesis is far more radical than the Hardin-Swets view.

same or different across time, e.g., in large numbers of trials. As I will use these terms, when we say that two objects appear the same to you (under certain conditions), normally this is shorthand for saying that the objects would appear the same to you were you to compare them (under those conditions). Or, if you prefer: the objects would be appearing the same to you were you to be judging them. And they would appear (be appearing) the same to you just in case you would judge (would be judging) them the same were you judging them.[7]

Maybe the sorites monger can reconstruct his paradox if the following scenarios are possible:

> (A-S1) For some time *t*, competent perceiver *S*, and series of objects $O_1 \ldots O_n$: were *S* to compare O_1 and O_2 at *t*, she would judge them (they would appear) the same; and were *S* to compare O_2 and O_3 at *t*, she would judge them the same; and so forth. But were *S* to compare O_1 and O_n at *t*, she would judge them different.

> (A-S2) For some time *t*, competent perceiver *S*, and series of objects $O_1 \ldots O_n$: At *t*, were *S* to compare O_1 and O_2, and then O_2 and O_3, and then O_3 and O_4, etc., and then O_1 and O_n, *seriatim*, she would judge the two members of every pair except O_1 and O_n the same, but would judge O_1 and O_n different. In other words, the members of every pair except O_1 and O_n would appear the same, but O_1 and O_n would appear different.

Actually I'm not certain about A-S1; but as far as I can see, a series of objects related in the way specified by A-S2 would instantiate a so-called phenomenal continuum (for *S* at *t*). What emerges, however, is that a phenomenal continuum may not be adequate to generate a sorites paradox for 'red' (e.g). Specifically, the possibility of a single time *t* at which the objects $O_1 \ldots O_n$ do or would receive the judgments described in A-S1 or A-S2 is not obviously sufficient to guarantee that if one of those objects *is* red, so are its neighbors. The possibility of such a time and pattern of judgments may be sufficient only to guarantee that if one of the objects *looks* red at *t*, so do its neighbors. Looking red is an "occasional" or "episodic" property; being red is not. Being red consists in (something like) looking a certain way under normal conditions, an enduring or dispositional property. I don't know whether the truth of A-S1 or A-S2 is sufficient to generate a sorites paradox; but we shouldn't be surprised if a *phenomenal* continuum turns out to generate a paradox only for 'looks red', not for 'red'. After all, looking red is the phenomenal property. The sorites monger should not be dissatisfied with this result, since the phenomenal sorites, employing a series in which neighboring items appear the same at a given time, is surely what theorists of vagueness have had in mind in saying that observational predicates generate a specially lethal version of the paradox. To sum up, observational vague words may well generate the most intractable form of the sorites, but it probably employs an appear-same series rather than an I-series, and as a result, the words in question may be "hyper-observational" ones like 'looks red', rather than 'is red'.

Before turning to my second question, about non-transitivity, I want to mention briefly a different line of attack against the possibility of an I-series. Borrowing

[7] See again note 3.

a strategy from Goodman (1951), Burns observes that no matter how small the (non-zero) physical difference between two stimuli, there will always be some third stimulus that appears the same as one but different from the other.[8] On her view, any two physically different stimuli are thus *indirectly* discriminable, as one might put it. Concerning stimuli *a, b, c* that form an Armstrong triad, Burns writes:

> We might argue that. . .the [determinate shade] predicate S', which applies to *a*, also applies to *b* only if there are no differences to be observed between *a* and *b* that are relevant to questions about their phenomenal shade. There is a relevant observable difference between *a* and *b* in [the present] visual context. . .since one but not the other is indiscernible in shade from *c*. . ..So we may refuse to apply the one shade predicate to *b* since *c* is not that shade, and matches in shade with other objects is one determining feature for the application of predicates of precise shade (1994: 37).[9]

The trouble with Burns's clever argument is that an I-series sorites paradox requires only a series in which neighboring items are "directly" pairwise indiscriminable, i.e., indiscriminable on the basis of a "good straight look". So she is effectively attacking a straw man.

Next I want to examine the claim that indiscriminability is non-transitive.

5.3 Non-transitivity and Phenomenal Continua

The idea that indiscriminability is non-transitive has largely been taken for granted in the philosophical literature. Burns takes it to be "a fact about human perception that there are such non-transitively matching triads" (1994: 37). Dummett thinks that the non-transitivity of indiscriminability renders the use of observational predicates incoherent (1976: 324). And according to Wright,

> [i]t is. . .familiar that we may construct a series of suitable, homogeneously coloured patches, in such a way as to give the impression of a smooth transition from red to orange, where each patch is *indiscriminable* in colour from those immediately next to it; it is the non-transitivity of indiscriminability which generates this possibility.

As Wright sees it, the existence of so-called phenomenal continua shows that indiscriminability or match *must* be non-transitive:

> Suppose that we are to construct a series of colour patches, ranging from red through to orange, among which indiscriminability is to behave transitively. We are given a supply of appropriate patches from which to make selections, an initial red patch C_1, and the instruction that each successive patch must either match its predecessor or be more like it than is

[8] See also Dummett, 1975.

[9] I-series are also thought to give rise to sorites paradoxes for determinate quality predicates such as 'red$_{19}$' and 'loud$_4$'. For example, suppose that in Burns's Armstrong triad, *a* is red$_{19}$ and *c* is red$_{20}$. The following argument then seems valid:

(1) *a* is red$_{19}$.
(2) Anything that is indiscriminable from something that is red$_{19}$ is itself red$_{19}$.
(3) Therefore *c* is red$_{19}$.

> any other patch not matching it which we later use. Under these conditions it is plain that we cannot generate any change in colour by selecting successive matching patches; since indiscriminability is to be transitive, it will follow that if each C_i in the first n selections matches its predecessor, that C_n matches C_1. The only way to generate a change in colour will be to select a non-matching patch (1976: 344–345).

In light of our discussion in the preceding section, I recommend that we read Wright and these other philosophers as referring to the "occasional" relation of appearing the same, not to indiscriminability as such, and that we take a phenomenal continuum to be a progression existing at a time *t* from an item that *appears* (e.g.) red to an item that *appears* (e.g.) orange, rather than from one that is red to one that is orange. The question before us, then, is whether the relation of appearing the same is non-transitive.

Consider an Armstrong triad of three patches *A, B,* and *C* that are homogenously colored and identical in size and shape but slightly different in the wavelengths of light they reflect. Suppose you were told that *A* matches *B* in infrared light, *B* matches *C* in incandescent light, and *A* matches *C* in the noonday sun. That is: *A* and *B* would look the same if you compared them in infrared light, *B* and *C* would look the same in incandescent light, and *A* and *C* would look different in the sun. Would you be persuaded that you had found a counterexample to the transitivity of 'matches' or 'looks the same'? Presumably not. You would want to know how the three pairs look, how they would be judged, under (some) uniform viewing conditions: in the same light, from the same angle of sight, and so forth. Hence if the appears-same relation is to be non-transitive, then at the least, a non-transitive pattern of same/different comparisons must be (psychologically? nomologically? logically?) possible with respect to a series of objects $O_1 \ldots O_n$ *presented simultaneously*. Otherwise one or more of the objects might appear different in their different comparisons; for instance, O_2 might appear different when presented with O_1 than when presented with O_3.

Wright's argument for non-transitivity (above) may seem irresistible; but the non-transitivity claim has its detractors. Raffman (2000) hypothesizes that even simultaneous presentation of all objects in an appear-same series does not guarantee that the appearance of those objects remains constant across their pairwise comparisons. For instance, in our series of 20 colored patches, simultaneous presentation does not guarantee that patch #2 looks the same when compared to patch #1 as when compared to patch #3, even though all three are in view throughout. Raffman hypothesizes that the two comparisons are made in distinct attentional episodes and that the appearance of patch #2 may shift as a result:

> Intuitively speaking, just as variation in the lighting conditions (infrared? incandescent?) or the subject's visual system (does he have a migraine? is he on drugs? has he gone blind?) from comparison to comparison can alter how the patches look, so too can variation in something as fine-grained as *what the subject is attending to*. Just as the light, the size and spatial arrangement of the patches, and the subject *inter alia* must be consistent across the [different] comparisons, so must the subject's focus of attention (25).

Until this possibility is ruled out, she contends, a claim of non-transitivity is not justified.

Taking a different but related tack, Graff questions whether the stimuli in a phenomenal continuum really do appear the same. She writes that we

> should not be misled into thinking that just because it may be convenient to describe a change as apparently continuous, that it really is that way" (18)....
>
> [There may be a] change in appearance...too slight...for us to *notice* it. We *judge* the [colors of the patches to look the same], but our judgment about the character of our experience is mistaken" (23).

By 'unnoticed' Graff seems to mean either (roughly) 'unconscious' or 'unattended', or both. I am not certain of the right reading. Be that as it may, she concludes that insofar as unnoticed changes in the way things appear are possible, the arguments for non-transitivity do not go through. At bottom, both Graff and Raffman are raising the possibility of unnoticed changes in the appearances of items in an appear-same series.

I think the Graff and Raffman essays aim in the right direction, but I'd like to have a more decisive (less purely hypothetical) case against the non-transitivity claim. That is what I will try to provide in the remainder of this chapter. Unlike Graff, I take it to be a datum that phenomenal continua exist, i.e., that there exist series of items (objects, stimuli) that effect an apparently continuous change on a given perceptual dimension such as hue or loudness. And against Wright, I will suggest that an appear-same series or phenomenal continuum can exist, is psychologically possible, even if *appears the same* is not non-transitive.

5.4 Unattended Phenomenal Differences: An Experiment

The thought that there can be unnoticed or unattended phenomenal changes may be understood in at least two ways:

(1) Two (or more) stimuli can appear different but by such a small amount that we don't, indeed can't, notice it.
(2) A single stimulus can change (shift) its appearance but by such a small amount that we don't, indeed can't, notice it.

Graff seems to intend (1), whereas my argument against non-transitivity will rely on a defense of (2). To find out whether (2) is true, I and two colleagues in psychology at Ohio State University, Del Lindsey and Angela Brown, designed and ran an experiment to test the hypothesis that the appearances of the stimuli in a look-same hue series do not in fact remain constant from one comparison to the next, even when all are presented simultaneously and viewing conditions are otherwise uniform throughout. The experiment will be described in full in a manuscript submitted independently for publication; here I will discuss only, and briefly, the parts of it that are of philosophical relevance to the topic of appear-same sorites paradoxes.

Lindsey constructed a series of 20 patches of light forming a hue progression between two slightly different shades of green. Each two consecutive patches in the

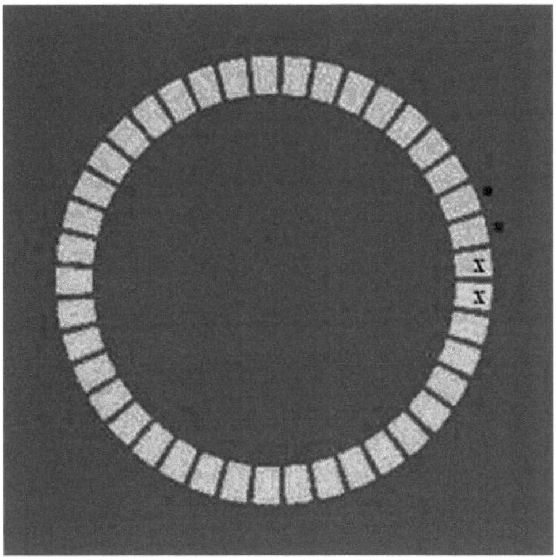

Fig. 5.1 Stimuli in the experiment. The endpoints of the series (clearly discriminable *shades of green*) are indicated with '*x*'

series differed in hue by less than the discrimination threshold or just noticeable difference of our most sensitive subject.[10] Twenty-one redundant patches were then added to the series so that every other pair of consecutive patches contained physically identical stimuli; in other words, every other patch was physically identical to its predecessor.[11] The 41 stimuli were then presented on a computer monitor in the circular arrangement shown in Fig. 5.1. (The two endpoints of the series, which looked slightly but clearly different in hue to all of the subjects, were the two patches marked 'x'. Nothing hinges on their position.)

The subjects in the experiment were ten philosophy and psychology faculty, students, and staff at Ohio State University, including several faculty and graduate students in psychology of vision. The subject's task on each trial had two parts. First, she was to make a "same"/"different" judgment of the hues of two consecutive patches (cued by two black dots as shown in Fig. 5.1). If she judged the patches different, the next trial would begin immediately and she would be cued to judge the next pair of patches. If she judged them the same, a disk of colored light appeared in the center of the circle, as illustrated in Fig. 5.2 below. The subject then adjusted the hue of the disk by moving the computer mouse back and forth until the disk matched the hue of the two patches. (The starting hue of the disk was randomized.) The disk then disappeared and the next trial began. In this way the subject judged each pair of patches *seriatim* – #1/#2, #2/#3, #3/#4. . .#40/#41 – and adjusted the hue of the disk accordingly. Subjects were taken around the circle twice.

[10]We had established the thresholds of our subjects in an earlier pilot experiment, requiring correct detection on 75% of trials.

[11]These identical pairs were used in "catch" trials that tested for false alarms, i.e., judgments of "different" made about identical stimuli.

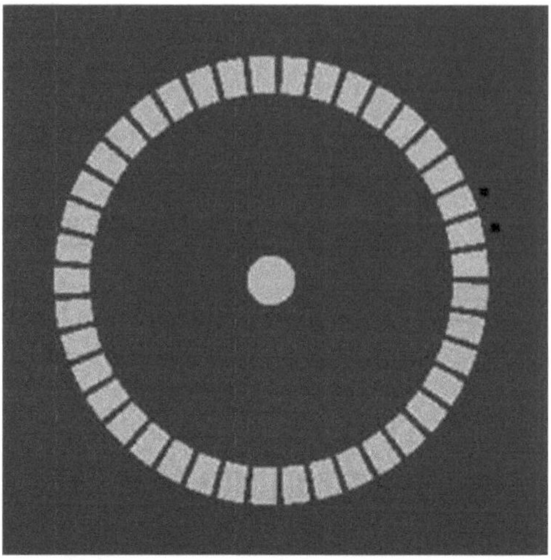

Fig. 5.2 Subjects' task was to match the hue of the central disk to the hue of each pair of patches judged same

What we found was that although all of the patches were in view throughout, subjects' settings of the disk progressed more or less systematically with the wavelengths of the patches, even though the members of the pairs in question had been judged "same".[12] In other words, subjects matched the pair #2/#3 to a longer wavelength than the pair #1/#2, the pair #3/#4 to a longer wavelength than the pair #2/#3, and so on. Data from one subject are pictured in Fig. 5.3. On the *y*-axis is the

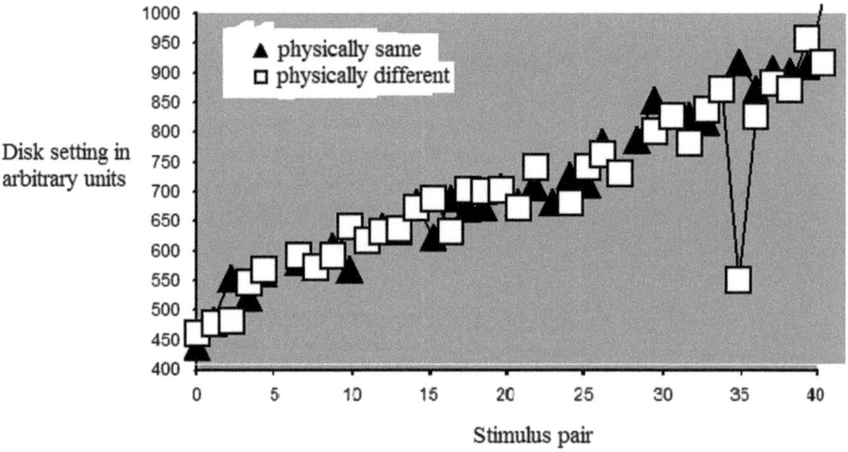

Fig. 5.3 Disk setting (in arbitrary units) for successive stimulus pairs

---

[12]For ease of discussion here I use the term 'wavelength', but it is strictly speaking incorrect. Rather, the stimuli were mixtures of broadband lights, and neither the primaries nor the mixtures have a defined wavelength.

wavelength setting of the disk (in arbitrary units), and on the x-axis is the number of the stimulus pair to which the disk was being matched. Black triangles indicate "catch" trials in which the stimuli in a pair were physically identical; white squares indicate trials in which stimuli were physically different. Since the graph shows the disk settings, the data points (squares and triangles) represent all and only trials in which the members of a pair were judged "same". (The graph contains more than 41 data points because subjects went around the circle twice; hence pairs that were judged "same" both times received two disk settings.) The graph shows a reasonably steady progression of the disk setting as the subject progresses through the pairs of patches, for both the physically identical and physically different pairs. (This result suggests that subjects may have been matching the hue of the disk to the average physical value of the two patches in each pair.)

How should we interpret this finding? One obvious hypothesis – indeed it is difficult to think of an alternative – is that the patches were shifting their hue appearance, were looking different, in their different pairings, but by such a small increment that although subjects were able to detect it, they were unable to attend to or notice (be conscious of?) it, and so were unable to report it. Granted, necessarily the experiment could not test the scenario described in A-S1, but it did test the A-S2 scenario; and I think we can safely draw an analogous conclusion with respect to A-S1. The experimental finding may also provide support for the idea, advanced in Raffman 2000, that among the factors that determine how a stimulus looks in respect of hue, there is one's attentional focus, and this varies from comparison to comparison even when all of the stimuli are in view simultaneously. Attentional focus – a purely internal factor – must be included among the factors that determine how things appear in respect of hue. Dummett and Wright both anticipate the occurrence of unnoticed phenomenal shifts in a phenomenal continuum. Dummett writes:

> [T]he non-transitivity of matching requires that not *every* feature of colour patches can be a directly observational one; colour patches evidently allow of changes, whether these changes are described as changes *in* colour or not, of a kind which cannot be directly discerned. So we have no alternative but to admit a gap among such items between seeming not to have changed in any respect, and actually not having done so.

Wright:

> [C]olour predicates [are evidently] tolerant with respect to changes which cannot be directly discerned in objects which undergo them; an object may suffer such a change without it being possible to discover that it has done so save by comparing it with something else....[W]e do not have ready to hand a concept in terms of which we can describe what these changes essentially are....[W]e are lacking, for example, a notion standing to the concept of shade as that of real position stands to phenomenal position.

Wright and Dummett take such shifts or changes of apparent hue to be necessitated by the non-transitivity of the appear-same relation; whereas if what I have been saying here is correct, then the shifts in fact defeat a claim of non-transitivity. These authors are correct, however, to point out the difficulty of describing our experience – the phenomenology – of these subtle differences. I surely do not know how to do it. What I do know is that however we describe these shifts, in *some* sense of 'look' the patches looked different in their different pairwise comparisons. Consequently, *contra* Wright, a phenomenal continuum can exist even if "indiscriminability" or looking the same is not non-transitive. What a phenomenal continuum seems to require are two things: that the hues of objects be unstable or shiftable, and that at least some instances of their instability, though detected by us, go unnoticed.[13] While our experience in such cases is difficult, perhaps impossible to describe, we needn't conclude that it is incoherent.

Perhaps the defender of non-transitivity will respond by requiring that the comparisons of the patches be made in a single attentional act. He might propose that non-transitivity can be exhibited only by series short enough to be encompassed in a single such act. Now it is likely impossible for human perceivers to attend to more than two, or possibly three, stimuli at a time, in the way required to make a same/different judgment. But forget that limitation and suppose that we can attend to three neighboring stimuli, and make two same/different judgments, at a single time. In order for non-transitivity to be exhibited in this condition, at least one of the patches must *be looking the same* in respect of hue as two other patches that *are looking different*. And that really does seem impossible, maybe even incoherent. On this point I think Jackson has it right:

> [T]he suggestion that *A* might look to be the same colour as *B*, *B* might look to be the same colour as *C*, while *A* looks to be a different colour from *C*, *to one and the same person at one and the same time*, is *inconsistent*. As *A* and *C* *ex hypothesi* look to be different colours, looking to be the same colour as *A* will be distinct from looking to be the same colour as *C*; therefore, the suggestion involves one object *B*, looking to have two different colours at the same time to the same person, which is impossible (1975: 114).

As a matter of fact, vision scientist Glenn Fry predicts that if we could make two such comparisons at the same time, all three patches would look the same.[14] The similarities among the patches would swamp the differences and the visual system would refuse to make any distinctions. If that is right, then still there would be no evidence of non-transitivity.

It may be that in order to present the appearance of continuous phenomenal change, a series of stimuli must contain more members than we can attend to simultaneously. If there are creatures whose attentional capacity exceeds our own, creatures who can attend to, say, 10 patches at a time, then their phenomenal continua will need to be that much longer. For that matter, you and I may differ in the number of items required for a series to present a phenomenal continuum.

---

[13] My own view is that colors – both determinate shades and broader determinables like 'magenta' and 'red' – are rather like hats that visible objects can put on and take off depending upon a variety of factors such as viewing context and the state of the viewer's visual system. I can't say more here, however.

[14] In conversation. Glenn Fry was Regents Professor and Director of the School of Optometry at Ohio State University.

5.5 Conclusion

As far as vagueness is concerned, the tentative conclusion to be drawn from the experimental results is that a claim of non-transitivity for the look-same relation is unjustified. In that case we have no reason to think that either a phenomenal continuum or an appear-same sorites paradox requires that the appear-same ("indiscriminability") relation be non-transitive.

Regarding the difficulty of specifying identity conditions for determinate observational qualities, if the appear-same relation is not non-transitive, then the problems must have their source elsewhere. (My suspicion is that identity conditions for determinate shades can be given in terms of the look-same relation; but again, I will not try to make that case here.) Similarly, *contra* Dummett, there is no reason to believe that vague observational predicates are incoherent – or, at any rate, no reason to believe that their incoherence owes to the nontransitivity of the appear-same relation. Of course, the existence of sorites paradoxes for observational predicates may show that they are incoherent on independent grounds. But I doubt it.[15]

References

Armstrong, D. (1968), *A Materialist Theory of the Mind*, London: Routledge & Kegan Paul.
Burns, L. (1994), "Something to do with Vagueness" in Horgan 1994, pp. 23–48.
Dummett, M. (1975/1999), "Wang's Paradox". *Synthese* 30: 301–324. Reprinted in Keefe & Smith, 1999.
Goodman, N. (1951), *The Structure of Appearance*, Cambridge: Harvard University Press.
Graff, D. (2001), "Phenomenal Continua and the Sorites", *Mind* 110(440): 905–935.
Hardin, C.L. (1988), "Phenomenal Colors and Sorites", *Nous* 22: 213–234.
Hellie, B. (2005), "Noise and Perceptual Indiscriminability", *Mind* 114: 481–508.
Horgan, T. (ed.), (1994), *Spindel Conference* 1994: *Vagueness. Southern Journal of Philosophy* 33 [supplement].
Jackson, F. (1975), *Perception*. Cambridge: Cambridge University Press.
Keefe, R. and Smith, P. (1999), *Vagueness: A Reader*, Cambridge, MA: MIT Press.
Peacocke, C. (1992), *A Study of Concepts*, Cambridge, MA: MIT Press.
Raffman, D. (2000), "Is Perceptual Indiscriminability Non-transitive?", in Hill, C. (ed.), *Philosophical Topics* 28, 1: *Vagueness*.
Raffman, D. (2010), (ms). *Unruly Words: A Study of Vague Language.*
Swets, J.A. (ed.), (1964), *Signal Detectton and Recognition by Human Observers*, New York, NY: Wiley.
Williamson, T. (1990), *Identity and Discrimination*. Oxford: Basil Blackwell.
Wright, C. (1976). "Language Mastery and the Sorites Paradox", Orig. in Evans, G. and McDowell, J. (eds.), *Truth and Meaning*, Oxford: Clarendon Press, pp. 223–247. Reprinted in Keefe and Smith, pp. 151–173.

[15] See Raffman 2010 (ms), especially *Chapter 4*, for extended discussion.

Chapter 6
Vagueness and Linguistics

Robert van Rooij

6.1 Introduction

An expression is vague, if its meaning is not precise. For vagueness at the sentence-level this means that a vague sentence does not give rise to precise truth conditions. This is a problem for the standard theory of meaning within linguistics, because this theory presupposes that each sentence has a precise meaning with respect to each context of use. The philosophical discussion on 'vagueness' concentrates on the notion of *tolerance*. An expression is vague, or has a tolerant meaning, if it is insensitive to small changes in the objects to which it can be meaningfully predicated. The discussion of 'vagueness' in linguistics mostly focusses on the interpretation of so-called 'gradable adjectives'. Within that class a difference is made between relative adjectives like 'tall' and absolute adjectives like 'flat'. An important difference between these two types of adjectives is that in contrast to relative adjectives, absolute adjectives allow for *natural precisifications*: if a we fix a level of *granularity*, relative adjectives are still vague, but absolute adjectives are not. Still, also absolute adjectives give rise to vagueness. This suggests that vagueness also has something to do with what a natural, or appropriate, precisification is.

In this chapter I first discuss the nature of vagueness, and contrast it with notions such as ambiguity and context-dependence. In Section 6.3 I briefly discuss some reasons that could perhaps explain *why* vagueness is such a pervasive phenomenon in natural language. Section 6.4 reviews some more or less standard linguistic analyses of gradable adjectives. I will concentrate myself on approaches that take *comparison classes* into account. Because comparative constructions are ideally formed in terms of gradable adjectives, comparative ordering relations will be discussed as well. In Section 6.5 it will be argued that one specific ordering relation is crucial for any analysis of vagueness that wants to capture the notion of 'tolerance': semi-orders. I will focus my attention here on contextuallist' approaches that want to account for

R. van Rooij (✉)
Institute for Logic, Language and Computation, Oude Turfmarkt 141-147, 1012 GC Amsterdam
e-mail: R.A.M.vanRooij@uva.nl

G. Ronzitti (ed.), *Vagueness: A Guide*, Logic, Epistemology, and the Unity of Science 19, DOI 10.1007/978-94-007-0375-9_6,

the Sorites paradox, because these approaches are most popular within linguistics. In the final main section, I concentrate on what some people have called 'loose talk'. The main issue here is whether with loose use of language we say something that is strictly speaking false, but true enough in the particular conversational setting, or true, because the conversational setting loosens the requirements for a sentence to be true.

As a warning to the reader, I should emphasize that this chapter is not just an unbiased overview of work in linguistics on vagueness. Especially the extensive use of comparison classes throughout the paper, the view that positive uses of adjectives are primary to their comparative use, the claim that semi-orders are crucial to model tolerance, and the ordering relation between structures used to model coarser-grained talk are at best not very common.

6.2 What Is Vagueness?

Vagueness is a pervasive feature of natural language. Members of almost any lexical category can be vague. Prototypical vague expressions are *adjectives* like 'tall', 'fast', 'red', and 'adolescent'. The Sorites Paradox is the hallmark of vagueness and formulated in terms of a *noun*, 'heap'. But also many *adverbs* ('very', 'rather', 'probably', 'softly', 'well') and *quantifiers* ('many', 'a lot', 'a few') give rise to vagueness. In fact, no linguistic expression whose meaning involves perception and categorization can be entirely free of vagueness. This is true for *proper names* and *definite descriptions* ('Amsterdam', 'the border between Belgium and the Netherlands'), *verbs* like 'start', 'finish' and 'understand', but also for more abstract linguistic categories such as *tense* (past or future) and *aspect* (perfective or imperfective). If a vague term occurs in a complex expression, this complex expression is often vague as well. Because 'very' and 'a heap' are vague, the expressions 'very sick' and 'not a heap' are vague too. Some expressions turn vague expressions in complex expressions that are less vague. A measure phrase is a prototypical example (turning 'tall' into '3 feet tall'). Other expressions have the opposite effect: while '2 o'clock' is not vague, when we combine it with a hedging expression like 'approximately', 'about', 'almost', 'roughly', etc. it becomes vague. Lakoff (1973) gives a list of more than 60 hedging expressions, and discusses in what sense they differ in meaning.

Whether one is tall depends on a *unique* gradient contingent fact, one's height. Vagueness of being tall is then due to the fact that it is unclear whether one's height counts as being tall or not. There is another reason for vagueness, though. Whether one is a clever person depends, intuitively on more than one factor. If one scores well in some relevant respects but not in others one can be a borderline clever person. As discussed by Lakoff (1973), one can reduce this vagueness by using so-called *hedging* expressions like 'In some respects', 'to some extent', and 'in a sense'.

With some vague content words ('red') we associate a *prototype*, i.e., a typical representative. For those expressions, membership is a matter of prototype resemblance. But having a prototypical representative is neither a necessary ('tall', 'heavy'), nor a sufficient ('bird', 'grandmother') condition for being vague. Adverbs and quantifiers don't have prototypes at all, and an adjective like 'tall' presumably has no prototype because there is in general no natural upper bound to how tall things can be (Kamp and Partee, 1995). Although a pinguin is a much less prototypical bird than a robin, it is not less of a bird.

Vagueness in linguistics is a problem about the *meaning* of linguistic expressions. It seems natural to assume that to be a competent speaker of English one has to know what it means for 'John came' to be true or false. So, a minimal requirement for any theory of meaning seems to be that one knows the meaning of a declarative sentence if one knows under which circumstances it is, or would be true. According to truth conditional semantics – the most successful and productive linguistic theory of meaning we know so far – we should stick to this minimal requirement: identify the meaning of a declarative sentence with the *conditions*, or *circumstances* under which the sentence is true.

The phenomenon of vagueness poses a problem, or threat, to this initially appealingly simple picture of meaning.[1] Even if we know that John is 1.80 meters long, it is still not clear whether we should count 'John is tall' as being true or as being false. The phenomenon of *ambiguity* seems to pose a similar threat. The noun 'bank', for instance, can be interpreted in several ways: it is perhaps used most often to denote a financial institution, but it can also be used to denote the edge of a river (ambiguity). Assuming that the meaning expressed by a sentence is via Frege's *principle of compositionality* determined by the meanings of its constituent expressions (and the way they are combined syntactically), the sentence 'John went to the bank' can be used to express (at least) two very different meanings. There is an important difference between ambiguity and vagueness: an expression is ambiguous when it has more than one semantically unrelated meaning, and thus tends to come with separate dictionary entries. This in contrast with expressions that are vague.[2] Based on this intuition, Lakoff (1970) suggested a test to distinguish ambiguity from vagueness and underspecification based on V(erb) P(hrase) ellipsis. Suppose a sentence S has a finite number of interpretations. Lakoff proposed that we should continue the sentence with phrases like 'and Mary did too' or 'and Mary isn't either'. In case this new larger sentence has equally many interpretations as S itself, sentence S is ambiguous. Otherwise, the sentence is vague or underspecified. As an example, take the sentence 'John walked to the bank' containing the word 'bank'. Suppose that this sentence has two interpretations: (i) John walked to the building in which the financial institution is housed, and (ii) John walked to the edge of the river. Intuitively, the whole sentence 'John walked to the bank and Mary did too' also has two interpretations: (i) both John and Mary walked to the building in which the financial institution is housed, and (ii) both John and Mary walked to the edge of the river. In particular, it doesn't have an extra reading saying, for instance, that John walked to the edge of he river while Mary walked to the building in which

[1] There are other problems as well, but they are not relevant for this chapter.

[2] At the level or individual words, the contrast between ambiguity and vagueness can also be denoted by the distinction between *homonymy* and *polysemy*.

the financial institution is housed. Thus, 'John walked to the bank' is ambiguous. The reason is that the two meanings of 'bank' are not semantically related at all, so 'Mary did too' has to pick up the original meaning. Now consider the sentence 'John is not a bachelor'. Suppose that being a bachelor means that you have to be human, male, adult, and unmarried. Thus, our sentence can be true for four different reasons, and might thus be interpreted in four different ways. Now continue the sentence with 'and Mary isn't either'. Lakoff's test predicts that the original sentence was not ambiguous, because the new sentence can be true if John is not a bachelor because he is not an adult, while Mary is not a bachelor because she is not male. Thus, the whole sentence might be true for more than four different reasons.

Although 'John is not a bachelor' is not ambiguous, it is also not vague. Rather, it is a *general* sentence, on a par with an example like 'Katrin received *a degree*'. Just like the truth of the latter sentence does not specify the particular type of degree Katrin received, the truth of the former does not specify the reason why John is not a bachelor. In contrast to vague sentences, however, general sentences have determinate truth conditions, and do not pose a threat to truth conditional semantics.

Vagueness should also be contrasted with *context dependence*. Whether what is expressed by a sentence like 'I am Robert' is true or false obviously depends on who (of potentially infinitely many persons) utters it, a context dependent fact. Vagueness and context dependence are in principle independent properties, although they often co-occur. *Left* and *right* are context-dependent but not (very) vague, whereas nouns like *vegetable* and *bush* are vague but not (very) context dependent (Kamp and Partee, 1995). The fact that natural language is context dependent *complicates*, but does *not threaten* truth-conditional semantics.

A traditional way of thinking about vagueness is in terms of the *existence of borderline cases*. John is a borderline case of a tall man, if the sentence 'John is a tall man' is neither (clearly) true nor (clearly) false. The three-valued logic account of vagueness, as well as the core supervaluation theory-account[3] are based on exactly this idea. These theories assume that predicates like 'tall' and 'bald' do not give rise to a twofold, but rather to a threefold partition of objects: the positive ones, the negatives ones, and the borderline cases. But proponents of fuzzy logic like Lakoff (1973), and authors like Wright (1975), Kamp (1981) have argued that the existence of borderline cases is inadequate to characterize vagueness: although by assuming a threefold instead of a twofold distinction one rightly rejects the existence of a clear border between the positive and the negative cases, one still assumes the existence of an equally unnatural border between, for instance, the positive and the borderline cases. What seems to characterize vagueness, instead, is the fact that the denotation of vague terms lack sharp boundaries. In the words of Sainsbury (1991), they are 'boundaryless': there is no sharp boundary that marks the things which fall under it from the things that do not, and no sharp boundary which marks

[3]Roughly speaking, with the 'core' supervaluation theory account of vagueness, I mean the theory without something like Fine's (1975) treatment of higher-order vagueness.

the things which do definitely fall under it from those which do not definitely, and so on. Instead, all these boundaries are blurred. Fuzzy logicians model this by assuming an *infinite*, rather than a *finite* set of truth values. Arguably, however, this is not enough: even if we assume infinitely many truth values, there still has to be a sharp boundary between, for instance, those objects that do and those objects that don't have the relevant property P to degree 1.[4] According to Wright (1975) and Kamp (1981), instead, vagueness gives rise to *tolerance*: a vague predicate is insensitive to very small changes in the objects to which it can be meaningfully predicated. Obviously, on such a view, vagueness is intimately related with the Sorites paradox.

It is clear that the existence of borderline cases does not automatically lead to vagueness (what is vague about a clear threefold distinction?), but it is not so clear that only predicates that give rise to tolerance are vague. Gaifman (1997) discusses the predicate 'large number of fingers'. Because changes in fingers are in discrete units, there is hardly any scope for tolerance, and one finger can make the difference. Still, 5 and 6 are borderline cases of 'large number of fingers', and the predicate seems vague. One might propose that only those expressions give rise to tolerance that can be modified by a hedge, such as *about, sort of,* or *somewhat.* An obvious consequence of this suggestion is, however, that tolerance is the rule, rather than the exception.

Vagueness is standardly opposed to *precision.* Just as gradable adjectives like 'tall' and a quantity modifier like 'a lot' are prototypical vague expressions, mathematical adjectives like 'rectangular', and measure phrases like '1.80 m' are prototypically precise. But what does it mean for these latter expressions to be precise? On first thought it just means that they are precise, because they have an exact mathematical definition. However, if we want to use these terms to talk about observable objects, it is clear that these mathematical definitions would be useless: if they exist at all, we cannot possibly determine what are the rectangular objects in the precise geometrical sense, or objects that are exactly 1.80 m long. For this reason, one allows for a margin of measurement error, or a threshold, in physics and other sciences. Notice, however, that once we allow for a margin of error, we could almost immediately construct a Sorites-series, meaning that adjectives like 'rectangular' and measurement phrases like '1.80 m' give rise to tolerance. According to Wright, this should mean that these phrases are vague. Pinkal (1995) stressed that our use of 'precise' measure phrases in natural language give rise to tolerance just like in the language of physics, but now to a much larger extent. But this means that it is not clear what is left of the absolute opposition between precision and vagueness.

A central problem posed by the Sorites paradox is whether vague predicates really give rise to inconsistency. Another conceptual problem is why vagueness is

---

[4]Fuzzy logicians might respond by saying that with respect to a relative adjective like 'tall', no individual has this property to degree 1. But then, as noted by Williamson (p.c.), what to do with the sharp boundary between those objects that do and those objects that don't have the relevant property P to degree > 0.5?

so pervasive in natural languages. A linguistic, or logical, problem is that although sorite predicates give rise to vagueness, it seems that sorite predicates are not distinct from non-vague predicates with respect to their inferential power: from 'John is very tall', for instance, we conclude to the truth of 'John is tall' and they give rise to *valid syllogisms*: 'If some linguists are tall, and every linguist is smart, then some smart people are tall.' Moreover, vague terms can be used to express uncontroversial true statements like 'If John is an adult, he is a man' and vague adjectives like 'tall' are typically used in *comparatives* that give rise to precise truth conditions. Moreover, we can reason with that: If John is taller than Mary, and Mary is taller than Sue, then John is taller than Sue.

6.3 Why Vagueness?

It is standardly assumed that the existence of vagueness in natural language is *unavoidable* in ordinary discourse. Our powers of discrimination are limited and come with a margin of error, and it is just not always possible to draw sharp borderlines. Sometimes we cannot be more precise even if we would want to. And indeed, the pervasive vagueness of natural language has often been regarded as a deficiency, especially by scientists, logicians, and philosophers. However, it seems that the use of vague expressions is not such a bad thing, and might even be beneficial compared to their precise counterparts.

First, on the standard view communicative success is defined as a 1-1 correspondence between what the speaker intends and how the listener interprets it. Communicating with vague expressions is then predicted to be bad. But the above definition of communicative success is both unreasonably strict, and more than required. Communication can still be successful in case speaker's intention and hearer's interpretation have sufficient overlap. How much overlap is sufficient depends on what is at stake, and could be utility-based, as suggested by Parikh (1994).

Standard Gricean pragmatic explanations of the use of language assumes that communication is a cooperative affair. In such a situation it never does any harm to be as precise as possible (disregarding processing costs). Thus, being vague can never be advantageous. This is in accordance with a standard game theoretical result saying that messages with precise meanings can be communicated successfully only in case the preferences of speaker and listener coincide. However, this result is based on the assumption that communication is *noiseless*. Recently, some game theorists (e.g. Myerson, 1991; de Jaegher, 2003) have shown that once the preferences of speaker and listener are not completely aligned, we can sometimes *communicate more* with vague, imprecise, or noisy information than with precise information. Vague, or *indirect*, use of language might be beneficial as well in case the speaker is *unsure* about the preferences of the hearer. In such circumstances a speaker might intent some of his messages to be diversely interpretable by cooperative versus non-cooperative listeners.

It is sometimes argued that it is useful to have vague predicates like 'tall' in our language, because it allows us to use language in a *flexible* way. Obviously, 'tall' means something different with respect to men than with respect to basketball players, which means that it has a very flexible meaning. This does not show, however, that *vagueness* is useful: vagueness is not the same as context-dependence, and the argument is consistent with 'tall' having a precise meaning in each context. But not any function from contexts to precise meanings will do. The meaning of 'tall' should be *learnable* and *computable* by us as boundedly rational agents. One requirement seems to be that 'tall' should at least behave *consistent* across these contexts: It shouldn't be possible that in one context x is counted as tall, but y is not, while in another context where we still look at things from the same perspective, but where we take more or less individuals into account, it is the other way around. But consistency is not enough: for a predicate to be precise, it has to be learnable and computable what the extension of that predicate is in each context. Bosch (1983) argues this is too much to ask, because there are many potential contexts for which we wouldn't know how to distinguish the individuals to which we can apply the predicate from those to which we cannot.[5]

In the introduction I claimed that vagueness involves not only tolerance, but also the required level of fine-grainedness. It seems beneficial for both the speaker and the hearer to sometimes describe the world at a more coarse-grained level (see for instance Hobbs, 1985; Krifka, 2007). There is obviously something to this. Deciding which precise term to use may be harder than using a vague term. For the listener, information which is too specific may require more effort to analyze. Another reason for not always trying to be as precise as possible is that this would give rise to *instability*. As stressed by Pinkal (1995), in case one measures the height of a person in all too much detail, this measure might change from day to day, which is not very useful. Also, in case there exists no standard way to measure the length of a certain object (like a river), being too precise is only confusing if the method of measurement is not provided as well.

A final reason why vague expressions are so prevalent in natural language might be that vague expressions are very useful to make *value judgments*.[6] Even if you know that Quiza is 1.45 m long, you might still learn something new when I tell you that she is *tall* for a Martian. This is mostly the case because whether one is tall depends on a gradient contingent fact, one's height, and it is not always very clear whether this particular height counts as being tall or not (for a Martian). A man for whom it is not clear whether he is tall or not, is standardly called a *borderline case* of tallness. John might be a borderline tall man although the speaker knows his height either because there is divergence in usage among competent speakers, or

[5]Bosch (1983) refers here to Waisman's (1968) notion of 'open texture', the feeling that for outlandish cases we wouldn't know yet how to apply the predicate. I believe this notion is closely related with the notion of 'unforeseen contingencies' in economics.

[6]Franks Veltman stresses this in his inaugural lecture Veltman (2002).

because the speaker still hesitates to call him tall or not. Lewis (1969), for instance, adopts the former characterization and suggests that languages themselves are free of vagueness but that the linguistic conventions of a population, or the linguistic habits of a person, select not a point but a fuzzy region in the space of precise languages.[7] Proponents of the epistemic approach to vagueness (e.g. Williamson, 1994) and many adherents of the supervaluation theory (e.g. Fine, 1975; Kamp 1975; Keefe, 2000) go for the second alternative: English, or its valuation function, is, or can be made, precise, but agents don't know, or don't bother to care, exactly what this valuation function is. On such a view, borderline cases of 'tall' are individuals that some speakers of a language consistent with the linguistic convention of English consider to be tall, while others don't (on Lewis's meta-linguistic account), or individuals of which an agent doesn't know, or doesn't care much about, whether they count as being tall or not, although the agent knows their precise height.

A semantic valuation function normally only determines how the facts are (e.g. whether John's height is 1.80 or 1.70 m). One way to model the above intuition of borderline cases is to assume that a valuation function includes information about 'semantic' facts, and that a speaker takes several of such valuation functions to be possible. A valuation function includes information about semantic facts, if it not only says what John's height is, but also whether this particular height counts as being 'tall', i.e., whether somebody who is 1.80 m should be considered to be tall or not. On this view, valuation functions, or worlds, should thus fulfill two roles, and those roles are exactly the roles a world can play according to Stalnaker's (1978) two-dimensional view on language. If we fix the meanings of the expressions, a sentence expresses a meaning, represented by a set of worlds, and if the actual world is a member of this set, what is said by the sentence is true, false otherwise. But if what is expressed by a (token of a) sentence depends on context, we can think of the world (together with the expression token) as determining how the expressions should be interpreted, and then it might be that in different worlds something different is said (i.e. different meanings are expressed) by the same sentential token. In this way we might explain why it might be unclear to the hearers what the speaker meant by saying 'I like you': the hearers might be unsure about the context that determines the reference of 'you' that the speaker had in mind. In the same way one might argue that also the meaning of nouns and adjectives depends on the utterance context. But if worlds fulfill the two roles suggested above, it seems natural to assume that they always fulfill the two roles *at the same time*. It follows that if we interpret a sentential token of a sentence ϕ in world w of which we consider it possible that it is the actual world, we use w both to determine *what is said* by ϕ, (denoted by $[\![\phi]\!]_w$), and to determining whether what is said by ϕ in w is *true* in w, i.e., whether $w \in [\![\phi]\!]_w$. The set of worlds in which what is said by sentence ϕ is w is also true in w – denoted by $\{w \in W : w \in [\![\phi]\!]_w\}$ – is called the *diagonal*

[7] Lewis (1970) takes this analysis of vagueness to be very similar to (what is now called) a supervaluation account. Burns (1991) argues (unconvincingly, we think) that the two are very different.

proposition by Stalnaker (1978). The diagonal proposition expressed by a sentence can be used to explain the so-called *evaluative meaning* of vague predicates. As noted by Barker (2002),[8] if one says that 'John is tall', one can make two kinds of statements: a *descriptive* one saying that John is above the relevant cut-off point (if it is clear in a context what the cut-off point for being tall is) and a *metalinguistic* one saying that the cut-off point for being tall is below the height of John (if it is clear in a context what john's height is). The latter involves the evaluative meaning of 'tall' and can be accounted for straightforwardly in terms of diagonalization. There is nothing extraordinary about metalinguistic statements: identity statements can be used to express them as well. It is well known that identity statements can be used (i) to state the identity of meaning of the two terms, but also (ii) to fix the meaning of one term in terms of the meaning of the other. The second reading is prominent in a sentence like 'Deep throat is the person who was the source of Woodward and Bernstein's Watergate information', and should be understood metalinguistically.

6.4 Gradable Adjectives

Although we have seen in Section 6.2 that expressions of many lexical categories are vague, most research on vagueness concentrates on adjectives like 'tall' and 'wide'. In linguistics these adjectives are known as *gradable* adjectives and should be distinguished from non-gradable adjectives like 'pregnant' and 'even'. The latter adjectives do not give rise to (much) vagueness. There exist two major types of approaches to the analysis of gradable adjectives: degree-based approaches and delineation approaches. Degree-based approaches (e.g. Seuren, 1973; Cresswell, 1976; Bierwisch, 1984; von Stechow, 1984; Kennedy, 1999, 2007), analyze gradable adjectives as relations between individuals and degrees, where these degrees are thought of as scales associated with the dimension referred to by the adjective. Individuals can posses a property to a certain measurable degree. The truth conditions of sentences involving these adjectives are stated in terms of degrees. Delineation approaches (Lewis, 1970; Kamp, 1975; Klein 1980, 1991) analyze gradable adjectives like 'tall' as simple predicates, but assume that the extension of these terms are crucially context dependent. In this section we will discuss both types of approaches in somewhat more detail, and also see how they treat comparatives.

6.4.1 The Degree Based Account

According to the degree-based approaches, relative adjectives are analyzed as relations between individuals and degrees, where these degrees are associated with the dimension referred to by the adjective. Individuals can posses a property to a certain measurable degree, and the truth conditions of comparative and positive sentences are stated in terms of degrees. According to the most straightforward

[8] But see also Kyburg and Morreau (2000).

degree-based approach, the absolutive (1) is true iff the degree to which John is tall is (significantly) greater than a (contextually given) standard of height.[9] While the comparative (2) is true iff *the* degree to which John is tall is greater than *the* degree to which Mary is tall.

(1) John is tall.
(2) John is taller than Mary.

But this straightforward degree-based approach has a problem with examples where the scope of the comparative contains an indefinite ('any'), or existential modal:

(3) a. John is taller than anyone else.
 b. John is taller than allowed.

It is not easy to see how the above degree-based approach can account in a compositional way for the intuition that from (3-a), for instance, we infer that John is taller than *everybody* else, if we treat *any* as an indefinite. To account for this problem Seuren (1973) proposed that (2) 'John is taller than Mary' should be counted as true iff *there is* a degree d of tallness that John has but Mary does not: $\exists d[Tall(j,d) \wedge \neg Tall(m,d)]$.[10] In this formalization, $T(j,d)$ means that John's degree of tallness includes *at least d*. This analysis easily accounts for the intuition concerning (3-a) and (3-b), by representing them by (4-a), and (4-b) respectively (treating 'any' as an existential quantifier)[11]:

(4) a. $\exists d[T(j,d) \wedge \neg \exists x[x \neq j \wedge T(x,d)]]$.
 b. $\exists d[T(j,d) \wedge \neg \Diamond T(j,d)]$.

Unfortunately, Seuren's analysis of comparatives meets a serious problem: we can't immediately account for the fact that from the truth of (2) we conclude to (5) which involves its antonym[12]:

---

[9]For some adjectives, like 'tall' this standard is either defined as the (arithmetical or geometrical, possibly weighted) mean of the height of all individuals in the class, for others, like 'red' this standard can be thought of as the prototype representative of the class.

[10]The idea that the 'than'-clause of a comparative contains a negation goes back to Jespersen (1917).

[11]von Stechow (1984) proposed a somewhat different analysis to account for these sentences. It is fair to say that although von Stechow's analysis has been improved on recently, it is the classic paper on comparatives, and still contains the most complete discussion of the analyses on the subject.

[12]In an early, but still very relevant study on grading, Sapir (1944), makes a distinction between adjectives for which inferences like that between (2) and (5) go through, and adjectives for which they do not. In the first class are things like 'good'-'bad' and 'far'-'near', while in the second class are antonyms like 'brilliant'-'stupid': From 'John is it less/more brilliant than Mary' we conclude that both John and Mary are brilliant, and we can't continue this sentence with 'but both are stupid'.

(2) John is *taller* than Mary.
(5) Mary is *shorter* than John.

There seems to be an easy way to account for this problem, however: just assume that 'John is short' is true if and only if he is not tall. Unfortunately, accounting for antonyms in this way gives rise to a serious problem. The problem – which von Stechow (1984) attributes to Hoepelman – is that it is predicted that the following two sentences are equivalent:

(6) a. *John is tall and short.
b. *John is neither tall nor short.

Indeed, the approach predicts that (6-a) is represented as $T(j) \wedge \neg T(j)$, while (6-b) is represented as $\neg T(j) \wedge \neg\neg T(j)$, which have the same meaning, and denote a contradiction. Although (6-a) seems inappropriate for exactly this reading, (6-b) seems to express a contingent proposition. The obvious conclusion from these examples is that we should not analyze 'short' as 'not tall'. But if we can't do this, it is not clear anymore how to account for the inference from (2) to (5) without making extra *ad hoc* assumptions.[13]

von Stechow (1984) and Kennedy (1999) conclude that to account for this latter problem[14] we have to assume that degrees are *directional*. Fortunately, it appears that in the alternative delineation approach to gradable adjectives, the above problem need not show up.

6.4.2 The Delineation Approach

Lewis (1970) and Kamp (1975) make use of supervaluation theory to account for the vagueness of adjectives like 'tall' and 'bald'. These expressions are taken to have specific cutoff-points with respect to each classical valuation function, or world, but it is undetermined, or unknown, what the actual cutoff-point for English is. Thus, a positive adjective is considered to be a simple predicate the extension of which depends on a world-dependent cutoff-point. For an adjective like 'tall', they propose that 'John is taller than Mary' is true just in case the set of worlds in which John is tall is a proper *superset* of the set of worlds in which Mary is tall.[15]

This in contrast with the appropriate discourse 'From the point of view of America, France is on the *near* side of Europe, though actually *far*'.

[13]Proponents of the degree-based approach can propose that in comparatives 'short' means 'not tall', but not in the positive use of the predicates: 'John is short' doesn't mean the same as 'John is not tall'. They can account for this by making use of the POS-operator they use to account for positive use of adjectives.

[14]And for a related problem that you can't say 'John is 1.80 m *short*'.

[15]Well, this is Kamp's (1975) proposal in case at least one of the two is considered to be a borderline tall individual.

Because the proper superset relation gives rise to a strict partial order (irreflexive and transitive),[16] it is correctly predicted that the comparative gives rise to a strict partial order as well. Still, the resulting analysis is not completely satisfactory.

First of all, as noted by Kamp (1975), in order to make this analysis work for comparisons like 'taller than' that give rise to orders that are not only irreflexive and transitive but satisfy other properties as well, Kamp and Lewis have to make a crucial *meaning postulate* to constrain the possible cutoff-points of a vague predicate P in the worlds: for all individuals x and y: either '$P(x) \rightarrow P(y)$' must be true in all worlds, or '$P(y) \rightarrow P(x)$'.[17] Although the meaning postulate required by Kamp and Lewis is natural, it is questionable whether by assuming it, we not already assume that we take the comparative to be more basic than the positive use of the adjective. But if so, this proposal is not in the 'spirit' of the delineation approach after all.

Second, the analysis gives rise to the same problem as Seuren's (1973) analysis does: it cannot account for the equivalence of (6-a) and (6-b) without making ad hoc assumptions. As noted by von Stechow (1984), the reason is that the analyses of Kamp and Lewis are essentially the same as Seuren's degree-based analysis. Lewis (1970) and Kamp (1975) assume that the worlds differ from each other in their cutoff-points of vague predicates. The comparative 'John is taller than Mary' is considered to be true if and only if there is a cutoff-point for 'tall' such that John is above it, while Mary is not. The easiest way to think of the cutoff-point of 'tall' in a world is as a particular *number*, a *degree*. But then we can assume that the predicate denotes a relation between individuals and degrees, and the delineation approach just claims that the comparative is true iff John has a degree of tallness that Mary does not have. This, of course, is exactly Seuren's analysis of comparatives.

In the standard supervaluation theory used by Lewis and Kamp it is assumed that vague words like 'bald' simply have an extension in a world: each world has a unique cutoff-point from whereon individuals are not counted as bald anymore. But it might be, of course, that John can be counted as tall when we compare him with other men, but not tall when we compare him with (other) basketball players. Thus, whether someone of 1.80 m is tall or not depends (partly) on who that person is compared with. In case the adjective occurs in attributive position it is natural to assume that the comparison class is at least partly determined by the *noun* to which the adjective is attached. For John to be *a tall man* it must be that John is being tall for a man, but that doesn't mean that John is a tall basketball player. This suggests that whether we count an object to be *tall for an X*, we compare this object with the other objects that are X and decide whether the former object is tall. Because adjectives need not be attached to nouns, however, this can't be enough. That is why we will assume with Wheeler (1972) and Klein (1980) that

---

[16] A relation R is irreflexive iff for all objects $x \in I : \neg R(x,x)$. It is transitive iff for all objects $x, y, z \in I : R(x,y) \wedge R(y,z) \rightarrow R(x,z)$.

[17] Notice that by adopting this constraint we can reformulate the above analysis of comparisons in terms of existential quantification: John is taller than Mary is true in a supervaluation frame just in case there is a complete valuation function, or world, in which John is tall, but Mary is not.

every relative adjective should be interpreted with respect to a *comparison class*.[18] A comparison class is just a set of objects/individuals and is contextually given. In particular if the adjective stands alone, we might assume that the contextually given comparison class helps to determine what counts as being *tall*.[19] The truth of the positive sentence (1)

(1) John is tall.

depends on the contextually given comparison class: (1) is true with respect to comparison class c (in model M) iff John is counted as tall in this class (in model M). The proposition expressed by a comparative like (2) is context independent.[20]

(2) John is taller than Mary.

and the sentence is true iff there is a comparison class according to which John counts as tall, while Mary does not.[21] This analysis is obviously close to the Kamp/Lewis approach to comparatives and to Seuren's degree-based account. Indeed, one can easily show that Klein (1980) can account for (3-a), and (3-b) in almost exactly the same way as Seuren (1973) could. But Klein's (1980) analysis seems better suited to account for the fact that from (2) we conclude that Mary is shorter than John. We have concluded above that to account for this problem we are not allowed to analyze 'short' as 'not tall'. Fortunately, Klein (1980) doesn't need to analyze 'short' in this way in order to account for the equivalence of (2) and (5).

---

[18]Graff (2000) has argued that a comparison class should be an *intensional* instead of an extensional object. If we allow for individuals of different worlds to be part of the same comparison class, I don't think this crucially undermines Klein's proposal.

[19]Although it does not necessarily uniquely determine what counts as being *tall*. See the end of this section for some discussion.

[20]But see Section 6.6.

[21]Equatives can be analyzed in terms of comparison classes as well. Klein (1980) proposes that (i-a) should be interpreted as (i-b).

(i) a. John is *as tall as* Mary.
    b. In every context where Mary is tall, John is tall as well.

Klein (1980) notes that on this analysis, the negation of (i-a), i.e. (ii-a), is correctly predicted to be equivalent with (ii-b):

(ii) a. John is *not* as tall as Mary.
     b. Mary is taller than John.

Standard pragmatics can explain why in the context of question 'How tall is John?', (i-a) would come to mean that John and Mary are equally tall.

(5) Mary is *shorter* than John.

The reason is that if there is any comparison class in which John but not Mary counts as tall, this is also the case in the comparison class containing just John and Mary.[22] But this means, intuitively, that *in this context* Mary is short, while John is not. From this we can conclude that we can account for the intuition that (2) and (5) have the same truth conditions without assuming that we should analyze 'short' as meaning *not tall.*

Notice that both the degree-based and the delineation account assume that the meaning of comparatives are context independent, but that the meaning of sentences containing positive adjectives are context dependent. On the comparison-class approach context-dependence is (partly) accounted for by the selection of the relevant comparison class, while on the degree approach the truth conditions of a sentence like (1) depend on the contextually selected standard of height. In this sense, the two approaches are the same. But there are also four differences that (we feel) are in favor of the comparison-class approach.

First, degree-based approaches need something like comparison classes as well. Such approaches claim that a positive sentence like 'John is tall' is true iff the degree to which John is tall is (significantly) greater than a given standard of height. But, obviously, this standard for basketball players differs from the standard for men.

Second, the comparison-class account just assumes that the meaning of the comparative 'taller than' is a function of the meaning of 'tall'. This is much in line with Frege's principle of compositionality,[23] and also accounts for the fact that in a wide variety of languages the positive is formally unmarked in relation to the comparative (Klein, 1980). The degree-based approach, however, treats the comparative as basic, and states the truth conditions of a sentence involving a positive adjective like (1) by making use of the comparative relation 'taller than': John should be (significantly) taller than the norm, or normal size of individuals, or taller than indifferent, or taller than we expected him to be. But why then, does at least the vast majority of languages express the comparative in more terms than the positive?[24]

---

[22] Later we will see that this is guaranteed by van Benthem's (1982) Downward Difference constraint (DD). However, some authors have argued that objects indistinguishable with respect to a small comparison class, might be distinguishable with respect to a larger comparison class. According to proponents of this view (see Section 6.5.2), constraint (DD) is not valid.

[23] But see von Stechow (1984) for an argument saying that also the degree-based approach is in line with Frege's principle.

[24] Sapir (1944: 125) argues that we must regard grading from different points of view. "It is very important to realize that psychologically all comparatives are primary in relation to their corresponding absolutes ('positives') [...] Linguistic usage tends to start from the graded concept, e.g. *good* (= better than indifferent), *bad* (= worse than indifferent) [...] for the obvious reason that in experience it is the strikingly high-graded or low-graded concept that has significance, while the generalized concept which includes all the members of a graded series is arrived at by a gradual process of striking the balance between these graded terms. The purely logical, the psychological, and the linguistic orders of primacy, therefore, do not necessarily correspond." Perhaps this is so, but this doesn't mean that making use of a theory that reflects such a correspondence wouldn't be preferred.

The third obvious difference is that in contrast to the comparison-class approach, the degree approach makes essential use of *degrees* from the very beginning. Because we can only make sense of degrees once we adopt a system of full-blooded quantitative measurement, it is predicted that already for very simple comparatives like (2) it is crucial to make use of quantitative measurement. But this seems wrong: making comparisons precedes measurement and counting, both in science and in individual development. A child may observe and inform others, for instance, that an individual is *taller* than he was before, or that John is *taller* than Mary, before it is able to count or to handle a measure tape. Thus, it seems preferred to favor a system that is able to account for simple comparatives that doesn't make use of precise measures, i.e. degrees. Of course, one also has to make sense of measurement phrases, but it would be preferred to find a system that accounts for comparisons that doesn't explicitly mention measures. Moreover, the introduction of degrees should give rise to a system that is a *natural extension* of the theory of comparatives that doesn't make use of degrees.

Suppose that one already has degrees with respect to a gradable adjective 'P' at one's disposal. According to a degree-based analysis, a positive sentence of the form 'x is P' is now considered to be true iff x has property P to a degree higher than a contextually given cutoff-point. But one may wonder why anyone then would use the positive sentence at all? Why not immediately state the precise degree to which x has property P? One valid reason can be, of course, that the speaker doesn't know the precise degree. Another reason might be that by using the positive sentence the speaker can make a value judgement (see Section 6.3). However, it seems clear that there are more obvious reasons why the vague positive sentence is used. Consider expressions like 'probable' and 'useful'. They behave much like gradable adjectives. I take it that these types of expressions have been used (also to give value judgments) long before they have been given a measure-theoretic interpretation in the twentieth century. It is unnatural to claim that a speaker who uses such an expression believes that its positive use comes with a precise cardinal cutoff-point, but that he or she just doesn't know what this exact cutoff-point is. In fact, most economists in the nineteenth and early twentieth century used an expression like 'useful' even though they strongly *dis*believed that 'usefulness' could be given a precise measure-theoretic interpretation.

A final problem for the degree-based account is that it is unclear how it accounts for the vagueness of sentences that involve, for instance, *nouns*, and not relative adjectives. Of course, prototype-based approaches of the meanings of nouns make use of something like degrees: the degree to which an object is a (typical) bird is inversely related to the *distance* of this object to the prototypical bird. But if one uses degrees here, it is unclear why we don't have simple comparatives like 'x is more heap than y' that involve nouns.[25,26]

---

[25]Of course, we do have 'x is more *of* a heap than y', but that seems to have a somewhat different meaning (or not?).

[26]There exists a striking syntactic difference between common nouns like 'bank' on the one hand and verbs and adjectives like 'tall' on the other: whereas common nouns combine with a determiner to form a noun phrase, verbs and adjectives must be nominalized first, before they can play that

Comparison classes can not only be used to help to determine the meaning of adjectives like 'tall', they can be used to help determining the meaning of degree modifier like 'very' and 'fairly' as well (cf. Wheeler, 1972; Klein, 1980). Suppose John is considered to be tall with respect to comparison class c. Then we might say that John is *very* tall just in case John is considered to be tall among the tall ones in c, i.e., iff $John \in Tall(Tall(c))$. Similarly, we might say that John is *fairly* tall if he is tall, but not very tall. Assuming that predicates denote (in each model) functions from sets of individuals (i.e. comparison classes) to sets of individuals (i.e., comparison classes) is crucial for such an analysis of degree modifiers.

Klein (1980) argued that because the positive adjective 'tall' is formally unmarked in relation to the comparative 'taller than', the meaning of the latter should be a function of the meaning of the former. Before we will look at how the meaning of the comparative 'taller than' can be defined in terms of the meaning of the adjective 'tall', we will take a look at positive and comparative sentences involving *absolute* adjectives first, because it turns out that their behavior can be characterized easier.

6.4.3 Absolute Terms and Comparison Classes

Consider adjectives like 'full', 'flat', or 'straight'. Just like the meaning of 'tall', also the meaning of these adjectives is vague. These adjectives are also perfectly acceptable in comparatives: there is nothing wrong with saying that one surface is *flatter* than another, or that one bottle is *fuller* than another. In this respect they differ from adjectives like 'pregnant' and 'even', and are on a par with other gradable adjectives like 'tall'. However, as observed by Unger (1975) and also discussed by Rothstein and Winter (2004) and Kennedy and McNally (2005), while with relative adjectives one can easily say something like

(7) John is tall, but not the tallest/but somebody else is taller.
this can't be done (so naturally) with (maximal) absolute adjectives.[27]

(8) a. *My glass is *FULL*, but it could be fuller.
b. *This line is *STRAIGHT*, but you can make it straighter.

role. It has been argued that there corresponds a semantic difference with this syntactic difference: it is in general not determinate how to count things like 'the tall ones' or 'the red ones' (a red grapefruit, for instance, won't have the same color as a red tomato), nor is it determinate how a thing which is tall or is red must be individuated and reidentified. In contrast to what falls under a common noun like 'cat' or 'bank', the general terms 'tall' and 'red' do not *by themselves* determine units which could underlie the possibility of counting: arbitrary many parts of a red object are red objects again. Of course, we can count red things, but only once we have determined beforehand what counts as an individual thing. Notice, though, that some philosophers have argued that even for nouns like 'cats' it is unclear exactly what should be counted (see Lewis, 1993 for discussion).

[27] According to Unger, stress forces a precise interpretation of the absolute adjective.

What this contrast shows is that sentences with absolute adjectives generate entailments that sentences with relative adjectives lack: it is inconsistent to say that something is flatter than something that is flat.[28] Thus, from (9-a) we conclude (9-b) that the pavement is not flat:

(9) a. The desk is flatter than the pavement.
 b. The pavement is not flat.

Comparatives with relative adjectives, however, don't give rise to entailments at all:

(10) a. John is taller than Mary. $\not\Rightarrow$ John/Mary is tall/not tall.

The natural way to account for absolute adjectives in a degree-based approach is to assume with Kennedy and McNally (2005) and others that we start with a 'fuller than' or 'flatter than'-relation between degrees, but assume that in contrast to the 'taller than'-relation formed with the relative adjective 'tall', the 'fuller than' and 'flatter than'-relations have *maximal elements*. The positive use of the adjective has then this maximal degree as its cut-off point.

But now suppose that we would like to assume with Klein (1980) that not only comparatives with relative adjectives like 'taller than' should be defined in terms of its corresponding positive adjective, but that this also holds for 'flatter than'. How should we proceed? Intuitively – and in contrast to the meaning of *relative* adjectives –, the meaning of the positive use of 'flat' is context-*in*dependent. We will suggest that this means that in the positive use of 'flat', the adjective should always be interpreted with respect to the *maximal* comparison class: the whole domain. If 'flat' is used in a comparative, however, we will assume that its meaning is relativized to a *smaller* comparison class. However, 'flat' selects with respect to each comparison class intuitively its 'maximal' element.

Saying that the meaning of an adjective depends on a comparison class, and defining the comparative relation by saying that 'x is P-er than y' iff x has property P in comparison class $\{x, y\}$, but y is not enough to give a proper analysis of the comparative relation. The reason is that once we relativize the meaning of adjectives to comparison classes, this leaves room for the most diverse behavior. It might be, for instance, that although x is considered flat in set $\{x, y\}$ and y is not, x is not considered to be flat in set $\{x, y, z\}$, while y is. In order to assure that the meaning of the adjective in different comparison classes behaves properly, we have to constrain this behavior. Fortunately for us, the formal problem we face here is exactly the same as the problem discussed already by Arrow (1959) of how to derive a preference ordering relation from the assumption that the notion of *choice* is primitive. Assuming a choice function – a function that selects elements from each finite set of options –,

[28] Bolinger (1972) and others working on degree words observed another contrast between absolute and relative adjectives: while relative adjectives combine well with degree adverbs like 'very' and 'rather', absolute adjectives combine well with other adverbs like 'completely', 'almost', 'hardly', and 'nearly'.

Arrow showed how this can generate an ordering relation if we put some natural constraints on how this choice function should behave on different contexts. Let us define a *context structure*, M, to be a triple $\langle I, C, V\rangle$, where I is a non-empty set of individuals, the set of contexts, C, consists of all finite subsets of I, and the valuation V assigns to each context $c \in C$ and each property P those individuals in c which are to count as 'being P in c'. Say that $P(c)$ denotes the set of individuals in c that have property P with respect to c: $P(c) = \{x \in c : x \in V(P, c)\}$ (In the context of social choice theory, P is thought of as a choice function, selecting the *best* elements of c.) We follow Arrow by proposing the following principle of choice (C), and the cross-contextual constraints (A1) and (A2) to limit the possible variation:

$$(C)\ \forall c \in C : P(c) \neq \emptyset.$$
$$(A1)\ \text{If } c \subseteq c', \ \text{ then } c \cap P(c') \subseteq P(c).$$
$$(A2)\ \text{If } c \subseteq c' \text{ and } c \cap P(c') \neq \emptyset, \text{ then } P(c) \subseteq P(c').$$

If we say that 'x is P-er than y', $x >_P y$, iff$_{def}$ $x \in P(\{x, y\}) \wedge y \notin P(\{x, y\})$, Arrow (1959) shows that the comparative as defined above gives rise to a *weak order*. A structure $\langle I, R\rangle$, with R a binary relation on I, is a weak order just in case R is irreflexive (IR), transitive (TR), and almost connected (AC).

Definition 1 A weak order is a structure $\langle I, R\rangle$, with R a binary relation on I that satisfies the following conditions:

$$(\text{IR})\ \forall x : \neg R(x, x).$$
$$(\text{TR})\ \forall x, y, z : (R(x, y) \wedge R(y, z)) \rightarrow R(x, z).$$
$$(\text{AC})\ \forall x, y, z : R(x, y) \rightarrow (R(x, z) \vee R(z, y)).$$

We can now define the relations 'being as P as', '$\sim_P$', and 'being at least as P as', '$\geq_P$', as follows: $x \sim_P y$ iff$_{def}$ neither $x >_P y$ nor $y >_P x$, and $x \geq_P y$ iff$_{def}$ $x >_P y$ or $x \sim_P y$. The relation '$\sim_P$' is predicted to be an equivalence relation, while '$\geq_P$' is predicted to be reflexive, transitive, and strongly connected (meaning that $\forall x, y : x \geq_P y \vee y \geq_P x$).[29]

Although weak orders seem appropriate for the analysis of comparatives,[30] by just looking at the comparison class involving the desk and the pavement, we can't account for the contrast between the acceptability of (11-a) versus the (at least according to Unger (1975)) unacceptability of (11-b):

(11) a. The desk is not flat, but it is flatter than the pavement.
b. *The pavement is FLAT, but the desk is flatter.

---

[29]It is standard in the literature to also denote a structure $\langle I, \geq_P\rangle$ with '$\geq_P$' reflexive, transitive, and strongly connected by a weak order.

[30]The reader probably doubts whether weak orders are also appropriate for the analysis of vagueness. Indeed, I will argue in Section 6.5 that for vagueness, we need semi-orders, rather than weak orders.

The asymmetry suggests that the comparison class involved in the first conjunct should play a role in the discourse as well: the comparison class c involved in the analysis of the conjunctive sentences (11-a) and (11-b), and thus their first clauses, should be a *superset* of the comparison involved in the analysis of the second conjunct, i.e. $c \supseteq \{d, p\}$. Thus, a comparative like 'The desk is flatter than the pavement' is true in context c iff (i) $\{d, p\} \subseteq c$ and (ii) $d \in Flat(\{d, p\}$, but $p \notin Flat(\{d, p\})$. With this extra constraint we predict by (A1) that from the truth of this sentence in c, we conclude that the pavement is not flat in c, because $\{d, p\} \cap Flat(c)$ is by (A1) required to be a subset of $\{d\}$. From this it follows that (11-b) denotes a contradiction. Sentence (11-a), however, does not denote a contradiction, because the desk can be flat compared to the pavement, without it being the case that the desk is flat when compared to the other members of $c \supseteq \{d, p\}$.

Kennedy and McNally (2005) and Kennedy (2007) observe that although all sentences involving absolute adjectives give rise to inferences, there exists an important distinction between the two opposing absolute adjectives 'dry' and 'wet': whereas 'dry' behaves the same as 'flat' with respect to their entailment behavior in comparatives, 'wet' behaves quite differently, and gives rise to a *positive* inference:

(12) a. The floor is drier than the table. $\rightarrow$ The table is not dry.
b. The floor is wetter than the table. $\rightarrow$ The floor is wet.

How can we account for this difference between 'dry' and 'wet'? Assuming that absolute adjectives satisfy axiom (A1) will prove useful here. But another distinction between relative and absolute adjectives is crucial as well. Cruse (1986) observes that in contrast to the case of relative adjectives, with antonym pairs involving absolute adjectives, the negation of one form (normally) entails the positive statement of the other (i.e., they are contradictory to one another)[31]:

(13) a. The door is not open. $\Rightarrow$ The door is closed.
b. The table is not wet. $\Rightarrow$ The table is dry.
c. The baby is not awake. $\Rightarrow$ The baby is asleep.

Based on this observation, we will assume that 'wet' is defined as 'not being dry'. It follows by axiom (A1) that if there is a subset c' of c in which the floor is not considered to be dry, the floor won't be considered dry in comparison class c either. So, we can conclude that the floor is wet in c.

But not only the inference pattern in comparatives with 'wet' is different from that of its antonym 'dry', the same is true for acceptable discourses. For adjectives like 'flat' and 'dry', we have seen above that (11-a) is appropriate, but (11-b) is not, and this was explained by our constraint on accessible comparison classes, and our assumption that absolute predicates obey constraint (A1). But the same constraint

[31] This is not always the case, it doesn't hold for the pair *full-empty*.

also explains the contrastive behavior of appropriate discourses for the adjective 'wet'.

(14) a. *?The floor is not wet, but wetter than the table.
b. The table is wet, but the floor is wetter.

The appropriateness of (14-b) is easily accounted for: the floor is not considered dry w.r.t. comparison class c. In the subset {table, floor} of c, however, objects not dry in c might be considered dry, and thus the floor might be dry with respect to {table, floor}, and thus not wet. This doesn't have to be the case for the table, and so (14-b) is predicted to be appropriate. As for the inappropriateness of (14-a), note that if the floor is not wet with respect to comparison class c, it can't be counted as wet in any subset c' of c either, which is enough to rule out (14-a).

Although this analysis of absolute adjectives is appealing, the analysis given above cannot explain yet another contrast between absolute and relative adjectives. As observed by Sedivy et al. (1999) and discussed by Kennedy (2007), there is nothing wrong with using a relative adjective as part of a definite description in a sentence like 'Please give me the *long* nail' to distinguish two nails neither of which is particularly long. The use of absolute adjectives in such definite descriptions is much less appropriate.[32] In terms of our framework, what this suggests is that the *use* of the *positive* absolute adjective (in contrast to the use of the adjective in a comparative) demands that the comparison class with respect to which the adjective is interpreted is simply the whole domain, and thus that only those individuals can be called 'flat', that are the flattest of all the individuals in the whole (context *in*dependent) domain. We will see in Section 6.6 how this analysis might still account for the vagueness of absolute adjectives.

6.4.4 Comparison Classes and Relative Adjectives

Let us now consider relative adjectives like 'tall' again. Just like for 'flat', we want to derive a weak ordering relation for 'tall' in terms of how this adjective behaves across comparison classes. However, it is easily seen that although 'tall' seems to obey axiom (A2), axiom (A1) is much too strong for relative adjectives: (A1) demands that if both x and y are considered to be tall in the context of $\{x, y, z\}$, both should considered to be tall in the context $\{x, y\}$ as well. But that is exactly what we don't want: in the latter context, we want it to be possible that only x, or only y, is considered to be tall. We should conclude that if we want to characterize the behavior of relative adjectives, we should give up on (A1). Unfortunately, by just constraints (C) and (A2) we cannot guarantee that the comparative behaves as desired. In particular, we cannot guarantee that it behaves as almost connected ((C) assures that the relation 'at least as P as' is complete, while (A2) assures that the comparative behaves as a strict partial order, i.e., irreflexive and transitive).

[32]It should be noted, though, that Kennedy (2007) bases this general claim on the difference between the behavior of 'long' versus 'full'. But the absolute adjective 'full' behaves crucially different from other claimed absolute adjectives, in that its antonym 'empty' is not contradictory with 'full'. This might well be a crucial difference.

To assure that the comparative behaves as desired, we add to (C) and (A2) the Upward Difference-constraint (UD), proposed by van Benthem (1982). To state this constraint, we define the notion of a difference pair: $\langle x, y \rangle \in D_P(c)$ iff$_{def}$ $x \in P(c)$ and $y \in (c - P(c))$. Now we can define the constraint:

$$\text{(UD) } c \subseteq c' \text{ and } D_P(c') = \emptyset, \text{ then } D_P(c) = \emptyset.$$

In fact, van Benthem (1982) states the following constraints: No Reversal (NR), Upward Difference (UD), and Downward Difference (DD) (where c^2 abbreviates $c \times c$):

$$\text{(NR) } \neg\exists c, c' \in C, x, y \in I : \langle x, y \rangle \in D_P(c) \wedge \langle y, x \rangle \in D_P(c').$$
$$\text{(UD) } c \subseteq c' \text{ and } D_P(c') = \emptyset, \text{ then } D_P(c) = \emptyset.$$
$$\text{(DD) } c \subseteq c' \text{ and } D_P(c) = \emptyset, \text{ then } D_P(c') \cap c^2 = \emptyset.$$

van Benthem (1982) shows that if constraints (NR), (UD) and (UD) are satisfied, the relations '$\geq_P$', '$\sim_P$' and '$>_P$' as defined before still have the same properties as before: '$\geq_P$' is reflexive, transitive, and strongly connected; '$\sim_P$' is still predicted to be an equivalence relation, while the comparative '$>_P$' is still predicted to be (i) irreflexive, (ii) transitive, and (iii) almost connected, just as in the case of absolute adjectives. For adjectives like 'tall', this seems just what we want.

It is important to realize that the above conditions constrain, but do *not* (at all) *uniquely determine* the behavior of the relevant predicate P across comparative classes. First, it might be that different context structures give rise to quite different ordering relations '$>_P$'. But even if two context structures gives rise to the same '$>_P$'-ordering, predicate P might still behave quite differently in those two models on larger comparison classes. This is due to the fact that to prove that '$>_P$' behaves as desired, we look at comparison classes of at most 3 elements. Once we have larger subsets of I, there are at least two context structures that give rise to the same ordering that satisfy the above constraints. Thus, whether a particular individual of a given comparison class counts as a P-individual or not might still depend on the context structure M.[33] This is as it should be, if we want to account for the observation of Kamp (1975) and Graff (2000) that even if the comparison class is identified, the meaning of the adjective might still depend on context. Graff (2000) observes, for instance, that with a sentence like 'Fido is old for a dog', where the comparison class is made explicit, one can not only attribute elderliness to Fido, but also extreme longevity.[34]

'Tall' is known as a *one-dimensional* adjective. Kamp (1975) calls an adjective one-dimensional if we can associate with the adjective a unique measurable aspect that membership depends upon. Examples of one-dimensional adjectives are 'tall',

[33] In terms of the analysis of value judgments sketched in Section 6.3, one might think of each context structure M as a precise valuation function. Although all these structures give rise to the same ordering relation, they give the predicate that gives rise to this ordering relation different extensions with respect to the same comparison classes.

[34] As argued by many opponents of analyses like ours, making the meaning of the adjective context dependent doesn't eliminate its vagueness. The phrase 'old for a dog' is just as vague as the adjective 'old' is. Thus, making the meaning of P, the positive form, dependent on both a comparison class and a structure M is not enough. We will come back to this in Section 6.5.

'heavy' and 'hot'. For the adjective 'tall', for instance, this aspect is 'height', for 'heavy' it is 'weight', and for 'hot' it is 'temperature'. These adjectives can easily be modified by adverbs of degree like 'very' and 'quite': '*very* tall', '*quite* heavy'; easily undergo comparative formation ('tall*er*', 'heavi*er*', 'warm*er*'), and superlative formation ('tall*est*', 'heavi*est*', 'hott*est*'). One-dimensional adjectives have only one contrary predicate: its antonym. According to Kamp (1975), most adjectives are *more-dimensional*. The extensions of color adjectives like 'blue', for instance, are determined by three dimensions: its *brightness*, *hue*, and *saturation*. This is still relatively unproblematic. For other more-dimensional adjectives, things are less clear. There is no unique way to determine, for instance, whether John is *cleverer* than Mary: it doesn't depend only on the ability of solving problems, and even if it did, it is not clear how the problem solving abilities in different contexts should be weighed against each other. Adjectives like 'large' and its antonym 'small' behaves just like 'clever': it is unclear whether it is its height, its volume, or its surface, or a combination of these which decides whether an object is large.

Important for us is that for more-dimensional adjectives P, the assumption that the comparative 'P-er than' is almost-connected is problematic. The reason is that such adjectives induce orderings that give rise to *incomparability* (cf. Klein, 1980),[35] and thus do not have a unique antonym.[36] Let us assume, for the sake of argument, that there are only two properties/dimensions associated with being clever: an ability to manipulate numbers, and an ability to manipulate people. Let us say that John is cleverer than Mary iff John is better both in manipulating numbers and in manipulating people. But now consider Sue. Sue is worse than John in manipulating numbers but better in manipulating people. Thus, neither John is cleverer than Sue, nor Sue is cleverer than John. For the *cleverer than*-relation still being almost connected, it has to be the case that Sue is cleverer than Mary. But it is well possible that although Sue is better in manipulating people than Mary (and John), Mary is better than Sue in manipulating numbers. Thus, if one doesn't fix a particular dimension, one cannot claim that 'cleverer than' denotes a relation that is almost connected. To solve this problem one could simply claim that the comparative can only be used if one fixes a particular dimension. According to two other proposals, we can also compare in a multi-dimensional way, but if we do so, almost connectedness is not valid anymore. We can make sense of that by either giving up constraint (UD) and try to replace it with another one that still guarantees that '$>_P$' behaves

[35] The standard way to make the distinction between *indistinguishability* and *incomparability* is by starting with a structure like $\langle I, >_P, \sim_P\rangle$ where I is a set of objects, '$>_P$' a primitive preference relation, and '$\sim_P$' a primitive indistinguishability relation. Given such a structure, and the natural definition of '$<_P$' in terms of '$>_P$', it is possible that $>_P \cup \sim_P \cup <_P \neq I \times I$. Thus, it is possible that for two elements x and y of I, it is neither the case that $x >_P y$, nor $y >_P x$, nor $x \sim_P y$. In that case, we call x and y *incomparable*. Now it is easy to rule out incomparability: just demand that $>_P \cup \sim_P \cup <_P = I \times I$.

[36] For more-dimensional predicates, comparative formation is arguably more difficult as well. Kamp (1975), for instance, claims that 'This is bluer than that' is most of the time not a meaningful statement.

transitive. Another way to give up almost connectedness would be to give up the assumption that C consists of *all* finite subsets of I, but to demand for all $c, c' \in C$ that if c and c' have a non-empty intersection, then their union is an element of C as well.[37]

6.4.5 Degrees and Measures

Remember that Arrow (1959) and van Benthem (1982) showed that given their constraints on context structures, the comparative as defined by Klein (1980) and others is (i) irreflexive, (ii) transitive, and (iii) almost connected, where R is almost connected iff $\forall x, y, z : xRy \rightarrow (xRz \vee zRy)$. Relations with these properties are well-known in semantics: Lewis' (1973) relation of comparative similarity is one of them. It is also wellknown that such relations R can be turned into *linear* orderings R^* of equivalence classes of individuals that are connected ($\forall v, z : vR^*z \vee zR^*v$). First, say that x is R-equivalent to y, $x \sim_R y$, iff$_{def}$ neither xRy nor yRx. Take $[x]_{\sim R}$ to be the equivalence class $\{y \in I | y \sim_R x\}$. Then we say that $[x]_{\sim_R} R^* [y]_{\sim_R}$ iff$_{def}$ xRy. Linear orderings like R^* form the basic input for any form of quantitative measurement, i.e., of *degrees*!

The idea of measurement theory (Krantz et al., 1971) is that we represent properties of and relations between elements of certain abstract ordering structures in terms of properties of and relations between real numbers that we already understand much better. A *quantitative* measure based on a linear ordering like $\langle I, >^* \rangle$ is a representation of the qualitative ordering relation (like *taller than*, represented by '$>^*$') in terms of the quantitative ordering relation *greater than* , '$>$', between real numbers. This measurement is defined in terms of a (homomorphic) function f that assigns each element of I to a real number such that $\forall x, y \in I : x >^* y$ if and only if $f(y) > f(z)$. In general, there are many alternative mappings to f that would numerically represent the qualitative relation $>^*$ equally well. However, this mapping f is *unique up to a certain group of transformations*. For instance, the mappings f and g to the (ordered) set of real numbers represent the same (*ordinal*) ordering structure $\langle I, >^* \rangle$ in case they can be related by a *monotone transformation*: for any $x, y \in I : f(x) > f(y)$ iff $g(x) > g(y)$. To faithfully represent *more informative* ordering structures, the different mappings should be unique up to a *more limited* group of transformations. For instance, suppose that the ordering structure can make sense not only of sentences like 'x is taller than y', but also of things like 'x is taller than y by more than v is taller than w'. For a mapping f to represent this latter type of information, it should be the case that $f(x) - f(y) > f(v) - f(w)$. Two mappings f and g faithfully represent the same such an ordering structure, iff f and g are the same up to a *positive linear*, or *affine, transformation*, i.e., for any $x \in I : g(x) = \alpha(f(x)) + \beta$, where α, β are real numbers, and $\alpha > 0$. Indeed, it are linear transformations that

[37] See van Rooij (2011) for making precise these two approaches.

preserve such differences.[38] The number α represents the fact that the *unit* of measurement is arbitrary. The number β represents the fact that the ordering structure doesn't have a fixed zero-point. Quantitative measures that are unique up to such linear transformations are called *intensional magnitudes*. The best known intensional magnitude is 'warmth'. We can measure it in terms of degrees Celsius and degrees Fahrenheit, and it is well-known that we can transform the one to the other by means of a linear transformation: x degrees Celsius is $32 + \frac{9}{5}x$ degrees Fahrenheit. Notice that one degree Celsius warmer is not the same as one degree Fahrenheit warmer (but $\frac{9}{5}$ degrees Fahrenheit warmer), and that 0° C is not at all the same as 0° F, but rather as 32° F.

To account for measure phrases like 'John is 1.80 m tall', we need a theory of degrees that involves *addition*. Standard measurement theory gives us that for so-called *extensional* or *additive magnitudes*. Ordering structures that give rise to extensional measurement must come with an operation of *concatenation*, a specified procedure for joining two objects, denoted by '$\circ$'. Thus, the ordering structures must be of the form $\langle I, >^*, \circ\rangle$, where operation '$\circ$' satisfies certain conditions, like associativity. For mapping f to faithfully represent such an ordering structure it must be the case that for all $\forall x, y \in I : f(x \circ y) = f(x) + f(y)$ (of course, it must also holds that $x >^* y$ iff $f(x) > f(y)$). Just as before, this mapping is unique up to a certain group of transformations. The group of transformations are now all of the form $g(x) = \alpha f(x)$, with $\alpha > 0$. The existence of α means that the unit of measurement is still arbitrary, but the disappearance of the constant β used in intensional magnitudes reflects the idea that the zero is *not arbitrary* anymore.

A striking fact about natural language is that certain adjectives combine well with measure phrases while others do not. For instance, it is ok to say that John is 1.80 m *tall*, but it is not good to say that Mary is 5° *happy*. A natural explanation of this is to claim that while 'tall' denotes an additive magnitude, 'happy' denotes only an ordinal one. A more interesting example is a *negative adjective* like 'short'. The antonyms of positive adjectives generally don't allow for measure phrases in their 'bare' use (to say 'John is 1.80 m short' is inappropriate), but they combine well with measure phrases in comparatives: 'Mary is 2 cm shorter than John', and then they mean the same as 'John is 2 cm taller than Mary'. Sassoon (2008) has recently given an appealing explanation of this fact by claiming that negative adjectives like 'short' are not extensional, but *intensional* magnitudes. This makes a lot of sense: if l is a mapping from individuals to their height, one can define a mapping s from individuals to their 'shortness' in terms of it by means of a linear (though not positive) transformation: $\forall x \in I : s(x) = \alpha l(x) + \beta$. The existence of the β reflects the idea that 'shortness' doesn't have a zero-point. If one sets α to –1 – as one intuitively should –, this means that $s(x) = \beta - l(x)$, which explains many, if not all, of the striking linguistic data involving 'short' discussed by Kennedy (1999). But why does 'shortness' not have a zero-point? A natural answer would be that zero-point β

[38]Such mappings not only preserve differences, but also ratios between differences: $\frac{f(x)-f(y)}{f(v)-f(w)} = \frac{g(x)-g(y)}{g(v)-g(w)}$.

is simply the height of the longest object or individual, and that we don't know this height.[39]

6.5 Tolerance and the Sorites Paradox

In Section 6.4.2 we have argued that the meaning of P, the positive form, is dependent on a context dependent comparison class and on the context structure M. It is standardly argued, however, that this double context dependence is not enough. It still fails to explain the fact that the positive form of the predicate allows for tolerance and gives rise to the Sorites paradox. This problem will be addressed in this section.

6.5.1 Semi-orders

Consider a long series of people ordered in terms of their height. Of each of them you are asked whether they are tall or not. We assume that the variance between two subsequent persons is always *indistinguishable*. Now, if you decide that the first individual presented to you, the tallest, is tall, it seems only reasonable to judge the second individual to be tall as well, since you cannot distinguish their heigths. But, then, by the same token, the third person must be tall as well, and so on indefinitely. In particular, this makes also the last person tall, which is a counterintuitive conclusion, given that it is in contradiction with our intuition that this last, and shortest individual, is short, and thus not tall.

This so-called Sorites reasoning is elementary, based only on our intuition that the first individual is tall, the last short, and the following inductive premise, which seems unobjectable:

> **[P]** If you call one individual tall, and this individual is not visibly taller than another individual, you have to call the other one tall too.

---

[39] Schwarzchild (2005) noted that measure terms occur with some, but not all positive 'measure' adjectives. They occur in English with adjectives like 'old', 'tall', 'high', and 'thick', but not with 'warm', 'heavy', and 'big'. We can say, for instance, 'John is 5 years old', and 'The ice was 5 cm thick', but we don't say in English 'The water was 75° warm', 'The suitcase is 20 kg heavy', or 'The apartment is 1,000 ft^2 big'. We might try to account for this by saying that while adjectives like 'old' work on additive magnitudes, an adjective like 'warm' does not. Unfortunately, we can say things like 'It is twice as warm in Amsterdam as it is in Berlin'. Moreover, there are cross-linguistic differences. In German some of the counterparts of the inappropriate examples above are acceptable: 'Das Konzert war nur 40 Min lang', 'Der Koffer ist 20 Kilo schwer', and 'Die Wohnung ist 90 m^2 gross' are all appropriate. To account for this, Schwarzchild (2005) proposes a syntactic solution, but one might wonder whether a pragmatic solution is not more suitable. It seems that it is for some measure phrases much more natural to use the relative adjective than for others. It doesn't make a lot of sense for mph, or degrees, or kilos, because saying that John went 50 mph doesn't leave much room for the relevant (relative) adjective. The same for 'It is 50°', and 'The suitscase is 20 kg'. It is different with centimeters, because there are many adjectives measured in terms of centimeters, so adding tall, or wide, makes perfect sense.

Our above Sorites reasoning involved the predicate 'tall', but that was obviously not essential. Take any predicate P that gives rise to a complete ordering 'being at least as P than'. Let us assume that '$\sim_P$' is the indifference relation between individuals with respect to predicate P. Now we can state the inductive premise somewhat more formally as follows:

$$\textbf{[P]} \text{ For any } x, y \in I : (P(x) \wedge x \sim_P y) \rightarrow P(y).$$

If we assume that it is possible that $\exists x_1, \ldots, x_n : x_1 \sim_P x_2 \wedge \cdots \wedge x_{n-1} \sim_P x_n$, but $P(x_1)$ and $\neg P(x_n)$, the paradox will arise. Recall that if $P(x_1)$ and $\neg P(x_n)$, it is required that $x_1 >_P x_n$. In Section 6.4.2 we have defined the relation '$>_P$' in terms of the behavior of predicate P: $x >_P y$ iff $x \in P(\{x, y\})$ and $y \notin P(\{x, y\})$ and we will assume that $x \sim_P y$ holds iff$_{def}$ neither $x >_P y$ nor $y >_P x$. We can assure that '$>_P$' and '$\sim_P$' behave natural by putting constraints on the behavior of P across comparison classes. The constraints discussed in Sections 6.4.3 and 6.4.4, however, did not allow for the possibility that $\exists x_1, \ldots, x_n : x_1 \sim_P x_2 \wedge \cdots \wedge x_{n-1} \sim_P x_n$, but $P(x_1)$ and $\neg P(x_n)$. Fortunately, there is a well-known ordering with this property. According to this ordering the statement '$x >_P y$' means that x is *significantly* or *noticeably* greater than y, and the relation '$>_P$' is irreflexive and transitive, but need not be almost connected. The indistinguishability relation '$\sim_P$' is reflexive and symmetric, but need not be transitive. Thus, '$\sim_P$' does not give rise to an equivalence relation. The structure that results is what Luce (1956) calls a *semi-order*. A structure $\langle I, R\rangle$, with R a binary relation on I, is a semi-order just in case R is irreflexive (IR), satisfies the interval-order (IO) condition, and is semitransitive (STr).[40]

Definition 2 A semi-order is a structure $\langle I, R\rangle$, with R a binary relation on I that satisfies the following conditions:

(IR) $\forall x : \neg R(x, x)$.
(IO) $\forall x, y, v, w : (R(x, y) \wedge R(v, w)) \rightarrow (R(x, w) \vee R(v, y))$.
(STr) $\forall x, y, z, v : (R(x, y) \wedge R(y, z)) \rightarrow (R(x, v) \vee R(v, z))$.

Just as weak orders, also semi-orders can be given a measure theoretical interpretation. If P is the predicate 'tall', one can think of R as the semi-order relation (significantly) 'taller than', and say that '$x >_P y$' is true iff the height of x is higher than the height of y plus some fixed (small) real number ϵ. In the same way '$x \sim_P y$' is true if the difference in height between x and y is less than ϵ. In case $\epsilon = 0$, the semi-order is a weak order.[41]

[40] Any relation that is irreflexive and satisfies the interval-order condition is called an *interval order*. All interval orders are also transitive, meaning that they are stronger than strict partial orders.
[41] Cf. Scott and Suppes (1958).

6.5.2 Contextual Solutions to the Sorites Paradox

Because it is such an age-old problem, there exist many proposed solutions to the Sorites paradox. It is fair to say that within linguistics, the so-called *contextualist*' solution is most popular. The contextualist' solution is really a whole family of solutions, but in all of its versions it is crucially based on the assumption that the meaning (or extension) of vague expressions depends on context. As such, it is in line with standard linguistic accounts of comparatives (whether they be degree-based, or comparison class-based). The contextualist solution to the Sorites paradox was first proposed by Kamp (1981). Other proponents of this type of solution include Bosch (1983), Pinkal (1984), Veltman (1987), van Deemter (1995), Raffman (1994, 1996), Gaifman (1997), Soames (1999), Graff (2000), and Shapiro (2006). In the following I will first discuss the central ideas of most of these contextualist' solutions, and the problems they give rise to, in a rather condensed way. Afterwards, I will discuss my favorite contextual solution in somewhat more detail.

The standard reaction to the Sorites paradox taken by proponents of fuzzy logic and/or supervaluation theory is to say that the argument is valid, but that the inductive premise [**P**] (or one of its instantiations) is *false*. But why, then, does it at least *seem* to us that the inductive premise is true? According to the standard accounts of vagueness making use of fuzzy logic and supervaluation theory, this is so because the inductive premise is *almost* true (in fuzzy logic), true in almost all complete valuations (in supervaluation theory), or that almost all its instantiations are true.

Linguists (e.g. Kamp, 1975; Klein 1980; Kamp and Partee, 1995; Pinkal, 1995) typically don't like the fuzzy logic approach to vagueness, because they can't account for what Fine (1975) called 'penumbral' connections. The standard objection of supervaluationalists to the analysis of vagueness in terms of (standard) fuzzy logic is that 'John is *P or* he is not *P*' and 'John is *P and* he is not *P*' are not predicted to be tautological and contradictory, respectively. But this objection is less than convincing: if John is a borderline case of a tall man, what is wrong with saying, for instance, that he is to a certain extent tall and to a certain extent not tall? But other objections that also involve the assumed truth functionality are more serious: Suppose 'Bert is tall' is true to degree 0.5 and 'Fred is tall' is true to degree 0.4. This can only be the case, intuitively, if Bert is taller than Fred. Now consider (a) 'Fred is tall and Bert is tall' and (b) 'Fred is tall and Bert is not tall'. Adopting the standard fuzzy logic-treatment of negation, these sentences are predicted to have the same value (0.4, if also the standard 'min'-analysis of conjunction is adopted). But it seems that this is false: (a) can be true (to some extent), but if Fred is shorter than Bert, sentence (b) can, intuitively, be true to no positive degree.[42]

[42]As another example: consider the conditionals (c) 'If Fred is tall, Bert is tall' and (d) 'If Fred is tall, Bert is not tall'. If the values of these sentences depend only on the values of their parts, they should have the same value. But this prediction is wrong: while (c) is plausibly true, (d) is certainly wrong. In defense of fuzzy logic, one might claim that conjunction and negation should not be analyzed as standardly assumed by Lakoff (1973) for instance. In fact, there exist many

The treatment of vagueness and the Sorites paradox in supervaluation theory is not unproblematic either. It doesn't seem to have a good answer to the question what it means that the negation of [**P**], $\exists d, d'[d \sim_P d' \wedge P(d) \wedge \neg P(d')]$, is predicted to be supertrue. This statement seems to deny that there are borderline cases, and why aren't we able to say which one (or more) of its instances is not true.[43] This problem is related to Dummett's (1975) complaint: the use of complete refinements in supervaluation theory assumes that we *can* always make sharp cutoff-points: vagueness exists only because in daily life we are *too lazy* to make them. But this assumption seems to be wrong: vagueness exists, according to Dummett (1975), because we *cannot* make such sharp cutoff-points even if we wanted to. In terms of what we discussed above, this means that the relation '$>_P$' should be thought of as a semi-order, rather than as a weak order. But if this view is adopted, it is unnatural to claim that [**P**] is false.

Indeed, in contrast to the fuzzy logic and supervaluation theory treatments, the contextualist' solution of the Sorites paradox is based on the idea that [**P**] *must* be true, because this is a principle in accordance with the way we use language. We can think of [**P**] either as one universal sentence, or as a collection of individual conditional premises. Normally, this doesn't make any difference: the one universal sentence is classically equivalent with the collection of the individual instances. For many proponents of the contextualist' solution, however, this distinction is crucial. I will call [**P**] read as one universal sentence its *collective* reading. If [**P**] is really seen as a set of individual conditional premises, I will call it the *distributive* reading.

In his classic article, Dummett (1975) claimed that inductive premise [**P**] (in both of its readings) should be considered to be true, and not just indefinite or 'near to truth', because the corresponding inferences are essential for our reasoning with natural language concepts. Dummett's conclusion was that thus natural language is inconsistent. Kamp (1981) follows Dummett's claim with respect to the distributive reading of [**P**], but not his conclusion. To get around inconsistency, he (i) makes use of a sophisticated mechanism of *context change* and (ii) adopts a non-truth conditional analysis of conditional sentences, and proposes a weak, but non-standard notion of entailment. The idea of context change is that once it is explicitly accepted within the discourse that x has property P, for any vague predicate, the initial contextually given valuation function V changes into (possibly) new valuation function V' such that indistinguishable, or at least sufficiently similar individuals to x must be

alternative ways to analyze the connectives in fuzzy logic. Arguably, however, these alternatives are less natural than the standard one (cf. Dubois and Prade, 1980).

[43] Williamson (1994) proposed that we should replace [**P**] by the weaker statement [$\mathbf{P}_w$]: For any $x, y \in I : (\Box P(x) \wedge x \sim_P y) \rightarrow P(y)$, where '$\Box\phi$' means that ϕ is known. But, as Graff (2000) points out, this proposal does not explain why we are so inclined to believe [**P**]. Shapiro (2006) proposed to weaken [**P**] in yet another way. Making a difference between a classical '$\neg$' and a three-valued '$\dot{\neg}$' negation, his principle of tolerance [$\mathbf{P}_{ws}$] says that for any $x, y \in I : (P(x) \wedge x \sim_P y) \rightarrow \neg\dot{\neg}P(y)$. I believe we want something stronger than this.

counted as having property P as well according to new valuation function (and context) V'. In other words, what Kamp proposes is that each of the inductive premises is true in case its antecedent is verified, because of context change.

Although they can be seen as improvements on Kamp's initial proposal, the approaches by Pinkal (1984), Raffman (1994, 1996) and Soames (1999) are still very similar, in that they essentially assume that the interpretation of a vague predicate systematically changes as we proceed along a Sorites series. Stanley (2003) has argued that such contextual solutions to the Sorites paradox break down in its 'elliptical' version. In the sentence 'John likes you, and Bill does too', the occurrence of 'you' in the Verb Phrase ellipsis (henceforth, VP ellipsis) must be interpreted as referring to the same person picked out by the overt 'you' in the first clause. This fact not only holds for the pronoun 'you', but for all context dependent expressions. According to Stanley (2003) this means that if we assume that the content of a vague predicate changes as we proceed along a sorites series, the contextualist's solution cannot handle the paradox stated in its 'elliptical' version:

(15) If that_1 is tall, that_2 one is too, and if that_2 is, that_3 is too, . . ., that_n is too.

If the meaning of the word 'tall' is context dependent, it cannot shift its denotation in any of the different conditionals in (15), which means – according to Stanley (2003) – that the standard formulation of the contextualist's solution can't solve all versions of the Sorites paradox.

In his argumentation, Stanley (2003) crucially assumes that 'context-dependence' means 'indexical'. But there exists a well-known argument due to Klein (1980) that the context dependence of the meaning of a word like 'tall' should *not* be indexical. Counterintuitive predictions result, Klein argued, if we would make that assumption. Look at the following example (16-a) due to Ludlow (1989):

(16) a. That elephant is large and that flea is too.
b. That elephant is large for an elephant and that flea is large for an elephant.

In case the adjective 'large' is treated as an indexical, the intuitively natural sentence (16-a) would be interpreted as something like (16-b), which is absurd. Klein (1980) and Ludlow (1989) conclude that the meaning of the adjective should not (in general) remain constant under VP ellipsis. Together with the assumption that VP ellipsis remains constant for indexical expressions, one has to conclude that adjectives like 'tall' and 'large' are not indexical.[44] But if the meaning of the adjective is

---

[44]This means that comparison classes are not scope-less (cf. Ludlow, 1989). Soames (1999) treats gradable adjectives as indexical, nevertheless. But also he might have good reasons for doing so, because even for indexicals constancy under VP ellipsis is disputable. Ellis (2004) gave the following example suggesting that this is not the case:

> Thirty friends are standing in the middle of a very large field. One of them has the following idea: 'Why don't we each go and stand in any place we choose, and see where everyone goes. Jill, you go first.'. Jill walks a good distance away from the group and shouts, 'I'm

not purely indexical, what is the property that remains constant under VP-ellipsis? One proposal would be that the comparison class with respect to which the adjective is interpreted can be dependent on the subject term involved. Thus, in (16-a) the property could be $\lambda x.L(x,f(x))$, where x is an individual variable, while f is a context dependent function from individuals to comparison classes.[45] Confronted with a Sorites series of objects $x_1, ..., x_n$ as in example (15), the constant meaning of the predicate is $\lambda x.T(x,f(x))$, and the context-dependent (partial) function f could be recursively defined as follows: $f(x_1) = \{x_1, x_n\}$, and $f(x_{i+1}) = f(x_i) \cup \{x_{i+1}\}$.

While most contextualists follow Kamp in validating the distributive reading of [**P**] by means of context change, they normally seek to improve on (ii) by making the resulting logic more classical. The latter is normally done by changing the notions of context and indistinguishability that are involved. One proposal along these lines is sketched by Veltman and Muskens (described in Veltman, 1987). They make use of a construction first mentioned by Russell (1940), and elaborated by Luce (1956), Goodman (1966) and Dummett (1975), that makes the notion of 'indistinguishability' context dependent. According to this idea, a context can be modeled by a comparison class, and the elements of such a comparison class can be used by an observer as resources to distinguish between, for instance, the heigths of individuals. If x is indistinguishable from y, which in turn is indistinguishable from z, it might still be that x is distinguishable from z (i.e., the notion of 'indististinguishability' is not transitive). What is proposed is that if z is available in context, it can be used to *indirectly* distinguish x from y: because in contrast to y, x is (directly) distinguishable from z. Thus, it might be that in one context, x and y are not distinguishable, while they are so in a larger context. (The notion of 'indirectly distinguishability' is transitive, and gives rise to an equivalence relation.) Now Veltman & Muskens propose that [**P**] is true under its distributive reading, but only with respect to their new notion of *indirect* indistinguishability.

To use this construction to solve the Sorites paradox, they propose that in each point in the discourse, a unique comparison class is relevant for the interpretation of a sentence, and thus predicate, at that point. For each sentence (formula) this unique

going to stand here!' It's Tom's turn next, and being the tag-along Tom is, he goes straight for Jill and stands right next to her. Jill exclaims humorously, 'And I guess Tom is too!' Sally then goes and stands on the other side of Jill, who now says And apparently, so is Sally!' Then Bill goes and stands behind Jill ('and so is Bill'), and then Ann stands in front of Jill ('and Ann'). Each of the other twenty-nine people walks towards Jill and stands as close to her as s/he can without touching anyone else. In each case, Jill amusingly shouts 'And so is s-and-so!'

In this case, the interpretation of 'here', which appears in VP ellipsis, varies.

[45] This suggestion is close to one proposed by Kennedy (1999). He notes that something like this is needed to account for the intuition that for 'Everybody in my family is tall' to be true, we compare different members of my family to different sets: we compare men with other men, women with other women, and children with other children. Peter Bosch (p.c.) gave also the following example, which makes the same point: 'Everything in America is big: The cars, the buildings, and even the Turkeys.'

class is simply the set of individuals mentioned by this sentence. Now consider any instance of [**P**] of the form '$P(x) \rightarrow P(y)$' with x and y not directly distinguishable. Because only x and y are mentioned by this sentence, the relevant comparison class is just $\{x, y\}$. But with respect to this class, x is not *in*directly distinguishable from y either, and thus the premise is predicted to be true. This holds for all inductive premises, if treated separately.[46] But this doesn't mean that we can derive a contradiction. In order to do that we would have to conjoin all inductive premises into one large inductive premise. But by the way the comparison classes relevant for each sentence are determined, the relevant comparison class of this large conjoined premise will contain many individuals. In fact, it will contain more than enough individuals such that at least for some set $\{x, y\}$ whose elements are indistinguishable in context $\{x, y\}$, its elements will be distinguishable in this larger context. Thus, what is wrong in the Sorites reasoning, on this account, are not the individual inductive premises, but the way these premises have been put together to produce a contradiction.

Van Deemter (1995) highlights that what Veltman and Muskens effectively propose is that inductive premise [**P**] (on both its collective and its distributive reading) is actually *ambiguous* between two readings. According to one reading, we should read the premise as [$\mathbf{P}_1$]:

$$[\mathbf{P}_1] \text{ For any } x, y \in I, c \in C : (P(x, c) \wedge x \sim_P^{\{x,y\}} y \wedge y \in c) \rightarrow P(y, c).$$

It is clearly the case that if we formalize the inductive premise as [$\mathbf{P}_1$] and read it collectively, the Sorites paradox will arise. Thus, [$\mathbf{P}_1$] should be rejected on its collective reading. However, we can also read [**P**] in a different way such that it doesn't give rise to a contradiction. In fact, van Deemter (1995) claims that [**P**] seems so natural because we don't read it as [$\mathbf{P}_1$], but rather as [$\mathbf{P}_2$]:

$$[\mathbf{P}_2] \text{ For any } x, y \in I, c \in C : (P(x, c) \wedge x \sim_P^c y) \rightarrow P(y, c).$$

Notice that the only difference between [$\mathbf{P}_1$] and [$\mathbf{P}_2$] is that whereas [$\mathbf{P}_1$] assumes that the similarity, or indistinguishability relation only considers x and y, while for [$\mathbf{P}_2$] it might involve (many) more objects. We assume that $x \sim_P^c y$ is true for $x, y \in c$ if and only if the following statement is true: $x \in P(c)$ iff $y \in P(c)$. Notice that if c is a proper superset of $\{x, y\}$, i.e. $c \supset \{x, y\}$, it might be that $x \sim_P^{\{x,y\}} y$, but $x \not\sim_P^c y$. Comparison class c might have enough individuals available such that we can *indirectly* distinguish x from y. Now it is easy to see that this 'small' switch from $x \sim_P^{\{x,y\}} y$ to $x \sim_P^c y$ makes a crucial distinction: in contrast to [$\mathbf{P}_1$], [$\mathbf{P}_2$] is *analytically true*. Assume that the two statements in the antecedent of [$\mathbf{P}_2$] are true: $x \in P(c)$ and $x \in P(c)$ iff $y \in P(c)$. From this we can conclude immediately that $y \in P(c)$, which is what the consequent says. Thus, [$\mathbf{P}_2$] is true, because its

[46]In this respect, their analysis is very similar to the proposals of Raffman (1994, 1996) and Graff (2000).

antecedent is false for at least one pair of *directly* indistinguishable objects. Now, why does this new reading of the inductive premise not give rise to the Sorites paradox? The reason is obvious: it doesn't give any information on top of the first premise that $P(x_1)$ and $\neg P(x_n)$, so we cannot derive a contradiction. According to the above reasoning, the Sorites paradox arises due to an *equivocation* of comparison classes.

Appealing as this analysis might be, it is perhaps not exactly what we are looking for. The main worry is that the notion of 'indistinguishability' that Veltman and Muskens and van Deemter propose is disputable. One might argue that Dummett's (1975) and Kamp's (1981) argument in favor of **[P]** is crucially based on the assumption that 'distinguishability' should really be *directly* distinguishability. It is doubtful whether reading [$\mathbf{P}_2$] of **[P]** really implements Dummett's (1975) conviction that the latter is a regulative principle of our use of language.[47] We don't seem to hold **[P]** to be true if we are confronted with a Sorites series, just because its antecedent is false for at least one pair of objects. For it to be a *substantial* regulative principle of the way we use our language, it seems that we *should* read **[P]** as [$\mathbf{P}_1$]. But both Veltman and Muskens (1987) and van Deemter (1995) predict that [$\mathbf{P}_1$] on its collective reading is *false*.[48] But if we want to obey this principle, how, then, can we be saved from contradiction?

Dummett (1975) is mostly known for suggesting a rather pessimistic, or nihilistic, conclusion: real vagueness gives rise to contradiction. But in line with Wittgenstein's radically pragmatic solution to the problem posed by vagueness in his *Philosofische Untersuchungen*[49] he also suggests that *in practice* contradiction is avoided. In normal discourse, we talk about relatively few objects, all of which are easily discernible from the others. In those circumstances, **[P]** will not give rise to inconsistency, but serves its purpose quite well. Only in exceptional situations i.e., when we are confronted with long sequences of pairwise indistinguishable objects – do things go wrong. But in such situations, we should not be using vague predicates like 'tall' but precisely measurable predicates involving, in this case, millimeters. We will discus how a weak version of this reaction can be formalized naturally in terms of comparison classes. The idea is that it only makes sense to use a predicate P in a context – i.e. with respect to a comparison class –, if it helps to clearly demarcate the set of individuals that have property P from those who don't. Following Gaifman (1997), we will implement this idea by assuming that any subset of I can only be an element of the set of *pragmatically appropriate* comparison classes C just in case the gap between the last individual(s) that have property P and the first that do(es) not must be between individuals x and y such that x is clearly P-er than

47 In a very real sense, the solution Veltman and Muskens propose is based on the same intuition as the solution proposed by supervaluationalists: the Sorites paradox arises, because we equivocate 'similarity' with 'sameness'. But Dummett's point was to take the former notion more seriously.

48 For a related recent critique of contextualist's solutions to the Sorites paradox, see Keefe (2007).

49 See in particular section 85–87: 'A rule stands like a signpost ... The signpost in order in in normal circumstances it fulfils its purpose. See also Waismann's (1968) notion of 'open texture'.

y.[50] This is not the case if the graph of the relation '$\sim_P$' is closed in $c \times c$.[51] Indeed, it is exactly in those cases that the Sorites paradox arises.

How does such a proposal deal with the Sorites paradox? Well, it claims that *in all contexts in which P can be used appropriately*, [$\mathbf{P}_1$] is true (in both its distributive *and* its collective reading). If we assume in addition that the first element x_1 of a Sorites series is the absolute most P-individual, and the last element x_n the absolute least P-individual, it also claims that *in all contexts c in which it is appropriate to use predicate P in combination with* x_1 and x_n, '$P(x_1, c)$' is *true* and '$P(x_n, c)$' is *false*. Thus, in all *appropriate* contexts, the premises of the Sorites argument are considered to be true. Still, no contradiction can be derived, because using predicate P when *explicitly* confronted with set of objects that form a Sorites series is *inappropriate*. Thus, in contrast to the original contextualist approaches of Kamp (1981), Pinkal (1984), and others, the Sorites paradox is not avoided by assuming that the meaning (or extension) of the predicate changes as the discourse proceeds. Rather, the Sorites paradox is avoided by claiming that the use of predicate P is inappropriate when confronted with a Sorites series of objects.[52] As a result, Stanley's problem for earlier contextualist' solutions does not arise.[53,54]

In our approach, we analyze adjectives like 'tall' with respect to a comparison class. But neither in this nor the previous sections have we discussed how a sentence

---

[50] Also Graff (2000) has argued that not all sets of individuals can figure as appropriate comparison classes. Her reasoning, however, is quite different from ours. She argues, for instance, that comparison classes need to form a *kind*.

[51] Notice that also in discrete cases the relation '$\sim_P$' can be closed in $c \times c$. In just depends on how '$\sim_P$' is defined.

[52] Although Graff (2000) seems to adopt a version of the standard contextualist' approach to vagueness, her analysis can be thought of as being close to our pragmatic analysis as well. She makes two claims: (i) there exists cutoff-points, but (ii) if x is significantly P-er than z, $x >^!_P z$, and y is similar to x, it must be the case that y is significantly P-er than z as well, $y >^!_P z$. Although the similarity relation Graff (2000) seems to assume behaves like the similarity relation used in semi-orders, the relation '$>^!_P$' can obviously not be the corresponding relation of a semi-order. Instead, the relation '$>^!_P$' should have the properties of a *weak order*. In fact, if we start with a semi-order $\langle I, > \rangle$, we can define a weak order $\langle I^*, >^* \rangle$ that behaves just like the one Graff (2000) seems to assume. Given that '$\sim$' is defined in terms of '>' as usual, we can define a new relation '$\approx$' in terms of it: $x \approx y$ iff$_{def}$ $\exists \vec{z} \in I^n : x \sim z_1 \sim \cdots \sim z_n \sim y$. Obviously, '$\approx$' is an equivalence relation. In terms of '$\approx$' we define equivalence classes like $[x]_\approx$ as usual, and take I^* to be the set $\{[x]_\approx : x \in I\}$. Now we define the order relation $>^*$ between the elements of I^* as follows: $X >^* Y$ iff$_{def}$ $X \neq \emptyset \wedge Y \neq \emptyset \wedge \forall x \in X : \forall y \in Y : x > y$. One can show that '$>^*$' indeed is a weak order. Now, why is (our reformulation of) Graff's analysis close to our pragmatic analysis? The reason is that in order to assume that the first element of a Sorites series has property P but the last one has not, she has to assume (if our reformulation of her ideas is faithful) that I is not closed under '$\sim_P$', and thus that the series allows for a cutoff-point.

[53] On this proposal, Stanley's elliptical conjunction is claimed to be inappropriate. Or better, if we assume that [**P**] holds and that the property that remains constant under VP-ellipsis is $\lambda x.T(x, f(x))$, where f was defined as $f(x_1) = \{x_1, x_n\}$ and $f(x_{i+1}) = f(x_i) \cup \{x_{i+1}\}$, it is predicted that the sentence at the one but last step in the Sorites series is inappropriate.

[54] It turns out to be possible to characterize semi-orders in terms of the way relative adjectives behave with respect to *appropriate* comparison classes (see van Rooij, 2011).

like $P(x)$ should be interpreted with respect to model M and comparison class c in case 'x' does not denote an individual in c. One proposal would be to declare such a sentence neither true nor false. Another proposal would be to interpret the sentence not w.r.t. c but rather w.r.t. $c \cup \{x\}$. According to a yet different proposal, $P(x)$ should be true if there is a $y \in P_M(c)$ such that $M \models x >_P y$, and false otherwise. Now consider comparison class $c = \{x, y, z\}$ with $x \sim_P y$ and $y >_P z$. According to our account, we predict that x and y are considered to be P-individuals in c, while z is not. But now consider object $v \notin c$. Suppose that $x >_P v$, but $y \sim_P v$ and $v \sim_P z$. Should we count '$P(v)$' true with respect to M and c, or not? According to the second proposal mentioned above, we should not. But in that case, $M, c \models P(y) \wedge \neg P(v)$, although $y \sim_P v$. Notice that this is consistent with our approach, if we assume that *pragmatic* appropriateness conditions are *independent* of *semantic* truth conditions:[55] although '$P(y) \wedge \neg P(v)$' is true, it is not appropriate to assert it.

We have seen above that each context structure $M = \langle I, C, V \rangle$ gives rise to a relation of 'indistinguishability'. Now I would like to argue that this latter notion should be considered more generally: $x \sim_P y$ iff there is no *relevant* difference between x and y concerning property P.[56] But, obviously, whether the P-distinction between x and y is relevant or not depends on context: on the *goals* of the participants of the discourse. Graff (2000) even suggests that the existence of vagueness in natural language is partly a consequence of the vagueness of our purposes. To argue in favor of this view, she points out that it depends on Smith's purpose whether we are inclined to accept the following *sorites sentence*: 'For any n, if n grains of coffee are enough for Smith's purpose, then so are $n - 1$.' Normally we are, but if very *fine distinctions* may tip the balance, things differ.[57] This suggests that in case fine distinctions matter, fewer individuals should be considered to stand in the tolerance relation '$\sim_P$', while the relation '$>_P$' should contain more pairs of individuals. We will see in Section 6.6 that what Graff (2000) has in mind is closely related to many other phenomena.

6.5.3 Boundaryless Concepts and Higher Order Vagueness

Vagueness is traditionally defined by the possession of borderline cases. More recently, it has been argued that this is not sufficient: a predicate might have borderline cases without being vague. What characterizes predicates as being vague, according to this alternative view, is the fact that these predicates have no clear borderline cases. A predicate is vague, if it lacks sharp boundaries. One way to model such *boundaryless* concepts is by making use of semi-orders. Just assume

---

[55]This is generally assumed in two-dimensional theories of presuppositions and conversational implicatures.

[56]Luce's (1956) intention was not to just model the notion of 'indistinguishability', but rather that of a more general notion of 'indifference'. Also Pinkal (1995) and others have argued that tolerance should be based on 'indifference' rather than 'indistinguishability'.

[57]See Pinkal (1984, 1995) for a similar argument.

that the relation '$\sim_P$' is closed under $I \times I$. In such a case, the topmost P individuals would semantically (definitely) fall under the extension of P, while the bottommost P-individuals would semantically (definitely) not fall under the extension of P.[58] But whenever we want to look for the dividing line between the P- and the $\neg P$ individuals, we can't find it: For any two consecutive individuals x and y, if we focus on only those two individuals, we won't find a significantly enough difference between them to draw here the dividing line. But this is not only true for the dividing line between P and $\neg P$ individuals, but also for dividing lines between, for instance, the *definitely* P individuals and the not definitely P individuals, etc.

The view that vague concepts are boundaryless is closely related with the view that vague expressions give rise to *higher-order vagueness*.[59] According to this view, there is not only no clear (1st-order) borderline between the (clearly) P versus the (clearly) non P-individuals, there is also no clear (2nd-order) borderline between the clearly P versus the 1st-order borderline cases of P individuals, etc. This phenomenon is known as *higher-order vagueness*. Williamson (1994) and others have argued that one can account for higher-order vagueness within a modal logic, if one takes the accessibility relation in terms of which one defines the meaning of 'definitely' or 'clearly' to be *reflexive* and *symmetric*, but *not transitive*. Making use of semi-orders, it is quite easy to do this. Let us assume that W is the set of worlds, and that '$>_P$' is an ordering between the elements of W such that $\langle W, >_P \rangle$ is a semi-order. One can think of $w >_P v$ to be true iff the cutoff-point for being a P-individual in w is (significantly) higher than that cutoff-point in v. Now define an accessibility relation R between worlds as follows: v is accessible from w, i.e. wRv, iff neither $w >_P v$ nor $v >_P w$. From Section 6.5.1 we know that relation R must be reflexive, and symmetric, but need not be transitive. Intuitively, we can say that wRv iff the cutoff-points according to which one has property P in w and v differ in at most a fixed margin ϵ. Let us now add a *definitely* operator 'Δ' to the language. We say that '$\Delta\phi$' is true iff 'ϕ' is true on all R-accessible worlds. Now we say that x is a 1st-order borderline case of P-ness iff '$\neg \Delta P(x) \wedge \neg \Delta \neg P(x)$' is true. Similarly, we say that x is a 2nd-order borderline case of P-ness if '$\neg \Delta \Delta P(x) \wedge \neg \Delta \neg \Delta P(x)$' is true, etcetera.

Fine (1975) and Keefe (2000) propose a rather different account of higher-order vagueness. They suggest that to account for higher-order vagueness we have to realize that what counts as an admissible (total) valuation is itself vague. I just want to suggest a very simple – and no doubt simplistic – way to implement their basic idea.

Fine (1975) and Keefe (2000) make use of both partial and total valuations functions. Recall that both partial and total valuation functions are interpretation functions of a *language* with respect to a *domain* of quantification. Suppose that a language $\mathcal{L}$ contains individual constants of all and only all individuals of domain I. In contrast to the partial valuation function, the total valuation functions do not

---

[58] I have argued above that in such a case it doesn't make sense to *use* predicate P *in context* I. This doesn't rule out, of course, that P can be used appropriately with respect to comparison classes smaller than I.

[59] Whether the assuming that predicate P give rise to (unlimited) higher order vagueness fully captures the intuition that the concept denoted by P is boundaryless is controversial, however.

allow for gaps – i.e., individuals in I that neither have property P nor property $\neg P$. Each individual that can be referred to by an individual constant, or quantified over, has property P or has not. Thus, according to each total valuation, there is a clear borderline between the individuals that have and the individuals that do not have property P. But now suppose that we (slightly) adjust the model by *extending its domain*, and that we adjust the language accordingly by introducing some new individual constants that can refer to those individuals. Now it will be the case that a valuation function that was total with respect to $\mathcal{L}$ and I is only partial with respect to the new language $\mathcal{L}'$ and new domain I'. Of course, these new partial functions can in turn be extended by new total functions, or valuations. But now the same game can be played again, and perhaps so indefinitely. Perhaps the most natural way to extend a domain, is to think of (some of) its elements as (something like) measures, or *degrees*. According to one model, we measure the height of individuals up to a decimeter precise, while at another up to a centimeter, or a millimeter precise. You will object that in this way we are not really talking about vagueness anymore, but about levels of *granularity*. But, then, perhaps vagueness is crucially related with granularity.

6.6 Vagueness and Granularity

In a series of papers (e.g. Hobbs, 1985) Hobbs argues that both in reasoning and in natural language use it is crucial that we conceptualize and describe the world at different levels of granularity. A road, for instance, can be viewed as a line, a surface, or a volume. The level of granularity that we make use of depends on what is relevant. When we are planning a trip, we view the road as a line. When we are driving on it, we view it as a surface, and when we hit a pothole, it becomes a volume to us. In our use of natural language we even employ this fact by being able to describe the same phenomenon at different levels of granularity within the same discourse. Thus, we sometimes explicitly shift perspective, i.e., shift the level of granularity to describe the same situation. This is perhaps most obviously the case when we talk about time and space. Consider examples (17) and (18):

(17) It is two o'clock. In fact, it is 2 min after two.
(18) The point of this pencil is actually an irregular surface with several peaks (Asher and Vieu, 1995).

In (17) we shift to describing a time-point in a more specific way, while in (18) we shift from a description of a pencil point as a point to its being a surface.

6.6.1 Absolute Terms Revisited

At the end of Section 6.4.3 we have suggested that with the positive use of absolute adjectives like 'full', 'flat', and 'straight', the only relevant comparison class can be the set of *all* objects, i.e. *I*. In this way, we can also account for the fact that in contrast to *relative* adjectives like 'tall', absolute adjectives don't give rise to the Sorites paradox with distinguishable objects, because the second premise is quite naturally judged to be false (cf. Kennedy, 2007).

(19) a. P1. A theater in which every seat is occupied is full.
b. P2. Any theater with one fewer occupied seat than a full theater is full.
c. C. Therefore, any theater in which half of (none of, etc.) the seats are occupied is full.

It also accounts for Kennedy's (2007) observation that just like measure phrases, but in contrast to relative adjectives, absolute adjectives allow for natural precisifications.

(20) a. We need a 10 m long rod for the antenna, but this one is 1 mm short of 10 m, so unfortunately it won't work.
b. The rod for the antenna needs to be *straight*, but this one has a 1 mm bend in the middle, so unfortunately it won't work.
c. ?? We need a long rod for the antenna, but since *long* means 'greater than 10 m' and this one is 1 mm short of 10 m, unfortunately it won't work.

An unfortunate consequence of this analysis, or so it seems, is that we have to conclude that absolute adjectives can hardly ever be used. This, however, seems to contradict actual practice. Moreover, the analysis cannot explain why absolute adjectives like 'flat' and 'full' allow for valuable interpretation and give rise to the Sorites paradox: just how bumpless should a table be to be called 'flat'?, and how much liquid should a bottle contain before it can be called 'full'? Thus, the puzzle then is to explain our daily use of absolute terms, and why they give rise to vagueness. We will take over Lewis's (1979) suggestion here:

> Peter Unger has argued that hardly anything is flat. Take something you claim is flat; he will find something else and you get to agree that it is even flatter. You think the pavement is flat – but how can you deny that your desk is flatter? But ''flat'' is an *absolute term*: it is inconsistent to say that something is flatter than something that is flat. Having agreed that your desk is flatter than the pavement, you must concede that the pavement is not flat after all. Perhaps you now claim that your desk is flat; but doubtless Unger think of something that you will agree is even flatter than your desk. And so it goes.
>
> [...] The right response to Unger, I suggest, is that he is changing the score on you. When he says that the desk is flatter than the pavement, what he says is acceptable only under raised standards of precision.

Lewis suggests that although Holland has hills, a sentence like 'Holland is flat' can still be used truly and appropriately in daily conversations, because whether the sentence can be used appropriately or not might depend on a contextually determined *standard of precision*.

6.6.2 Standards of Precision

Until now we have assumed that the comparison-class account always works with a *fixed* model, or context structure $M = \langle I, C, V \rangle$. We have seen that on the basis of such a context structure we can define an ordering relation, like '*P-er than*' or '$>_P$', between individuals, and in terms of the relation '*being as P as*' or '$\sim_P$'. In a different context structure M', however, the relations '$>_P$' and '$\sim_P$' might come out very differently. In particular, it might be that according to a different context structure, the resulting comparative relation '$>_P$' is more fine-grained.[60]

Let us now look at a *set* of context structures $\mathcal{M}$. Let us say that in all context structures M, M' of $\mathcal{M}$, the set of individuals, I, and the set of contexts, C, is the same: $I_M = I_{M'}$ and $C_M = C_{M'}$. This means that M and M' of $\mathcal{M}$ only differ with respect to their valuation functions, $V_M \neq V_{M'}$. Now we can define a *refinement* relation between models M and M' as follows: we say that model M' is a refinement of model M with respect to predicate P only if $\exists x, y \in I, M \models x \sim_P y$, but $M' \not\models x \sim_P y$. So, M' is more fine-grained than M with respect to predicate P iff there is at least one pair of individuals equally P in M that is not equally P in M'. There is a natural constraint on the ordering between models: if Mary is taller than Sue, but shorter than John in fine-grained model M', it cannot be the case that John and Sue are counted as equally tall in the more coarse-grained model M, but still taller than Mary. Formally: M' is a refinement of M w.r.t. P only if $\forall x, y, z \in I$: if $M' \models x \geq_P y \wedge y \geq_P z$ and $M \models x \sim_P z$, then $M \models x \sim_P y \wedge y \sim_P z$. This follows if we define refinements w.r.t. predicate P as follows: M' is a refinement of M with respect to P, $M \leq_P M'$, iff $V_M(>_P) \subseteq V_{M'}(>_P)$. Notice that if $V_M(>_P) \subseteq V_{M'}(>_P)$, it follows that $V_M(\sim_P) \supseteq V_{M'}(\sim_P)$, which is what we desired. Moreover, it follows that in more coarse-grained models, the relation 'being at least as P' will be larger: $M \leq_P M'$ only if $V_M(\geq_P) \supseteq V_{M'}(\geq_P)$.

---

[60]In Section 6.4 we have assumed that although statements involving predicates like 'tall' occurring positively are vague, comparatives are *not*. The vagueness of 'tall' was accounted for by interpreting sentences where the predicate is used positively with respect to a contextually given comparison class. Comparatives were not vague, because for their interpretation we existentially quantified over comparison classes. It is quite common among linguists to assume that comparatives are not vague. Philosophers like Kamp (1975), Williamson (1994) and Keefe (2000), however, have claimed otherwise. Kamp (1975) noted already that comparatives associated with more-dimensional predicates – for example 'cleverer than' – are typically vague. They have borderline cases: pairs of people about whom there is no fact of the matter about who is cleverer, or whether they are equally clever. This is particularly common when comparing people who are clever in different ways. Keefe (2000), argues that there can also be borderline cases of one-dimensional comparatives. She argues that although there is a single dimension of height, people cannot always be exactly placed on it and assigned an exact height. For what exactly should count as the top of one's head? Consequently there may also be borderline cases of *taller than*. Even more interesting from our point of view is the fact that *taller than* can also be vague due to indeterminacy over exactly what should count as a point (or an equivalence class) in the tallness ordering: individuals whose height is 2 μm apart normally count as equally tall, although this would not be the case in contexts in which every micro-millimeter is important.

Consider now the following two sentences.

(21) a. John is 2 meters tall.
b. John is *exactly* 2 meters tall.

Both sentences are true if and only if the (maximal) height of John is the height denoted by the phrase '2 m tall'. Intuitively, however, (21-a) would count in more contexts as being true, or appropriate, than (21-b), if John is a little bit more than 2.00 m tall, e.g. if he is 2.02 m tall. The question is how we should account for this latter difference. Part of the answer to this question involves the issue whether even (21-a) can be *true* in case John is 2.02 m tall, or whether in such a case, (21-a) is (strictly speaking) false, but still appropriate, because *close enough to the truth.*[61]

Lasersohn (1999) argues that in case John is 2.02 m tall, (21-a) is false. In fact, (21-a) and (21-b) are claimed to be semantically equivalent. Still, sentence (21-a) can be used felicitously, because minor kinds of falsehood are pragmatically permissible. The distinction between 2.00 and 2.02 m may not be relevant to the purposes of our discourse, so we can ignore it, counting the sentence as close enough to the truth for its context, even though not really true. But if (21-a) is true iff John is 2.00 m tall, how should we then account for the above mentioned contrast between (21-a) and (21-b)? Lasersohn proposes that the function of 'exactly' is to put higher demands on the situations under which a sentence is pragmatically felicitous, i.e., under which circumstances (21-a) – the sentence without the word 'exactly' – counts as close enough to the truth.

To formally account for this idea, Lasersohn associates with each expression not only its denotation, but also a context dependent set of items understood to differ from the denotation only in ways which are pragmatically ignorable in that context. This set is called the *pragmatic halo* of the item. The pragmatic halo of a complex expression is determined compositionally from the pragmatic halos of its parts.[62] Assuming that we should analyze pragmatic vagueness in terms of pragmatic halos, (if α is an element of the pragmatic halo of expression $\mathcal{A}$ of type $\langle b, a\rangle$, and β an element of the pragmatic halo of expression $\mathcal{B}$ of type b, then $\alpha(\beta)$ is an element of the pragmatic halo of expression $\mathcal{AB}$ of type a). Obviously, the actual denotation, or meaning, of an expression is also an element of the expression's pragmatic halo, and for some types of expressions (e.g. logical words, presumably) this is the only element of the set. The result of this is that a sentence might be 'true' in its halo, although the sentence is actually (in its denotation) false. Now Lasersohn says that ϕ is close enough to the truth in a context iff one of the elements of ϕ's pragmatic

[61] In a recent paper, Sauerland and Penka (2007) studied the difference between modifiers like 'exactly' and 'definitely'. Both could be used to modify measure phrases, but they do so in different ways: 'exactly' says something about how precise the measure phrase should be interpreted, while 'definitely' measures the speaker's epistemic certainty. This is corroborated by the fact that the adjective 'tall' can be modified by 'definitely' but not by 'exactly'.

[62] It is questionable whether compositionality should be assumed here, and it contrasts standard Gricean treatments of other pragmatic phenomena.

halo in this context is true. To account for the distinction between (21-a) and (21-b), Lasersohn (1999) claims that the function of 'exactly' is to *contract* the halo. The result of this contraction is that if the proposition expressed by 'John is 2.02 meters tall' is an element of the pragmatic halo of (21-a), this proposition need no longer be an element of the pragmatic halo of (21-b). As a result, although (21-a) will be false, but true enough in the context, (21-b) is neither true, nor true enough in that context.

Lasersohn (1999) assumes that (21-a) is true iff John is exactly 2.00 m tall. He assumes that the phrase '2 m' has a context-independent semantic interpretation, such that semantically this is never compatible with 2.02 m. But what is this context-independent semantic interpretation of '2 m'? Presumably, or at least the only one that seems consistent with his general methodology, Lasersohn's answer would be that this interpretation can never be compatible with 1 millimeter, or even 1 micro-millimeter, higher than 2.00 m. Lasersohn assumes a context independent fixed measure of height, which is such that it is practically, or even physically, impossible to refine it. But this means that measure phrases like '2 m' denote (physically) non-extensive points, which has the result that a sentence like (21-a) is (almost) necessarily false (on an exactly-reading of the measure phrase). On this line of reasoning, the actual denotation of an expression in the end doesn't really count, and the only thing that matters is the pragmatic halo. This conclusion suggests that the assumptions Lasersohn makes are questionable. But it gives rise to an empirical problem as well: Suppose that up to the minimal point we can measure, John and Mary are equally tall. There is nothing incomprehensible about my saying: 'but had we had a better measurement instrument, we would have found out after all that John is taller than Mary'. Because Lasersohn predicts it be incomprehensible, he seems to make an empirically incorrect prediction.

Lasersohn crucially assumes that measure phrases are interpreted with respect to a *fixed* underlying structure of heights. The obvious alternative – an alternative assumed by Lewis (1979) and I guess by most semanticists –, is to assume that the underlying height-structure is not fixed in advance, but determined by context. One context can require a more fine-grained measurement than another, and what counts as a particular height in one context, counts as an interval of heights in a context that requires more fine-grained measurements. On this alternative view, context determines the underlying measure structure, or level of fine-grainedness, with respect to which sentences should be interpreted, and there is no need for pragmatic halos. Pragmatics is not independent of semantics, but rather helps to determine whether a sentence is true or false. But this means that (21-a) can be true in one context where John is 2.02 m, but false at another. Now, what is the function of the word 'exactly' in (21-b)? Like Lasersohn (1999), we would like to claim that its function is most of all pragmatic. But where for Lasersohn its function is to contract the pragmatic halo, we claim that it is an indication of the fine-grainedness of the underlying structure. If (21-a) is true with respect to an underlying structure where 2.02 m is not distinguished from 2.00 m tall, the use of 'exactly' in (21-b) may indicate that the speaker has a richer measurement structure in mind.

We have assumed that in a more coarse grained model, measure phrases denote *intervals* rather than points of a more fine-grained model. But how do the intervals denoted by different measurement phrases relate to each other? Until now we have assumed the simplest view – perhaps suggested by the phrase 'granularity'. Also in the coarse-grained model, a measure phrase denotes an equivalence class, but such an equivalence class now contains more elements of I than in a fine-grained model. Thus, just like the fine-grained model, also the coarse-grained model is a weak order. This picture might be somewhat simplistic, though. In Section 6.2 we saw already that in physics one assumes that measure phrases allow for a margin of error. But then one can assume that these phrases denote intervals, and this almost immediately means that the denotations of two different measure phrases might overlap, and that there are areas where it is unclear which of two measure phrases can be truly attributed to the points in this area, if not both. Assuming that all measure phrases allow for the same margin of error, the resulting structure will be a semi-order. If different measure phrases might allow for different margins of error, the resulting structure will be an interval order. A structure $\langle I, R\rangle$, with R a binary relation on I, is an interval order just in case R is irreflexive (IR) and satisfies the interval-order (IO) condition.

Definition 3 An interval order is a structure $\langle I, R\rangle$, with R a binary relation on I that satisfies the following conditions:

$$(IR)\ \forall x : \neg R(x,x).$$
$$(IO)\ \forall x,y,v,w : (R(x,y) \wedge R(v,w)) \rightarrow (R(x,w) \vee R(v,y)).$$

In Section 6.6.2 we have defined the refinement relation between models with respect to relation R as follows: M' is an R-refinement of M iff $V_M(R) \subset V_{M'}(R)$. We have seen that this works in case 'R' denotes a weak order in both models M and M'. However, it is the appropriate definition as well in case it denotes, for instance, an interval order in both models, or if it denotes an interval order in model M and a semi-order, or a weak order in model M'. It is well known that we can think of a linear order as a refinement of a weak order: every linear order is a weak order, but not every weak order is a linear order. But in the same way, interval orders are refinements of strict partial orders, semi-orders are refinements of interval orders, and weak orders are refinements of semi-orders.

Interval orders are relevant for the analysis of vagueness. In most discussions on vagueness where an indifference, or margin of error principle is involved, this indifference, or margin of error, is standardly taken to be the same for all expressions.[63] Jerry Hobbs and Manfred Krifka have recently argued that we should give up this assumption. Hobbs (2000) observes that if there are 920 people at the meeting, the following sentence is intuitively false, if $X = 980$, but possibly true, in case $X = 1{,}000$:

[63] But see Williamson (1994) for some discussion.

(22) There are *about* X people at the meeting.

This is surprising, because '1,000' is higher than '980', and the latter instantiation of X seems thus closer to the truth. To account for these intuitions, also Hobbs suggests that different objects in the same model need not necessarily have the same grain-size. This is exactly what we see in interval orders. Krifka (2007) has argued that something very similar happens even without the use of an approximator like 'about'.

It is well-known that (21-a) allows for much more variation than (23):

(21-a) John is 2 meters tall.
(23) John is 2.02 meters tall.

Whereas (21-a) can be true (or appropriate) in case John is exactly 2.03 m tall, (23) cannot. Krifka (2007) argues that because '2.02 m' is a more complex expression than '2 m', it has a more complex meaning (derived by Horn's division of pragmatic labor). One way to account for this observation is to assume that the complexity of the meaning involves the fine-grainedness of the underlying structure of measurement. Although the denotations of '2 m' and '2.02 m' each denotes a point in the measure system used for the interpretation of the sentence (21-a) and (23), respectively, what denotes a point in the measurement system underlying (21-a) denotes an interval (i.e., a set of more fine-grained points) in the measuring system underlying (23). That's why, according to this analysis, the expression '2 m' is more vague than the expression '2.02 m'. On this analysis, the underlying ordering relation is always a weak order. But there is another way to account for the same intuition. According to this alternative analysis, both '2 m' and '2.02 m' have a denotation *in the same* (coarser-'grained') *model M'* such that (21-a) is true in case John is exactly 2.03 m tall, while (23) is not. This can be accounted for by assuming that numbers denote *intervals*, but that some intervals might be proper parts of others, i.e., that we look at *interval orders*. In our case, what is denoted by '2.02 m' in coarse-'grained' model M' is an interval that is a proper part of the interval denoted by the phrase '2 m' in model M'.

6.6.3 Granularity and Relevance

Our way to relate different models in terms of a coarsening relation made use of a standard technique. We assume an ordering relation and define an equivalence relation in terms of it. In a coarser-grained model we just let an equivalence class of individuals of the fine-grained model be represented by a single individual. We did this (in Sections 6.4.5 and 6.6.2) by means of the ordering *taller than*. Another classical case (e.g. Kamp, 1979) is to define intervals as equivalence classes of simultaneous events defined in terms of the temporal inclusion relation. To define a coarsening relation between models, however, we don't need to start with such an ordering.

Hobbs (1985) argues that to represent or conceptualize the world at a coarser-grained level, we can just restrict ourselves by looking only at the *relevant* predicates of our original language. Consider a model $M = \langle I, V \rangle$ for the first-order language $\mathcal{L}$, and take $\mathcal{L}'$ to be a sublanguage of $\mathcal{L}$ containing only its 'relevant' predicates. In terms of the monadic predicates of $\mathcal{L}'$ we can now define an equivalence relation '$\sim_{\mathcal{L}'}$' with respect to language $\mathcal{L}'$: $a \sim_{\mathcal{L}'} b$ iff $a, b \in I_M$ and for all monadic predicates P of $\mathcal{L}'$: $M \models P(a) \Leftrightarrow M \models P(b)$. In terms of this equivalence relation, Hobbs (1985) proposed to construct a coarse-grained model M' as follows: (i) the domain $I_{M'}$ is just the set of equivalence classes $I_{M'} = \{\{y \in I : y \sim_{\mathcal{L}'} x\} : x \in I_M\}$, and (ii) the valuation function is such that for all monadic predicates $P \in \mathcal{L}'$, $M' \models P([a])$ iff $M \models P(a)$, where $[a]$ denotes the equivalence class containing $a \in I_M$.[64] Except for examples like (17) and (18), Hobbs (1985) suggests that in this way we can also account for some examples discussed by Nunberg (1985).

Nunberg (1985) has argued that an account of definite reference and the use of the phrase 'the same' is greatly simplified if we assume that people construct models of what is going on at different levels of granularity. An intuitive account of definite reference says that 'my P' refers to the *unique* (relevant) individual with property P owned by me. An example like 'My leg hurts' seems an obvious counterexample, however, because people have (usually) two legs. Nunberg (1985) suggests that the distinction between the two legs is not pragmatically relevant and can be represented by a single object in a more coarse-grained model, and thus satisfying the uniqueness requirement after all. Perhaps slightly less controversial is his proposed use of levels of granularity to give a semantics for 'the same'. It is obvious that we can use this phrase to denote not only *token*-identity, but *type*-identity as well. Thus, we can say

(24) I own a Ford Falcon. The same car is owned by Enzo.

meaning that Enzo and I owned the same *type* of car, not the same *token*. Nunberg (1985) and Hobbs (1985) suggest to account for *type*-identity as identity at a more coarse-grained level of description. In this way, they propose, we can account for the fact that we cannot say 'A Ford Falcon was heading south on U.S. 101, went out of control, and crashed into the same car' to mean that it hit another Ford Falcon. The reason is that *type*-level identity is just indistinguishability, but only restricted to distinguishable predicates that are *relevant*.[65]

Hobbs' suggestion is very appealing. Unfortunately, Lasersohn (2000) showed that the truth definition at the coarse-grained level proposed by Hobbs (1985) does not capture the intuitive motivation. It is clear that discourse (24) should be interpreted with respect to a coarse-grained model. According to Hobbs' construction, $M' \leq M$ just in case if for every monadic predicate $P \in \mathcal{L}'$, if $P([a])$ is true in coarse-grained model M', it has to be the case that $P(b)$ is true in fine-grained model M,

[64] van Lambalgen (2001) noted that this construction needs to be generalized, because it does not generalize to predicates of higher arity.

[65] According to Tim Williamson (p.c.), a sentence like 'Enzo owns two of the same car' is ok. This would be problematic for the Nunberg/Hobbs proposal.

for *every* $b \in [a]$. However, it is clear that in (24) the predicates 'Owned by me' and 'Owned by Enzo' are relevant, and thus part of $\mathcal{L}'$. Because in M' it is the same car that has both of these properties, Hobbs' construction predicts that every token of this car should have both properties in M as well. This, however, is obviously not the case. Lasersohn (2000) concludes that we should thus not account for the type-token distinction in terms of levels of granularity. Lasersohn might well be right with this conclusion, but this doesn't mean that Hobbs' (1985) project could not be saved by modifying Hobbs' ordering relation between models of different grain. Instead of making use of *universal* quantification as proposed by Hobbs (1985), we *could* make use of *existential* quantification. In that case we should not *define* the domain of the coarse-grained model M' in terms of equivalence classes of M as suggested by Hobbs, but rather take it to be a primitive domain. Moreover, we assume a surjective function f from the domain of M, I_M, to the domain of coarser-grained model M', $I_{M'}$,[66,67] that preserves (but not necessarily anti-preserves) each relevant predicate P: if $x \in P_M$, then $f(x) \in P_{M'}$, but if $x \notin P_M$, it need not be that $f(x) \notin P_{M'}$.[68] The other direction, however, follows by contraposition: if $x \notin P_{M'}$, then there is no $y \in f^{-1}(x)$ such that $y \in P_M$. In this case it is not problematic that the predicates 'Owned by me' and 'Owned by Enzo' are relevant, and thus part of $\mathcal{L}'$. It is just important that their negatives like 'Not owned by me' and 'Not owned by Enzo' are not part of $\mathcal{L}'$. To capture the idea of simplification, or coarsening, it is natural to assume that f is *not injective*: it might be that $f(x) = f(y)$, although $x \neq y$. Of course, we want refinements to preserve all the predicates and relations of the restricted language $\mathcal{L}'$, but this preservation is now stated as follows: $M' \leq_{\mathcal{L}'} M$ just in case if $x \in P_{M'}$, then $\exists y \in f^{-1}(x) \in P_M$, for each $P \in \mathcal{L}'$.[69] To a certain extent, the refinement relation used here is similar to the refinement relation used in supervaluation theory. But these refinement relations are obviously not the same: in contrast to what we assumed now, in supervaluation theory one assumes a one-to-one relation between the objects that exist in the different models.[70]

---

[66] A function f from D to D' is surjective iff the range of f is D'.

[67] If one desires, one can think of this function as a counterpart function used in quantified modal logic.

[68] Technically, f is just a homomorphism from M to M'. In general, homomorphisms don't preserve negative sentences.

[69] In general, the truth conditions of sentences in course-grained model M' are defined in terms of their truth conditions in fine-grained model M as follows:

$$\begin{array}{lll} M', g \models P(x) & \text{iff} & \exists d \in f^{-1}([\![x]\!]^{M',g}) : M, g[^x/_d] \models P(x) \\ M', g \models \neg\phi & \text{iff} & M', g \not\models \phi \\ M', g \models \phi \wedge \psi & \text{iff} & M', g \models \phi \text{ and } M', g \models \psi \\ M', g \models \forall x\phi & \text{iff} & \text{for all } d \in I_{M'} : M', g[^x/_d] \models \phi. \end{array}$$

Notice that $M', g \models \neg P(x)$ iff $\forall d \in f^{-1}([\![x]\!]^{M',g}) : M, g[^x/_d] \not\models P(x)$.

[70] Instead, the system described here is much closer to the 'inverse system' used by van der Does and van Lambalgen (2000) to account for the logic of vision.

The question how to relate the truth conditions of the same sentence with respect to models of different levels of granularity is a deep one, and I am not aware of any *general* satisfying answer. The question is closely connected with the issue in tense logic how to relate truth conditions of sentences with respect to *intervals* or events, to that of models that take *instants* to be basic. For 'John slept' to be true in interval i, is it enough that he slept at *some* instant in i, or should he have been sleeping in *most*, or even *all* instants in i? Although the first proposal seems very weak, Kamp (1979) convincingly argued that the latter proposal is much too strong for a sentence like 'John wrote an article'. Kamp concludes that we should not reduce judgments about intervals to judgments about instants. More in general, according to a tradition going back to Russell (1914) and Wiener (1914), and taken up by Kamp (1979), van Benthem (1982), and Thomason (1984), we should rather try to reduce our talk about instants to talk about intervals and events: absolute time does not exists independently of our experiences and is at best a construction our of them.[71] Notice how much this view differs not only from Lasersohn's (1999) position, but also from all those analyses that propose to account for the meaning of 'tall' in terms of exact cutoff-points.

6.7 Conclusion

In this chapter I focussed my discussion on relative adjectives. The meaning of a relative adjective is context dependent. I accounted for this context dependence by assuming that such adjectives should be interpreted with respect to so-called comparison classes. In terms of the interpretation of adjectives with respect to comparison classes, I characterized the difference between relative and absolute adjectives in terms a difference of constraints these two types of adjectives have to fulfill. More importantly, I have argued that the notion of 'tolerance' can be accounted in terms of Luce's semi-orders. Semi-orders, in turn, can be characterized in terms of constraints on comparison classes as well. I have argued that the level of tolerance a predicate allows for depends on the context of use.[72] If the stakes are higher, a predicate allows for less tolerance. The level of tolerance, in turn, determines how precise one can be. In this way, the discussion in Section 6.6 is linked closely to the discussion in Section 6.5.

In this chapter I focussed on the context dependence and vagueness of *adjectives*, and tried not to make use of numbers, like degrees, or probabilities. I suggested that many other vague expressions can be analyzed by make use of the same tools, but I don't think it can do all of the work. The most natural way to account for vague quantifiers like 'many' and 'few' (cf. Fernando and Kamp, 1996), and the use of adjectives in *exclamatives* like 'How tall you are!' (Graff, 2000), for instance, seems

---

[71] In fact, this tradition goes back all the way to Leibniz. Technically, the actual world, the *ding an sich*, is seen as the inverse limit.

[72] In a sense this is just what Parikh (1994) argued for as well.

to be by making use of probabilities. Whether we are forced to take probabilities into account to account for such cases remains to be seen.

Acknowledgement I would like to thank Johan van Benthem, David Etlin, Ewan Klein, Frank Veltman, and Tim Williamson for commenting on (sometimes much) earlier versions of this chapter. Thanks also to Chris Kennedy, Manfred Krifka, and Roger Schwarzchild for discussion.

References

Arrow, K. (1959), "Rational Choice Functions and Orderings", *Economica* 26: 121–127.

Asher, N. and Vieu, L. (1995), "Towards a Geometry of Common Sense: A Semantics and Complete Axiomatization of Mereotopology", *Proceedings of IJCAI-95*, Montreal, pp. 846–852.

Barker, C. (2002), "The Dynamics of Vagueness", *Linguistics and Philosophy* 25: 1–36.

Benthem, J. van (1982), "Later than Late: On the Logical Origin of the Temporal Order", *Pacific Philosophical Quarterly* 63: 193–203.

Bierwisch, M. (1984), "The Semantics of Gradation", in Bierwisch, M. and Lang, E. (eds.), *Dimensional Adjectives*, Berlin: Springer, pp. 71–262.

Bolinger, D. (1972), *Degree Words*, The Hague/Paris: Mouton.

Bosch, P. (1983), "'Vagueness' Is Context-Dependence. A Solution to the Sorites Paradox", in Ballmer, T. and Pinkal, M. (eds.), *Approaching Vagueness*, North-Holland Linguistic Series 50, Amsterdam: North Holland, pp. 189–210.

Burns, L.C. (1991), *Vagueness: An Investigation into Natural Language and the Sorites Paradox*, Dordrecht: Kluwer.

Cresswell, M. (1976), "The Semantics of Degree", in Partee, B., et al. (eds.), *Montague Grammar*, New York, NY: Academic Press, pp. 261–292.

Cruse, D.A. (1986), *Lexical Semantics*, Cambridge: Cambridge University Press.

Deemter, K. van (1995), "The Sorites Fallacy and the Context-Dependence of Vague Predicates", in Kanazawa, M., et al. (eds.), *Quantifiers, Deduction, and Context*, Stanford, CA: CSLI Publications, pp. 59–86.

Does, J. van der and Lambalgen, M. van (2000), "A Logic of Vision", *Linguistics and Philosophy* 23: 1–92.

Dubois, D. and Prade, H. (1980), *Fuzzy Sets and Systems. Theory and Applications*, New York, NY: Academic Press.

Dummett, M. (1975), "Wang's Paradox", *Synthese* 30: 301–324.

Ellis, J. (2004), "Context, Indexicals, and the Sorites", *Analysis* 64: 362–364.

Fernando, T. and Kamp, H. (1996), *Proceedings of Salt 6.*

Fine, K. (1975), "Vagueness, Truth and Logic", *Synthese* 30: 265–300.

Gaifman, H. (1997), "Vagueness, Tolerance and Contextual Logic", manuscript, Columbia University.

Goodman, N. (1966), *The Structure of Appearance*, Indianapolis, IN: Bobbs-Merill Publishing.

Graff, D. (2000), "Shifting Sands: An Interest Relative Theory of Vagueness", *Philosophical Topics* 28: 45–81.

Hobbs, J. (1985), "Granularity", *Proceedings of the International Joint Conference on Artificial Intelligence (IJCAI-85).*

Hobbs, J. (2000), "Half Orders of Magnitude", manuscript.

Jaegher, K. de (2003), "'A Game-Theoretic Rational for Vagueness", *Linguistics and Philosophy* 26: 637–659.

Jespersen, O. (1917), "Negation in English and Other Languages", in *Selected Writings of Otto Jespersen*, London and Tokyo: Allen and Unwin and Sejo Publishing Co., Ltd.

Kamp, H. (1975), "Two Theories of Adjectives", in Keenan, E. (ed.), *Formal Semantics of Natural Language*, Cambridge: Cambridge University Press, pp. 123–155.

Kamp, H. (1979), "Events, Instants and Temporal ", in Bäerle, R., et al. (eds.), *Semantics from Different Points of View*, Berlin: Springer, pp. 376–417.

Kamp, H. (1981), "The Paradox of the Heap", in Mönnich, U. (ed.), *Aspects of Philosophical Logic*, Dordrecht: D. Reidel, pp. 225–277.

Kamp, H. and Partee, B. (1995), "Prototype Theory and Compositionality", *Cognition*, 57: 129–191.

Keefe, R. (2000), *Theories of Vagueness*, Cambridge: Cambridge University Press.

Keefe, R. (2007), "Vagueness Without Context Change", *Mind* 116: 462.

Kennedy, C. (1999), *Projecting the Adjective: The Syntax and Semantics of Gradability and Comparison*. New York, NY: Garland Press.

Kennedy, C. (2007), "Vagueness and Grammar: The Semantics of Relative and Absolute Gradable Adjectives", *Linguistics and Philosophy* 30: 1–45.

Kennedy, C. and McNally, L. (2005), "Scale Structure and the Semantic Typology of Gradable Predicates", *Language* 81: 1–37.

Klein, E. (1980), "The Semantics of Positive and Comparative Adjectives", *Linguistics and Philosophy* 4: 1–45.

Klein, E. (1991), "Comparatives", in von Stechow, A. and Wunderlich, D. (eds.), *Semantik: Ein internationales Handbuch der zeitgenössischen Forschung*, Berlin: Walter de Gruyter.

Krantz, D., Duncan Luce, R., Suppes, P., and Tversky, T. (1971), *Foundations of Measurement, Vol. 1*, New York and London: Academic Press.

Krifka, M. (2007), "Approximate Interpretation of Number Words: A Case of Strategic Communication", in Bouma, G., et al. (eds.), *Cognitive Foundations of Interpretation*, Proceedings of the KNAW colloquium, Amsterdam, pp. 111–126.

Kyburg, A. and Morreau, M. (2000), "Fitting Worlds: Vague Language in Context", *Linguistics and Philosophy* 23: 577–597.

Lakoff, G. (1970), "A Note on Vagueness and Ambiguity", *Linguistic Inquiry* 1: 357–359.

Lakoff, G. (1973), "Hedges: A Study in Meaning Criteria and the Logic of Fuzzy Concepts", *Journal of Philosophical Logic* 2: 458–508.

Lambalgen, M. van (2001), "Conditional Quantification, or Poor Man's Probability", *Journal of Logic and Computation* 11: 295–335.

Lasersohn, P. (1999), "Pragmatic Halos", *Language* 75: 522–551.

Lasersohn, P. (2000), "*Same*, Models and Representations", in Jackson, B. and Matthew, T. (eds.), *Proceedings from SALT X*, Ithaca, NY: CLC Publications, pp. 83–97.

Lewis, D. (1969), *Convention*, Cambridge, MA: Harvard University Press.

Lewis, D. (1970), "General Semantics", *Synthese* 22: 18–67.

Lewis, D. (1973), *Counterfactuals*, Oxford: Blackwell.

Lewis, D. (1979), "Scorekeeping in a Language Game", *Journal of Philosophical Logic* 8: 339–359.

Lewis, D. (1993), "Many, but Almost One", in Campbell, K., et al. (eds.), *Ontology, Causality, and Mind: Essays on the Philosophy of D.M. Armstrong*, Cambridge: Cambridge University Press.

Luce, R.D. (1956), "Semiorders and a Theory of Utility Discrimination", *Econometrica* 24: 178–191.

Ludlow, P. (1989), "Implicit Comparison Classes", *Linguistics and Philosophy* 12: 519–533.

Myerson, R.B. (1991), *Game Theory: Analysis of Conflict*, Cambridge, MA: Harvard University Press.

Nunberg, G. (1985), "Individuation in Context", *Proceedings of WCCFL*, Santa Cruz, CA, pp. 203–217.

Parikh, R. (1994), "Vagueness and Utility: The Semantics of Common Nouns", *Linguistics and Philosophy* 17: 521–535.

Pinkal, M. (1984), "Consistency and Context Change: The Sorites Paradox", in Landman, F. and Veltman, F. (eds.), *Varieties of Formal Semantics, Proceedings of the Fourth Amsterdam Colloquium*, Groningen-Amsterdam Studies in Semantics, Dordrecht: Foris Publications.

Pinkal, M. (1995), *Logic and Lexicon*, Studies in Linguistics and Philosophy, Dordrecht: Kluwer.

Raffman, D. (1994), "Vagueness Without Paradox", *The Philosophical Review* 103, 41–74.

Raffman, D. (1996), "Vagueness and Context-Relativity", *Philosophical Studies* 81: 175–192.

Rooij, R. van (2011), "Revealed Preference and Satisficing Behavior", Synthese, to appear.

Rothstein, C. and Winter, Y. (2004), "Total Adjectives vs. Partial Adjectives", *Natural Language Semantics* 12: 259–288.

Russell, B. (1914), *Our Knowledge of the External World*, Chicago, IL: Norton.

Russell, B. (1940), *An Inquiry into Meaning and Truth*, London: George Allen and Unwin.

Sapir, E. (1944), "Grading: A Study in Semantics", *Philosophy of Science* 11: 93–116.

Sassoon, G. (2008), *Vagueness, Gradability and Typicality*, PhD thesis, Tel Aviv University.

Sauerland, U. and Penka, D. (2007), "Scalar vs. Epistemic Vagueness", in M. Gibson and T. Friedman (eds.), *Proceedings SALT 17*, Ithaca, NY: CLC Publications.

Scott, D. and Suppes, P. (1958), "Foundational Aspects of Theories of Measurement", *Journal of Symbolic Logic* 23: 113–128.

Schwarzchild, R. (2005), "Measure Phrases as Modifiers of Adjectives", *Recherches Linguisticus de Vincenenes* 35: 207–228.

Sedivy, J. Tannenhaus, M., Chambers, C., and Carlson, G. (1999), "Achieving Incremental Semantic Interpretation through Contextual Representation", *Cognition* 71: 109–147.

Seuren, P. (1973), "The Comparative", in Kiefer, F. and Ruwet, N. (eds.), *Generative Grammar in Europe*, Dordrecht: Reidel, pp. 528–564.

Shapiro, S. (2006), *Vagueness in Context*, Oxford: Clarendon Press.

Stalnaker, R. (1978), "Assertion", in Cole, P. (ed.), *Syntax and Semantics, Vol. 9: Pragmatics*, New York, NY: Academic Press, pp. 315–332.

Stanley, J. (2003), "Context, Interest Relativity, and the Sorites", *Analysis*, 63: 269–280

Soames, S. (1999), *Understanding Truth*, New York, NY: Oxford University Press.

Stechow, A. von (1984), "Comparing Semantic Theories of Comparison", *Journal of Semantics* 3: 1–77.

Suppes, P. and Zinnes, J.L. (1963), "Basic Measurement Theory", in Luce, R.D., Bush, R.R., and Galanter, E. (eds.), *Handbook of Mathematical Psychology*, New York, NY: Willey.

Thomason, R. (1984), "On Constructing Instants from Events", *Journal of Philosophical Logic* 13: 85–96.

Unger, P. (1975), *Ignorance*, Oxford: Clarendon Press.

Veltman, F. (1987), *Syllabus Logische Analyse 2: Vaagheid*, Amsterdam: Universiteit van Amsterdam.

Veltman, F. (2002), *Het verschil tussen vaag en precies*, Inaugurial lecture, Amsterdam: Amsterdam University Press.

Waismann, F. (1968), "Verifiability", in Flew, A. (ed.), *Logic and Language*, Oxford: Basic Blackwell.

Wheeler, S.C. (1972), "Attributives and Their Modifiers", *Nous* 6: 310–334.

Wiener, N. (1914), "A Contribution to the Theory of Relative Position", *Proceedings of the Cambridge Philosophical Society* 17: 441–449.

Williamson, T. (1994), *Vagueness*, London: Rootledge.

Wright, C. (1975), "On the Coherence of Vague Predicates", *Synthese* 30: 325–365.

Chapter 7
Vagueness and Law

Timothy Endicott

Where it seems that the law does not draw a boundary, it would seem impossible for a human being to identify one. Yet the law trains officials for that very purpose, and appoints them to judge and to regulate that which it leaves undetermined, as rightly as they can.

Aristotle, *Politics* III.16

In that brief remark, Aristotle identified a reflexivity in the nature of law: law regulates the resolution of its own indeterminacies. That reflexive characteristic of law distinguishes vagueness in law from vagueness in some other contexts.

After explaining two respects in which law is reflexive (Section 7.1), this chapter will point out that vagueness in law is typically *extravagant*, in a sense to be explained (Section 7.2), and that extravagant vagueness is a *necessary* feature of legal systems (Section 7.3). Some philosophers of law and philosophers of language claim that bivalence is a property of statements in the domains that concern them (the domain of law in the former case, the whole domain of meaningful discourse in the latter). Section 7.4 is an argument that the bivalence claim should be rejected. In philosophy of law, the motivation underlying the bivalence claim is an urge to assert the principle that the law must be capable of standing against arbitrary use of political power. The challenge – if the bivalence claim is rejected – is to articulate that principle in a way that is compatible with the possibility of indeterminacy in the application of vague laws.

Vague laws are laws that can accurately be stated in vague language. And they are typically[1] *made* by the use of vague language by a lawmaker. Here are some examples:

T. Endicott (✉)
Professor of Legal Philosophy, Balliol College, Oxford University, Oxford, UK
e-mail: timothy.endicott@law.ox.ac.uk

[1]But not necessarily. If a lawmaker uses precise language, the law that is made will be vague if, for example, there is a rule of the system that the application of the law is subject to equitable considerations.

G. Ronzitti (ed.), *Vagueness: A Guide*, Logic, Epistemology, and the Unity of Science 19, DOI 10.1007/978-94-007-0375-9_7,

- The English doctrine that a duty of care in negligence only arises if it is 'fair, just and reasonable' that the law should impose such a duty on the defendant.[2]
- A prohibition on 'torture' and 'inhuman or degrading treatment or punishment'.[3]
- A police power to order a concert to be called off if the music 'is likely to cause serious distress to the inhabitants of the locality'.[4]
- A rule authorizing a monopolies commission to investigate mergers between two companies, if the merger affects the supply of goods or services in 'a substantial part' of the country.[5]
- A rule that a copyright is not infringed by copying, unless the user copies the whole or a 'substantial part' of the original work.[6]
- A criminal offence of causing a child to be 'neglected, abandoned, or exposed, in a manner likely to cause him unnecessary suffering or injury to health' (Children and Young Persons Act, 1933 s.1(1)).[7]

The lawmaker's language may acquire a technical meaning (either by stipulation in an enactment, or by custom in the legal system), and the lawyer may need to interpret an enactment in light of other rules of the system (and will, of course, need to apply other rules of the system even to decide whether a purported lawmaker had authority to make the law that it has purported to make). Even though the relation between the lawmaker's language and the content of the law involves those complexities and others, the use of extremely vague language by lawmakers (in the above examples, and in so many others) results in vague law. After the lawyer's interpretative work is done, the English law of negligence, torture, public nuisance, copyright, and child neglect can only be stated in terms that are roughly as vague as the terms of the legislative enactments and common law precedents given above.

Legal philosophers have addressed the vagueness of law by focusing, as Aristotle did, on the role of officials trained to resolve disputes over cases in which the correct application of the law is unclear. Is it always the responsibility of those officials (a responsibility that they may or may not discharge successfully) to give effect to the rights of the parties? Then those rights may be controversial and unclear, but their requirements in each case must be fully determined by the interpretative resources available to a good judge. Or does the resolution of disputes over the law sometimes require the resolution of an indeterminacy in the rights of the parties? Then there are some cases in which a decision either way would be compatible with the law,

---

[2] *Caparo v Dickman* [1990] 2 AC 605 at 618.

[3] European Convention on Human Rights 1950, Article 3. Cf. the prohibition on 'cruel and unusual punishments' in the Eighth Amendment to the United States Constitution.

[4] Criminal Justice and Public Order Act 1994, c 33, s 63(1); discussed in Endicott (2000: ch. 4).

[5] *R v Monopolies and Mergers Commission, ex p South Yorkshire Transport* [1993] 1 WLR 23.

[6] Copyright, Designs and Patents Act 1988, s 16(3)(a). The vagueness of that rule, and its role in copyright protection, are discussed in Endicott and Spence (2005).

[7] Discussed in Endicott (2005: ch. 1, 27–48).

and we need to ask whether decision making in such cases is doomed to be merely arbitrary.

The competition between those two accounts of adjudication has been a central debate in modern philosophy of law.[8] The first three sections of this chapter set the scene for a discussion of the views of the proponents of each view (in Section 7.4.1), by explaining the context in which vague laws are made and applied. Sections 7.2 and 7.3 show that if vagueness is a problem for the rule of law, it is a very serious problem.

Vagueness in law is only a particular instance of vagueness in human discourse. The ideal of the rule of law – which is itself constitutive of the concept of law – is related to principles of communication that are essential to a sound theory of the meaning of linguistic utterances in general. So the philosopher of language may have something to gain from a reflection on the use of language in law. The conclusion of this chapter comments on relations between the debate in philosophy of law, and the debates over bivalence in philosophy of logic and philosophy of language.

7.1 Law Is Reflexive

Law is reflexive in two respects that are important for an understanding of vagueness in language. First, the law regulates the meaning and application of its own language. Second, it authorizes institutions (I will call them 'courts') to resolve disputes as to its own content and application, in a rule-governed way.

There are other reflexivities. Law constitutes and regulates the institutions that make law. It regulates the identification of sources of law. It provides and regulates legal processes for pursuing remedies for legal wrongs. It confers legal powers to create legal rights.[9] And then, legal systems very commonly use the resolution of disputes as a technique for regulating the meaning and application of their language, through a rule of precedent.[10] That common form of lawmaking is related to the initial two forms of reflexivity that are important for our purposes. Vague laws give a form of power to courts. That power could be used on every occasion without reference to the ways in which other disputes have been decided, but because it is characteristic of law to regulate itself, courts characteristically make law when they resolve a dispute.

Because of these reflexive features of law, the effect of legislation in vague language is:

---

[8]Some legal theorists – particularly in the twentieth century – took the view that legal rights and duties are pervasively indeterminate, so that an adjudicative decision can never (or, perhaps, can hardly ever) give effect to the rights of the parties. That view will not be addressed here; for a survey of radical indeterminacy claims see Endicott (2000: ch. 2).

[9]As Kelsen said, law regulates its own creation (Kelsen, 1991: 124, 126, 132).

[10]This technique is characteristic of the common law tradition, but it is also a common and very important feature of civil law systems.

1. determined by the rules of the system that determine the effect of language used in legislation, and
2. subject to the jurisdiction of institutions authorized to determine the content of the law and its application (courts), and
3. capable of being developed through lawmaking decisions of courts in applying legislation.

These reflexive features of law generate a serious challenge for understanding the rule of law, which Aristotle identified:

> **The rule of law problem:** if law appoints persons 'to regulate that which it leaves undetermined', how can we be ruled by law rather than by persons?

The rule of law problem may seem all the worse, if vagueness in law is extravagant (Section 7.2), and if it is a necessary feature of legal systems (Section 7.3). This chapter aims to offer a response to the rule of law problem, and to suggest implications for the philosophy of language.

7.2 Vagueness in Law Is Extravagant

In their arguments over the sorites paradox, philosophers of logic use words like 'heap' or 'bald' as illustrations. Lawmakers do not generally use vague descriptive terms like those, when they can be avoided,[11] and they are certainly not the most notable vague terms in law. And lawmakers never use *slightly* vague expressions such as 'almost seventeen years old'.[12] When the law is vague, its vagueness is usually much more extravagant than the vagueness of those terms. If an expression is vague, then there are cases in which it is not clear (even when we know the meaning of the expression and the facts of the situation) whether the expression applies or not. Even when we know how old a person is, it may be unclear whether it is true that she is almost seventeen, or whether it is true that she is a child. Let's call such a case a 'borderline case'. Of course, not every case is a borderline case. And it is actually a critically important feature of vague terms that we can make sense of the lack of clarity in a borderline case by reference to the cases in which the applicability of the expression is perfectly clear. So although it is clear at age five that a person is a child, and clear at age fifty that she is not a child, there will be points on a timeline at which it is unclear whether she is a child, or not. We can treat the timeline as a *dimension*. I will use the term 'dimension' for a line on which borderline cases separate cases to which a vague term clearly applies, from cases to

---

[11] They often cannot be avoided, and the law of taxation provides examples of fierce disputes over the application of a vague term such as 'trade': see *Edwards v Bairstow* [1956] AC 14.

[12] But that is not to say that there is no trivial vagueness in law. The most common sort of trivial vagueness arises from *de minimis* principles – that is, legal doctrines preventing sanctions against or remedies for trivial breaches of the law. The lack of clarity in the application of general *de minimis* (as to what counts as trivial) is itself rather trivial.

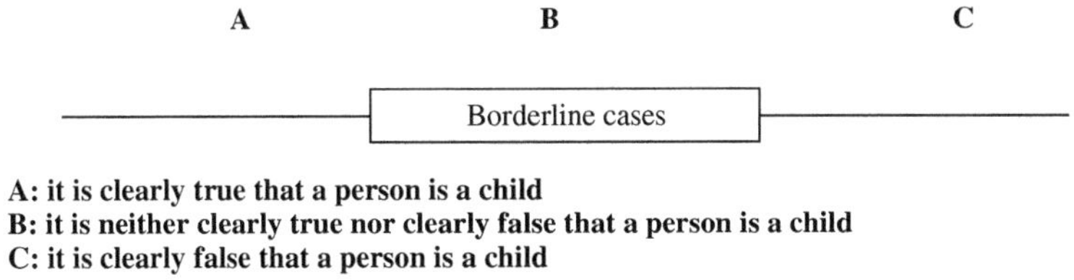

Fig. 7.1 Vagueness – 'child'

which it clearly does not apply. A single small increment between two cases along a dimension cannot justify us in applying a vague term in one case, and withholding it in the next case. In Fig. 7.1, the dimension for application of 'child' is a timeline.

As a depiction of the applicability of a vague expression, Fig. 7.1 has some dangerous features:

a. It makes it look as if there is a precise boundary to the range of borderline cases, when in fact it is not clear where the borderline cases start and stop (we could draw a further range of second-order borderline cases to indicate that unclarity, but then we would need third-order borderline cases too. . .).
b. There are few vague terms whose applicability can fairly be represented by a single dimension. The applicability of 'tall' or 'heavy' can be mapped on a single dimension, perhaps, but childhood ends at different times for different children because it involves maturity and not simply age. Moreover, various dimensions may be incommensurable: that is, there may be no rational basis for any precise way of calculating the relative impact of changes in each dimension on the applicability of the term. Colour terms such as 'blue' are incommensurable in their application, because there are multiple dimensions (e.g. wavelength and brightness) with no metric that gives us reason to say for every shade of turquoise that it is or is not more truly blue than a particular shade of teal. Incommensurabilities in the respects in which an action can be reasonable are, perhaps, the most important source of the extravagant vagueness in legal language (such as 'reasonable' in its various legal uses) that will be discussed below.[13]
c. The figure does not disclose the fact that the context in which a term is applied makes a difference to its correct application. In fact, some philosophers of logic concerned have tried to resolve the sorites paradox by pointing out the dependence of correct application on context (see chapter by Hyde).

Figure 7.1, nevertheless, gives a faithful representation of one feature of vague expressions: for all of them, it is possible to identify a dimension along which cases can be plotted, in such a way that a small increment along the dimension will not give a person reason to apply the term in one case and reason not to apply the term in the next case. That is possible for terms whose applicability depends on two or

[13]On whether incommensurability is a form of vagueness, see Broome (1997).

more incommensurable factors, and it even applies to terms whose applicability is immensurable. A factor determining the applicability of a term is immensurable if it cannot be measured. It cannot be measured if there are no units of it that we can count. So, for example, there are no units of niceness, and although one thing may be nicer than another, the meaning of the comparative 'nicer' is not given by the ordering of any measurable criterion in the way that the meaning of 'taller' is given by the ordering of a criterion of height. Yet even for terms like 'nice', it is possible to identify a dimension, and to construct a figure like Fig. 7.1, if only by using a timeline running from a time at which something (a flan? a person?) was clearly nice, to a time at which it is clearly not nice, through a gradual process of change (the change must, of course, be a change in respects relevant to its niceness).

Increments along such a dimension generate a sorites paradox, if we treat them as supporting the conditional premise that if the expression applies in one case, it applies in the next case. Philosophers sometimes describe this feature of vague expressions by using indiscriminable increments: increments (in, e.g., a colour spectrum) so tiny that a person cannot tell the difference between one case and the next. But when an expression is extremely vague, the increments may be quite substantial. And there may even be substantial unclarity as to where the unclear cases lie on the dimension. We may disagree in resolving the borderline cases, and we may disagree as to which cases are borderline cases. If an expression is extravagantly vague, it is possible for two competent users of the language, who understand the facts of each case, to take such different views that there is not even any overlap between the cases that each disputant would identify as borderline.[14] If everyone who uses the word 'child' agrees that, say, some 15-year-old in some context is a borderline case of a child, then 'child' (in that context) is *not* extravagantly vague, even if various speakers would draw boundaries between the clear cases and the borderline cases at different points. We might say that the 15-year-old is a paradigm borderline case: a model agreed by all speakers, that could be used to explain what a borderline case is.

But there are often no paradigm borderline cases for the application of a vague term. Consider Fig. 7.2, in which the area of the United Kingdom affected by a merger provides the dimension for application of the vague legislative term, 'substantial part of the United Kingdom'.

Extravagant vagueness offers the possibility for deep controversy over the application of the law. At point x, each of the disputants will think that the other is misclassifying a clear case of a substantial part of the country as clearly not substantial, or a part of the country that is clearly not substantial as clearly substantial. And it is just this sort of disagreement that is most common in legal practice. Note that, from the mere fact that two competent users of the language take such different

[14]Are the expressions 'bald' and 'child' extravagantly vague in this sense? Perhaps they are, and for present purposes I cannot rule out the possibility that all vague terms are extravagantly vague. Even if that is true, there may still be important differences between the vagueness of terms such as 'bald', and terms such as 'substantial' that are both evaluative, and massively context-dependent in their application.

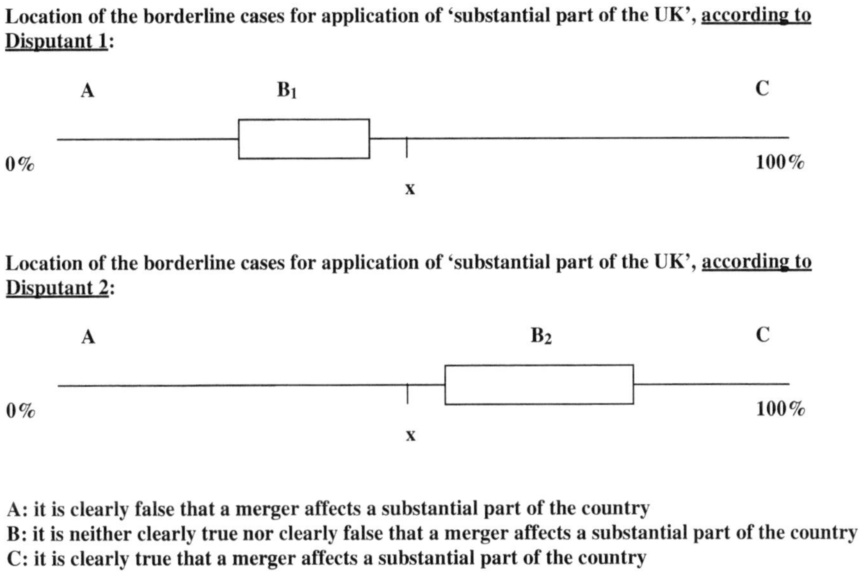

Fig. 7.2 Extravagant vagueness – 'substantial part of the United Kingdom'

views, we can draw no conclusions whatsoever as to whether an area *is* a substantial part of the UK, or as to whether there is a determinate answer to the question. It may seem tempting to say that the nature of the disagreement shows that x is a borderline case, because competent users of the language disagree on whether to characterize it as substantial. But nothing in the scenario would support that rash conclusion. There is no rule of our language that neither of us is right if we have this sort of disagreement. Whether x is a substantial part of the country is a question that cannot be answered by a survey of speakers, and a survey of speakers in itself cannot even show us that there is no determinate answer to the question.

7.3 Extravagant Vagueness and the Regulation of the Life of a Community

Vagueness is an intrinsic feature of law. Here are four reasons for that conclusion.

7.3.1 The Need for Vague Legislation

Every legal system regulates the life of a community in ways that can only be achieved through vague regulation.[15] The easiest way to see this point is to consider the control of traffic. It is done with more precision today than it was in the

[15]See Endicott (2001).

nineteenth century, when legislation made it an offence to drive a vehicle 'in a wanton or furious manner'.[16] Today, the law of many countries uses precise speed limits to control driving that is furious in one respect, and uses precise blood alcohol levels to control driving that is wanton in one respect. Twenty-first-century technology makes it possible to impose standards that offer precise guidance to drivers and to officials in some aspects of traffic control. Yet no legal system has eliminated, or even tried to eliminate, vagueness in traffic regulation, and no system every will. Every system has rules like the vague Canadian Criminal Code prohibition on operating a motor vehicle 'in a manner that is dangerous to the public'.[17] The reason is the vast variety of ways of using a vehicle that create unacceptable risks to other road users. Driving while intoxicated and driving too fast are two salient ways of creating such risks, and it is possible to control them through precise standards. But it would not be possible to create a precise list of everything dangerous that a person might do with a vehicle, for two reasons: none of us could foresee all such behaviour, and even the foreseeable sorts of driving that ought to be prohibited are too diverse for a lawmaker to compile a list of precise descriptions of them. The lawmaker's reasonable response to this legislative need was to impose an extravagantly vague standard, writing into the Criminal Code the very objective of control (prohibition of dangerous use of a vehicle), rather than authoritatively specifying what comes within the objective.

The lawmaker's predicament is an inability to specify. They may delegate the task of specification by, for example, providing that a regulator or a court or an administrative official will have power to set standards. When they do not expressly allocate power to someone else to set standards, they need to impose a standard in spite of their inability to be specific. To do that, they must use extravagantly vague general terms.

This need for vagueness arises whenever a *diverse* pattern of human conduct needs to be regulated in a *general* way. Let us refer to this principle as 'the diversity principle': the principle that precise regulation cannot effectively be used to control a massively complex pattern of behaviour. Precise regulation is possible only when some measurable criterion, such as the speed of a vehicle, or the proportion of alcohol in a person's blood, bears an appropriate relation to a regulatory objective.[18]

The diversity principle is of importance not only in traffic regulation, but pervasively throughout the public and private law of every legal system. And wherever it is *essential* for the law to regulate a diverse field of human conduct, the diversity principle is a feature of the nature of law. So, for example, every legal system regulates intentional violence against persons. It is not a coincidence that all legal systems do that; they do it because the massively complex point of a legal system

[16]United Kingdom Offences Against the Person Act, 1861, s35; see ibid.

[17]Criminal Code of Canada, s 249. http://www.canlii.org/ca/sta/c-46/sec249.html.

[18]And even then, some degree of arbitrariness will be incurred by the precision of the regulation: see Endicott (2005).

includes (or you might say, the massively various array of purposes that justify the creation and sustenance of a legal system include) control on violence against the person. If a human community is to be regulated at all, it must be regulated in that respect. A system of rules that regulated only the height of garden hedges would not be a legal system, and a system that regulated property entitlements without regulating violence against the person would not be a legal system. We can say this much without undertaking any comprehensive outline of the purposes that a system must pursue if it is to qualify as a legal system.[19] If we embarked on that complex and open-ended undertaking, we would come up with many more aspects of the life of a community that must be regulated if the community is to be ruled by law, and that can only be regulated with extravagantly vague rules.

7.3.2 Vagueness in Interpretation

Although the application of extravagantly vague language is a massively important source of unclarity in particular cases, there are other sources of unclarity in the interpretation of the law that are at least as important.

Interpretation of legislation is the working out of the legal effect of the authoritative acts of a lawmaker. It is often best done by reference to the purposes of the law. The purposes of the law are vague, and so the principles of interpretation are vague. In particular, there are often diverse, incommensurably good purposes that may be pursued in the interpretation of legislation, and then the effect of the legislation will be vague, as a result.

Consider the rule giving a national monopolies commission authority to investigate mergers between two companies, if the merger affects the supply of goods or services in 'a substantial part' of the country. In *R v Monopolies and Mergers Commission, ex p South Yorkshire Transport* [1993] 1 WLR 23, the merging bus companies had routes that affected an area between Leeds and Derby that covered 1.65% of the land area of the United Kingdom (with 3.2% of the population). South Yorkshire Transport said that that was not a substantial part of the UK, so that the Commission should not have started an investigation.

In the leading judgment, Lord Mustill said that it was the court's job to identify 'the criterion for a judgment', even if 'opinions might legitimately differ' as to what the criterion ought to be.

To identify the criterion for a judgment is to interpret the law. The criterion that Lord Mustill established in *South Yorkshire Transport* was vague. He interpreted 'substantial part of the United Kingdom' to mean 'of such size, character and importance as to make it worth consideration for the purposes of the Act' (32), and he found that the Commission's decision that South Yorkshire was a substantial part of the UK was within the 'permissible field of judgment' (33) allowed by that criterion. It follows from the decision that there is a wide range of cases (and the range

---

[19] For a comprehensive (and therefore very abstract) outline, see Raz (1979: 167–177).

A substantial part of the United Kingdom?

is not sharply bounded) in which it would be lawful for the commission *either* to investigate or to refuse to investigate a merger.

There is no such thing as a precise general rule of interpretation; this is an application of the diversity principle. The effect of the vagueness of rules of interpretation is to compound vagueness in legislative language. And then the resulting massively complex questions may be answered in particular cases by legal doctrines, or by authoritative resolutions of an unclarity in previous decisions of the courts. Or they may not be answered or resolved by anything, and then they generate extravagant vagueness in the law.

7.3.3 Non-linguistic Vagueness in Customary Rules (and in the Framework Rules of the System in Particular)

Just as there are no precise general rules of interpretation, there are no precise general rules as to what differences between two cases are sufficient to justify different decisions. Therefore, the courts' general doctrines of precedent are always vague. It is a form of vagueness insofar as there is no *precise* doctrine in a legal system regulating the effect of precedents, or regulating the interpretation of statutes. This vagueness does not arise from the use of vague language to make law.[20] Like the vagueness of general principles of interpretation, this is a necessary feature of legal systems, because every legal system needs to regulate the effect of its own precedents and legislation, and the diversity principle means that that cannot be done with precise rules.

For a final example of framework vagueness in the law, consider the rules that regulate the relations between institutions in a system, such as the grounds of appeal from a lower court to a higher court, or the grounds of judicial review of executive decisions by a court. In the *South Yorkshire Transport* case, Lord Mustill said that if the criterion established by the court is vague,

> ...the court is entitled to substitute its own opinion for that of the person to whom the decision has been entrusted only if the decision is so aberrant that it cannot be classed as rational.[21]

The standard that the court adopted in answering the question of law in *South Yorkshire Transport* left the commission a very wide leeway; and because 'aberrant' is vague, it is a leeway with no sharp boundary.

The diversity principle applies here, too, and general standards of review of executive and lower court decisions are extravagantly vague. Those standards can give lower courts and executive agencies just as much leeway as an express discretion would give them. So, for example, Lord Donaldson MR held in *O'Kelly v Trusthouse Forte plc* [1984] QB 90 that if a tribunal has stated the law correctly, an appellate court can interfere with the application of the law to the facts only if 'no reasonable tribunal, properly directing itself on the relevant questions of law, could have reached the conclusion under appeal' (123). And in *Moyna v Work and Pensions Secretary* [2003] UKHL 44, Lord Hoffmann held that the court cannot overturn a decision 'whether the facts as found or admitted fall one side or the other of some conceptual line drawn by the law... unless it falls outside the bounds of reasonable judgment' [25].

7.3.4 Private Ordering

Every legal system ascribes legal effect to a wide variety of transactions for the purpose of ordering commercial and other relations, and for the purpose of arranging ownership of real and personal property. That juridification of private arrangements cannot be carried out unless the system is prepared to give legal effect to vague standards that the parties have set for themselves and for each other. This is not just

---

[20]Though it is, of course, reflected in vagueness in the language with which a good lawyer would express the doctrines of the effect of precedent or the interpretation of statutes.

[21][1993] 1 WLR 23, 32.

because people are prone to a mistake of making vague provision for the disposition of their affairs; people often have good reason to impose vague obligations on each other. The standard contract for sale of goods is the paradigm example: every such contract provides for the goods to be of satisfactory quality, and it is not generally possible to provide a precise criterion of quality.[22]

The upshot of these three points is not only that vagueness is an intrinsic feature of law,[23] but that extravagant vagueness is an intrinsic feature of law.

7.4 Discretion and the Rule of Law Problem

> For how is the concept of a game bounded? What still counts as a game and what no longer does? Can you give the boundary? No. You can *draw* one; for none has so far been drawn. (But that never troubled you before when you used the word "game".)
>
> -Wittgenstein, *Philosophical Investigations* 68

In law, the fact that no boundary has been drawn does trouble people. Parties to a dispute over the application of vague laws argue about the application of words that are as vague as the word 'game', but the dispute may have very serious consequences for them. And then, if a boundary has not been given to the application of a vague law, the parties seem to be at the mercy of whatever official gets to draw one. We have seen that the effect of vague laws can be similar to the effect of express discretions. Consider the rules for control of executive officials and lower courts by higher courts, discussed above: if the law is vague (as in the 'substantial part of the United Kingdom' doctrine for the monopolies commission), and the courts control the decisions of the commission by quashing them only if they are aberrant, then the effect is much as if the executive agency had an express discretion controlled only by restrained (and vague) doctrines of responsible government. The 'permissible field of judgment' is very substantial. And where the initial decision maker is the court rather than an executive agency, then *its* permissible field of judgment is very substantial, if the law is extravagantly vague. The effect of extravagant vagueness in law is an extravagant allocation of discretion to executive or judicial officials of the system.

As H.L.A. Hart put it in 1962:

> In every legal system a large and important field is left open for the exercise of discretion by courts and other officials in rendering initially vague standards determinate, in resolving the uncertainties of statutes, or in developing and qualifying rules only broadly communicated by authoritative precedents.[24]

---

[22] For this reason, statutory regulation of the sale of goods also provides vague standards for the quality of goods: Sale and Supply of Goods Act 1893 (c 71) s 14(2): 'merchantable quality'; Sale and Supply of Goods Act 1994 (c 35) s 1 'satisfactory quality'.

[23] Note: this does *not* imply that every law is vague! There are many precise laws. But vagueness is an intrinsic feature of law because a legal system necessarily includes vague rules.

[24] Hart (1994: 136).

Note that Hart pointed out a similarity between the vagueness of rules laid down in vague language, and the characteristic vagueness of customary rules (see above Section 7.3.3). In the case of vague legislation, '...the language of the rule seems now only to mark out an authoritative example, namely that constituted by the plain case'.[25] In an unclear case for the application of a 'general term', '...there are reasons both for and against our use of a general term, and no firm convention or general agreement dictates its use, or, on the other hand, its rejection by the person concerned to classify. If in such cases doubts are to be resolved, something in the nature of a choice between open alternatives must be made by whoever is to resolve them.'[26]

This approach to the role of vagueness in law has been very influential. But if we agree with Hart, then the rule of law problem may come to seem paradoxical. The rule of law requires vague forms of regulation, yet vagueness means that some cases are not ruled by law; and *extravagant* vagueness means that *many* cases are not ruled by law, and the necessity of extravagant vagueness in law means that many cases *cannot* be ruled by law. The law itself deprives us, across a wide but indeterminate range of cases, of the predictability, consistency, and control over official conduct that seemed to be the marks of the rule of law. The rule of law seems to be incompatible with itself. Now the rule of law problem seems to be a rule of law paradox. What can we do about it?

7.4.1 Bivalence in Law

We could try to solve the paradox by insisting that there is a unique correct answer to every question of the content of the law, and to every question of its application to a particular case. That is, we could assert bivalence for all legal statements. This solution may seem attractive, because as John Finnis has said, it is a 'working postulate' in any legal order that there are no gaps: that the system provides the resources for a determinate resolution to every problem that may arise for legal decision.[27] It is an important working postulate, too, because it is crucial to the rule of law that disputes should be resolved, and should (generally) be given a precise resolution. A criminal prosecution, an action in tort, a claim that a licence is valid, all call for bivalent resolutions (guilty or not guilty, liable or not liable, valid or not valid[28]).

---

[25] *Ib* 127.

[26] *Ib*.

[27] Finnis (1980: 269, 279). See Endicott (2000) on 'juridical bivalence', at 72–75.

[28] Note that sentencing and the law of damages do not generally call for bivalent resolutions: that is, the court must determine a period for the sentence and an amount of damages. This feature of legal ordering itself creates a need for the resolution of vagueness: a conviction may call for nothing more determinate than a serious sentence, and a tort may be compensable with nothing more determinate than substantial damages, and a court needs to give a resolution that will tell the jailer a precise time at which to open the prison gates, and a resolution that will tell a defendant a precise sum of money to pay in compensation. When courts make vague orders (such as the United States Supreme Court's famous order in *Brown v Board of Education*, 349 US 294 (1955), that

But according to Finnis, 'There is no need to labour the point that this postulate is fictitious'.[29]

Given the essential role of extravagant vagueness in law, how could anyone disagree with Finnis's view that the postulate is fictitious? Some legal theorists have turned the working postulate into a theorem in the philosophy of law. They have done so because it seems the only way to solve the rule of law problem. And also because the extravagantly vague standards of the law are *so* vague that they seem not really to be vague at all.

Ronald Dworkin has been the most prominent advocate of the view that there is a unique legally correct solution to every legal dispute. He argued in the 1980s that legal principles can eliminate vagueness.[30] But general legal principles (even a closure principle such as, 'a person is to be convicted of an offence only if his conduct *clearly* satisfies the definition of the offence') are themselves vague, and the result is the compound vagueness that we saw in Section 7.3.2, above. There is no general reason to think that legal principles diminish the vagueness of legislation (because of extravagant vagueness, a closure principle may not even do so), and they cannot eliminate it.

Dworkin's more enduring strategy has been to claim that abstract normative terms such as 'just' and evaluative terms such as 'cruel' are not vague. Those terms appeal, in his view, to 'concepts that admit of different conceptions'.[31] It is true that those concepts admit of different conceptions (though concepts such as 'bald' and 'heap' and 'tall' admit of different conceptions, too). But that fact does not support Dworkin's inference that such concepts are not vague. No competent conception of justice would yield sharp boundaries to its application.

In his most recent work on the subject, Dworkin insists that there is no justification for any general claim that indeterminacies arise in law because of vagueness, and suggests that there is a general reason for denying it:

> We make sense of them [indeterminacy claims], if there is any sense to make, by treating them as internal, substantive positions based, as firmly as any other, on positive theories or assumptions about the fundamental character of the domain to which they belong. In law, for example, the functional need for a decision is itself a factor, because any argument that the law is indeterminate about some issue must recognize the consequences of that being true, and take these into account.[32]

'The functional need for a decision' is the need that lies behind the working postulate that the law has no gaps. It is a need that gives a court reason to resolve a dispute even if there is no conclusive reason to choose one resolution rather than another. That need is not a reason for concluding that the law requires a particular resolution.

---

racial segregation should be ended in schools 'with all deliberate speed'), they incur a responsibility for continuing supervision to resolve any disputes over compliance.

[29] *Ib.*

[30] See, e.g., Dworkin (1985).

[31] Dworkin (1977: 103).

[32] Dworkin (1996: 137).

And the consequence of indeterminacy is only that the court must make a decision even though the law does not require a particular outcome.

Samantha Besson, too, argues against the view 'that abstract normative and evaluative concepts like justice or cruelty should be regarded as vague'.[33] She says that:

- disagreement over justice 'is not restricted to uncertainties about norms for the use of language, but expands into uncertainties about moral and political norms more generally',
- a term is only vague if it has undisputed paradigms, but 'justice and other evaluative concepts do not often have fixed paradigms that are undisputed and indisputable', and
- there may be no dimension (in the sense explained in Section 7.2, above) for the application of a term like 'justice'.[34]

The application of these terms certainly is controversial (in a way that the application of 'blue' or 'heap' is not), and value-laden. But uncertainties about the application of vague terms are not restricted to uncertainties about norms for the use of language. A dispute about whether a person is bald is no more or less a dispute about a norm for the use of language, than a dispute about whether an action is just. In both cases, a resolution of the dispute or doubt will entail a conclusion as to how a word ('just' or 'bald') is to be used, but neither dispute is merely a dispute about a word. As for undisputed paradigms, they are not essential to vagueness. If no one agrees on any clear case of a just action, that gives no reason to think that 'just' is not vague. It is vague if there are actions that are just and actions that are not just, and if there is no sharp boundary between the class of just actions and the class of actions that are not just. So the critical point in Besson's argument is whether there is any dimension, in the sense explained above, for the application of abstract normative evaluative expressions ('just', 'cruel', 'good', 'nice'...).

Suppose that justice demands monetary compensation to victims of an industrial accident, or to a person who has been falsely imprisoned. Or in fact, suppose that justice demands monetary compensation to anyone who has suffered, as a result of a wrong, a personal injury or a loss of liberty that cannot be repaired with a precise amount of money. Compensation of one pound would not do justice (it would be an insult). If a sum (whether it is one pound or more than one pound) is inadequate to do justice, merely adding another pound will not do justice either. Those claims are enough to generate sorites reasoning (and, incidentally, a sorites paradox – i.e.

[33] Besson (2005).

[34] Besson (2005: 76–77). Besson adds a suggestion that 'bivalent logic does not necessarily apply to justice'. She would presumably insist that there are logical relations among claims of justice, but she does not explain what alternative logic might apply, or how it would support the view that there is a single right answer to legal disputes.

Location of the borderline cases between an award of compensation that is less than justice requires, and an award of compensation is <u>not</u> less than justice requires, <u>according to Disputant 1</u>:

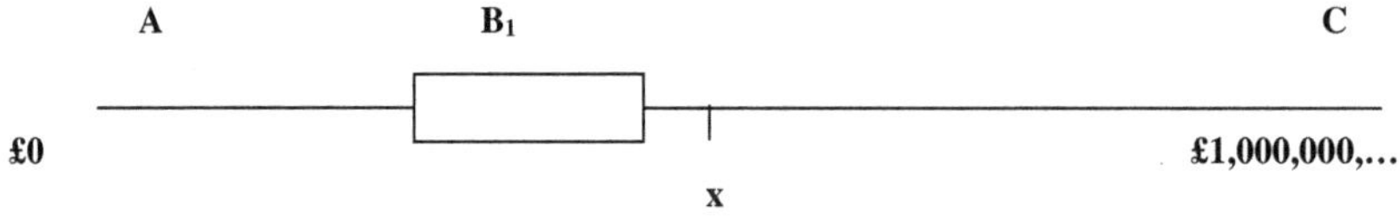

Location of the borderline cases between an award of compensation that is less than justice requires, and an award of compensation is <u>not</u> less than justice requires, <u>according to Disputant 2</u>:

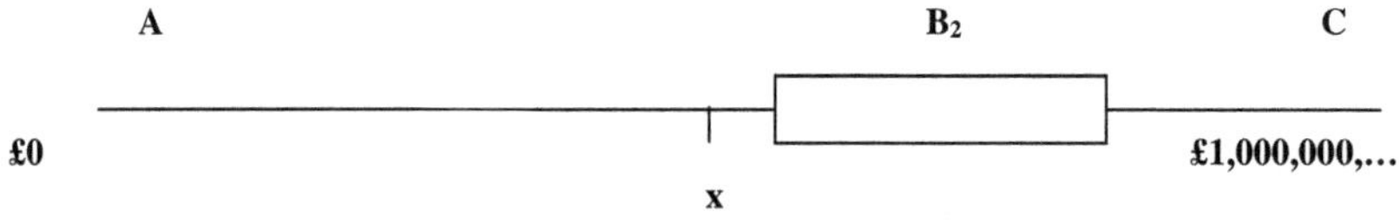

A: it is clearly true that an award of compensation is less than justice requires
B: it is neither clearly true nor clearly false that an award of compensation is less than justice requires
C: it is clearly false that an award of compensation is less than justice requires

Fig. 7.3 The extravagant vagueness of justice

a pseudo-proof that no amount of compensation is adequate). So it is possible to construct a dimension for justice (see Fig. 7.3).

Justice is an abstract concept, and there is, of course, no single dimension for its application in all contexts (as there is for the word 'tall'). And in some contexts the requirements of justice will be precise. But the concept of justice is vague because it is very often possible to construct a dimension for its application. It is, in fact, extravagantly vague, partly because there can be multiple incommensurable dimensions for its application in a particular context.

The just quantum of compensation for personal injuries is not only open to controversy (which Dworkin and Besson would insist upon). There is often no precise sum that justice demands. And there are many other questions of justice that yield no precise answer, such as the question of how unsound a criminal conviction must be before justice demands release of the prisoner. Of course there are many clear cases in which there is no doubt that an action is just (and many clear cases in which there is no doubt that an action is unjust) and there ought to be no disagreement, and the people who deny the truth in those paradigm cases are actually *rejecting* justice (perhaps while they are pretending to be just, or deceiving themselves, or even just making a fundamental mistake) rather than applying a conception of justice that competes with other people's conceptions. That human capacity to dispute the indisputable is compatible with the fact that the requirements of justice are vague.

7.4.2 Arbitrariness and the Rule of Law

If we do not try to solve the paradox by asserting bivalence for legal statements, what escape is there from the rule of law paradox? We will need an explanation how a community can be ruled by law, if the law often does not require a court to reach a particular resolution to a dispute. That calls for an understanding of arbitrary government.

As Wittgenstein said, we can draw a boundary for the application of a vague expression. We have a discretion. It is arbitrary, in a sense, to draw a boundary here or there. But it is arbitrary only in the sense that there is no reason to draw the boundary here and not to draw it there. If you draw a boundary (or, for that matter, if you decide to apply an expression in any particular borderline case), you make a decision as to how to apply the expression that is neither required nor forbidden by the meaning of the expression (that is, by the rule for its application). So it is not arbitrary in any pejorative sense.

A decision is arbitrary if it is reasonless. In a wide sense, a decision is arbitrary if it is not supported by reasons for reaching one decision rather than another. Sometimes it is entirely reasonable for decision-making to be unresponsive to such reasons: particularly when a decision is needed, and there *are no* reasons for reaching one decision rather than another. In a lottery, for example, there is no reason for one ticket to be chosen rather than another (and in fact, there is reason to choose a ticket at random and therefore, in the wide sense, arbitrarily). The wide sense of arbitrariness does not generate any rule of law problem: holding a lottery is not in itself an abandonment of the rule of law. A decision that is arbitrary in the wide sense does not count as arbitrary in the pejorative sense – the sense in which arbitrary government is opposed to the rule of law – if there is no reason for one decision rather than another. A decision is wrong if there is conclusive reason for a different decision to be made; a decision is arbitrary in the pejorative sense if it is not even based on reasons for reaching it, when it ought to be. So, for example, it would be arbitrary in the pejorative sense, if a random technique were used to decide whether to convict a defendant of a criminal charge.[35]

How large a part of the country must be affected by a merger, before it becomes lawful for the monopolies commission to investigate it? As Wittgenstein suggested, it would be arbitrary (in the wide sense) to say that the line is here or here. There would be no reason for it. But there may be a very good reason for it to be drawn,

---

[35]Most real examples of arbitrary government actually arise from a systemic failure of the law to control its own officials and institutions. A decision is arbitrary in the sense relevant to the rule of law, if it is one that other institutions can competently identify as not responding to the relevant considerations. A decision does not count as arbitrary government, if there is a good reason for leaving the decision-maker free to act the way that he or she wishes, without requiring any justification for the decision other than the fact that the decision maker made it. So, e.g., an executive power to detain persons without judicial control is an arbitrary governmental power. But the power of a legislature to impose taxes without judicial control is not an arbitrary power.

and then it must be drawn somewhere. Then the drawing of a line is not arbitrary in the pejorative sense.

The law resolves its own indeterminacies, and does not necessarily stop ruling the life of a community in virtue of the fact that courts must come up with answers to questions for which the law itself does not provide an answer. We only lose the rule of law if decision making is arbitrary in the pejorative sense.

7.5 Conclusion

The ideal of the rule of law is *not* an ideal of submission of all action to control by rules (to which no community could even approximate). For that reason, discretion on the part of officials (even the very wide 'permissible field of judgment' that they gain from extravagant vagueness in the law) is not necessarily contrary to the rule of law. Official discretion is contrary to the rule of law only if it is arbitrary in the pejorative sense. Wittgenstein implied this conclusion, in a remark about traffic regulation:

> The regulation of traffic in the streets permits and forbids certain actions on the part of drivers and pedestrians; but it does not attempt to guide the totality of their movements by prescription. And it would be senseless to talk of an 'ideal' ordering of traffic which should do that; in the first place we should have no idea what to imagine as this ideal. If someone wants to make traffic regulations stricter on some point or other, that does not mean that he wants to approximate to such an ideal. *Zettel* §440

That insight explains why there is not necessarily a failure in the rule of law when a court needs to decide a dispute, and the law provides no conclusive reason for a particular decision. There *is* a failure in the rule of law when (because of vagueness or for any other reason) the law does not communicate to the subjects of the law, and to the institutions of the legal system, standards that are sufficiently determinate for the actual purposes of legal regulation. Partly because the purposes of law are themselves vague, and are only partly permanent, and partly depend on the nature of the community and on the characteristics of the system itself, the rule of law is itself a vague and open-ended ideal. But the ideal does, as Lon Fuller pointed out, require that laws must be public, prospective, clear, non-contradictory, and stable.[36] That requires effective communication. And remember that Wittgenstein's reason for reflecting on the regulation of traffic was that he was trying to understand the extent of our need for determinate rules in communication in general.

Contrary to Jeremy Bentham's view, a law is not an assemblage of signs.[37] But it certainly is something that can be communicated by the use of signs. If it were not so, then the law would be incapable of ruling the life of the community. What is more, law is something that actually *is* communicated (this is the requirement of publicity in Fuller's account of the rule of law). If it were not so, then the law would

[36] Fuller (1969: ch. 2).

[37] Bentham (1782).

not actually rule the life of the community. So a community can only achieve the rule of law if its institutions communicate standards for the life of the community that are not too vague for their purposes.

Is there any need for philosophers of law to be concerned with recent arguments about vagueness in philosophy of logic? It may seem that the sorites paradox is a problem for philosophers of logic, and not for philosophers of such a messy and political matter as law. But it is only a problem for philosophers of logic because of their attempt to understand natural language as meaningful, and to understand inference as a rational, objectively justifiable act of the intellect. Insofar as philosophers of law seek to account for statements of law as meaningful, and for legal reasoning as a pursuit that can be carried out in a rational, objectively justifiable manner, it is as important for them as for anyone else to be able to solve or to resolve the paradox.

Is the epistemic theory of vagueness, in particular, of importance to the philosophy of law? That theory seeks to solve the paradox of the heap by claiming that there are no indeterminacies in the extension of vague terms. The solution entails that there is a sharp boundary to the application of every vague term (which may be unknown or even unknowable to the users of the term).

You may conclude that the philosophical dispute over the epistemic theory has no importance for the law, because the rule of law problem is a problem for the epistemic theory, too. For the problem (and the associated pseudo-paradox of the rule of law) can be restated in epistemic form by saying that the right answer to a legal dispute can be unknowable. An epistemic theorist will say that there is a sharp boundary to the concept of a substantial part of the United Kingdom. But because the vague legislation imposes an *unknowable* boundary, there will be many cases in the epistemic theorist's view, as in the indeterminacy theorist's view, in which the law cannot rule the court's decision. The indeterminacy theorist will say that there is no right answer; the epistemic theorist will say that the right answer is unknowable. Both will say that the court cannot be governed by the law when it resolves the dispute, and will need to invent a resolution to a dispute in a borderline case. The indeterminacy theorist will say that the decision makes new law where there was none before. The epistemic theorist will say that the decision may make new law that is contrary to the old law, insofar as the legal system gives legal force to the decision as changing the unknown boundary that had been set by the legislation.

Is it possible, though, that the considerations as to the role of vagueness in law show that the sorites paradox can be resolved (by showing that the paradoxical question is a badly formed question), and the epistemic theory refuted? We have learned the following insights from considering the vagueness of law:

- *extravagant vagueness*: vague evaluative language has a paradigmatic importance, which philosophers of logic have avoided discussing;
- *incommensurability* of grounds of application has a crucial importance for any understanding of the vagueness of many terms (which, again, has been neglected by philosophers of logic), and it seems to rule out the epistemic theory because it rules out sharp boundaries to the extension of vague concepts;

- there is a crucial similarity between problem of extension of a vague term, and problem of the drawing of *analogies* (see the discussion of Hart's work in Section 7.4, above), and it seems that good analogies have no sharp boundaries;
- it is possible to offer standards for the *non-arbitrary application* of a vague term.

But those considerations will not persuade the epistemic theorist.[38] The epistemic theorist will say that the point about extravagant vagueness only shows (1) that the extension of some terms is extravagantly unknowable, and (2) that if evaluative terms are meaningful, then there are sharp boundaries to the true extension of every evaluative term.[39] The epistemic theorist will deny that there is any genuine incommensurability in the grounds of application of any meaningful term.[40] The epistemic theorist will, moreover, insist that there is a sharp (unknowable) boundary to the class of analogies that are sufficiently close to call for the same treatment of two cases (just as there is a sharp unknowable boundary to the class of red objects). And the epistemic theorist will welcome an account of non-arbitrary decision-making in borderline cases as a way of solving the problem of how we can achieve the rule of law when the sharp boundaries to its application are unknowable. Perhaps the discussion of extravagant vagueness in law has this to offer to the philosophical debates over the epistemic theory of vagueness: it shows what the epistemic theory is up against.

References

Bentham, J. (1782), *Of Laws in General*, in Hart, H.L.A. (ed.), London: Athlone Press 1970.
Besson, S. (2005), *The Morality of Conflict: Reasonable Disagreement and the Law*, Oxford: Hart Publishing.
Broome, J. (1997), "Is Incommensurability Vagueness?" in Chang, R. (ed.), *Incommensurability, Incomparability, and Practical Reason*, Cambridge, MA: Harvard University Press, pp. 67–89.
Dworkin, R. (1977), *Taking Rights Seriously*, London: Duckworth.
Dworkin, R. (1985), "Is There Really No Right Answer in Hard Cases?" in *A Matter of Principle*, Cambridge, MA: Harvard University Press.
Dworkin, R. (1996), "Objectivity and Truth: You'd Better Believe It", *Philosophy and Public Affairs* 25: 87.
Endicott, T. (2000), *Vagueness in Law*, Oxford: Oxford University Press.
Endicott, T. (2001), "Law is Necessarily Vague", *Legal Theory* 7: 377–383.
Endicott, T. (2005), "The Value of Vagueness", in Bhatia, V.K., Engberg, J., Gotti, M., and Heller, D. (eds.), *Vagueness in Normative Texts*, Bern: Peter Lang, pp. 27–48.

---

[38] See Williams (2004).

[39] But if they were meaningless, there would be no meaningful descriptive terms, since the true extension of a vague descriptive term can only be explained in vague evaluative terms, such as: '"red" applies to those objects that are *sufficiently* similar in *relevant* respects to fire engines'.

[40] Or rather, they will say that incommensurability is epistemic: that is, that we do not and cannot know how to commensurate the various considerations that may be relevant to the application of a vague term.

Endicott, T. and Spence, M. (2005), "Vagueness in the Scope of Copyright", *Law Quarterly Review* 121: 657–680.
Finnis, J. (1980), *Natural Law and Natural Rights*, Oxford: Oxford University Press.
Fuller, L. (1969), *The Morality of Law*, 2nd edn, New Haven, CT: Yale University Press.
Hart, H.L.A. (1994), *The Concept of Law*, 2nd edn, Oxford: Oxford University Press.
Kelsen, H. (1991), *General Theory of Norms* (1945), in Hartney, M. (ed.), Oxford: Oxford University Press.
Raz, J. (1979). *The Authority of Law*, Oxford: Oxford University Press.
Williams, S.G. (2004), "Indeterminacy and the Rule of Law", *Oxford Journal of Legal Studies* 24: 539–562.

Index

G. Ronzitti (ed.), *Vagueness: A Guide*, Logic, Epistemology, and the Unity of Science 19, DOI 10.1007/978-94-007-0375-9,

MIX
Papier aus verantwortungsvollen Quellen
Paper from responsible sources
FSC® C105338

If you have any concerns about our products,
you can contact us on
ProductSafety@springernature.com

In case Publisher is established outside the EU,
the EU authorized representative is:
Springer Nature Customer Service Center GmbH
Europaplatz 3, 69115 Heidelberg, Germany

Printed by Libri Plureos GmbH
in Hamburg, Germany